How to Make Sense of God

John Wijngaards

Sheed & Ward
Kansas City

Sheed & Ward™ is a service of The National Catholic Reporter Publishing Company.

◆

Library of Congress Cataloguing-in-Publication Data

Wijngaards, J. N. M.
    How to make sense of God / John Wijngaards.
        p.   cm.
    Includes bibliographical references.
    ISBN: 1-55612-821-5 (pbk. : alk. paper)
    1. God. 2. Apologetics. I. Title.
BT102.W535 1995
239—dc20   95-24017
                                                                         CIP

◆

Published by: Sheed & Ward
                 115 E. Armour Blvd.
                 P.O. Box 419492
                 Kansas City, MO 64141-6492

Co-published with Housetop for the United Kingdom.
To order, call: (800) 333-7373

Cartoons by Tom Adcock.
Illustrations by Sheila Gosney.

Contents

Part Two. CREATION

The Ultimate Reality we owe our existence to, we call God.

Belief in creation makes sense.

Questions and Answers.

Part Three. CONSCIENCE

It is God in us who gives us our human dignity and freedom.

Conscience is our human reason responding to God.

Questions and Answers.

Part Four. ENCOUNTER

God is cosmic Mind.

Questions and Answers.

God makes contact with us and transforms our lives.

Question and Answer.

Part Five. LOVE

We need to do some serious thinking before blaming God for suffering.

Questions and Answers.

Because God is LOVE, God can fulfil our deepest aspirations.

How to keep in touch with God.

Foreword

This book has been written for you if you want to find out why believing in God makes sense."

Perhaps, you have come to the conclusion that in our scientific age there is no further need of a Creator God. You can get along well enough without some supernatural power dictating what you should or should not do. You cannot visualise a Governor in heaven meddling in our chaotic, fractured and unintelligible world. What need is there of God?, you ask.

Perhaps, you still cling to your cherished childhood beliefs and even attend the occasional Church service, but entertain nagging doubts. Are the traditional concepts of God still compatible with your pragmatic and secular way of living? Are your prayers really heard? Or do they just soothe some emotional need? What solid intellectual basis is there for what you would like to be true?

In this book I present my reasons for believing in God. Though I was baptised a Christian the day after I was born, faith has always been a search for me, and it continues to remain so. From when I was a teenager I have felt a tension between my passionate hunger for God and my unconditional enthusiasm for modern values such as scientific truth.

Much in this book is personal. I will not blame you for disagreeing with some of the arguments I put forward, or for laying a different emphasis than I have. In fact, when you take issue with my thoughts, and work out your own line of thinking, I will feel I have achieved my purpose.

How to find your way through this book

The argument I present in this book is rather long and complex. It moves through five stages: Mystery (*Do we need religion?*), Creation (*Has the world been brought about by*

God?), Conscience (*Does morality derive from God?*), Encounter (*Does God communicate with us?*) and Love (*What is the ultimate meaning of life?*)

Though there is some logic in this sequence, you may want to zoom in first on questions that affect you more directly; like *Why is there evil and suffering in this world? Does belief in God not destroy our human freedom?* and *How can we distinguish genuine religious experiences from spurious ones?*

To locate your priority questions, I suggest that you study the *Table of Contents* first. The titles of sections and chapters clearly indicate the subject matter dealt with in each. After perusing the topics that preoccupy you most, you may want a wider look. The various facets of belief in God form a coherent whole.

At regular intervals I have inserted a *question and answer* section to give scope to debate. Here you will find discussion on many specific objections and queries.

In the margins of the text I give cross-references. They are by no means complete.

I express sincere thanks to all who have read, and commented on, the manuscript of this book, in particular: Mrs. Annette Barker, Dr. David Barker, Dr. Edward Bailey, Dr. Fiona Bowie, Mr. Anthony Buckley, Dr. Michael Cleary, Mr. Peter Hermon, Dr. Michael Hornsby-Smith, Mr. Stanley John, Dr. Eamon Mulcahy, Mrs. Barbara Paskins, Mr. Eric Tabet, Prof. Dr. Noel Timms, Dr. Rosemary West and Miss Mary Willson. Representing, as they do, a wide range of expertise and religious belief, from conservative Christianity and postmodernist theology to agnosticism and atheistic humanism, they helped me greatly by their frank remarks. Responsibility for the final text is entirely my own.

A two-and-a-half-hour film has been produced based on this book. It is called *Journey to the Centre of Love*. It describes the story of two young people who search for God. The themes in the story run parallel to the themes I discuss in *How to Make Sense of God.* The film is also available on video. I recommend it as a way of enlivening the topics through powerful and dramatic images.

How to Make Sense of God is all about life and living it well. In the last analysis, it addresses the question of how we can make sense of ourselves.

John Wijngaards

Part One

Mystery

1.

Religion is all about the mystery of our life.

Since we are entering the realm of religion, it may be useful to remind ourselves how traditional religions functioned. What were these religions really about?

They tried to answer fundamental questions that still confront each person in our world:

Who am I?

Where do I come from?

Why am I here?

What is the meaning of my life?

What am I really worth?

How can I find fulfilment and happiness?

Why do I need to suffer?

Traditional religions provided answers by placing us, human beings, within a wider, spiritual context. Everyday happenings made sense because they were part of a 'universe' of value and meaning.

Traditional religions in their various forms taught that everything that exists has been made by a God (or the gods). We have been created for a specific purpose. Our ultimate happiness lies in fulfilling our potential and conforming to the rights and duties enshrined in our nature. Friendship with God (or the gods) guarantees life beyond the grave; whether in reincarnation, nirvana or heaven. Egyptian religion may serve as an example.

Four thousand years ago, the Pharaoh of Egypt and his courtiers would recite this hymn to Amon-Râ in the Temple of Karnak:

Hail to you, Amon-Râ,
Lord of the thrones of the two countries

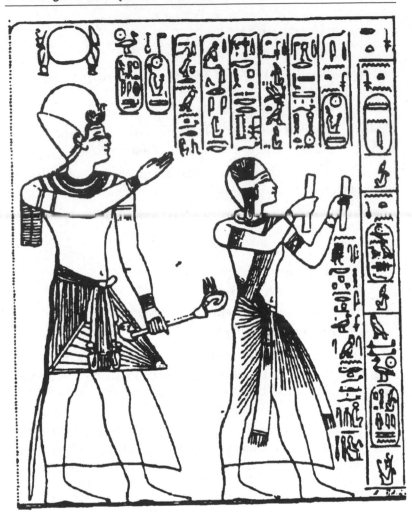

>   *of Upper and Lower Egypt,*
> *Eldest of heaven,*
> *Firstborn of earth,*
> *Lord of what is, present in all things,*
> *Master of truth*
>   *and father of the gods and goddesses,*
> *Who made human kind and created the animals,*
> *Who created fruit trees, grass and cattle,*

Who made what is below and what is above,
Hail to you![1]

Though many of the expressions are foreign to us, we have no difficulty entering into the religious contents of the prayer. We are attracted to it; and yet there are elements in Egyptian religion that worry and disturb us. The Egyptians attributed everything that happens in nature to divine powers. Their gods and goddesses were a strange lot.

Thoth   God of intelligence, depicted as an ibis; patron of artists, scribes and judges.

Ptah   The craftsman god, who resided in Memphis. He designed the shape of creatures at creation.

Isis   The 'great goddess,' depicted as a cow or as a mother suckling a child; source of fertility and life.

There were twenty other prominent gods and goddesses. And even granted that there was a slow transition to belief in one supreme God, the god Amon-Râ, people's lives were in reality dominated by hundreds of superstitions. There was the constant anxiety of trying to placate this or that divine power, to protect oneself by incantations, sacrifices and plain magic.

Religion for our time

Ancient religions, like the one practised by the Egyptians, cannot satisfy us any longer for two principal reasons: they rest on a world view which has been overtaken by our new scientific understanding; and they make people the slaves of fears and superstitions.

---

1   The hymn is found engraved on a statue of the Thirteenth Dynasty (1775 BC) and on a papyrus that dates from the Eighteenth Dynasty (1550-1350 BC). J. B. Pritchard, *Ancient Near Eastern Texts,* Princeton University Press, Princeton 1955, pp. 365-367 (I quoted only excerpts; the hymn is 106 lines long).

*"After a lifetime of aimless seeking –
this is the religion I want to join!"*

Traditional religions gave expression to the religious dimension of life. They were also right in trying to give people a framework that fitted the needs of the time. But they were a *human,* often all too human, attempt to formulate answers.

We, too, in our own day need a religious perspective, but we need one that is suited for our time. I for one am convinced that Christianity, if properly understood, does provide just such a perspective. But I also recognise that there are many historically dated and human aspects in all religious traditions, including in Christianity, which will simply not do for our situation today.

Read also ch.65
To find our true self we have to discover or re-discover our place in a mysterious universe. In other words: we need to recognise and re-affirm religion in our life.

2.

Yes, religions are shaped by human imagination, but they point at something real.

The German philosopher Ludwig Feuerbach (1804-1872) was struck by the fact that all nations in the world "make gods and goddesses in their own image." In his view, human beings observe certain qualities in themselves such as Reason, Will and Love which seem to be absolutes. People objectify them in imaginary, outside powers.

This is the origin of religion, Feuerbach said. It is really human nature which is 'divine'; the whole religious super-structure is an illusion, he said. Human beings need to be liberated from religion to find their true selves. He stated: "In religion man seeks contentment; religion is his highest good. But how could he find consolation and peace in God if God were an essentially different being?"

Feuerbach claims that there is nothing objective in religion. Religion is totally, utterly and exhaustively human. "I have reduced the supermundane, supernatural, and superhuman nature of God to the elements of human nature as its fundamental elements. The beginning, middle and end of religion is MAN."[1]

At first sight it looks as if Feuerbach is right. Consider, for instance, the ancient worship of the sun.

A god like us?

In many ancient religions the Sun was worshipped as a god: as Shamash for the Assyrians, as Râ and Aton for the Egyptians, as Sûria for the Hindus, as Ametarasu for the Japanese and as Mithras for a Persian sect in the Roman empire,

---

1 L. Feuerbach, *The Essence of Christianity*, Berlin 1845; transl. G. Eliot, New York 1957; here pp 45, 184.

each time in images that reflected the ideas of the particular worshippers.

The Sun god was of particular importance to the Aztecs (who lived in Mexico from 1200 - 1600 AD). They were convinced that the world order depended on the well-being of the Sun. Four previous worlds had already been destroyed because of the untimely death of their own "Sun." To ensure the continuation of the earth and society, the contemporary Sun had to be fed and protected.

When the earth had been plunged in darkness, after the collapse of the fourth world order, the Snake God *Quetzalcóatl* revived the human corpses by sprinkling them with his own blood. Another deity, weak and covered in ulcers, threw himself into a fire and became the new sun, called *Nahui-ollin*. He was so weak that he could not move until many other gods sacrificed themselves by offering their blood as food to him.

The Aztecs feared that the Sun might again collapse; in which case they would become an easy prey to the monsters of famine, the *Tzitzimime*, who would kill them mercilessly. Therefore they were anxious to sustain the Sun with gifts of blood. The blood came partly from acts of penance: piercing the tongue, ears and other organs, partly from human sacrifices. They even started wars for this purpose, to capture victims, and often hundreds of men and women would have their hearts taken out on a single day

We obviously have here an example of a religion gone wrong. Human behaviour and human weaknesses were projected onto the world of the gods, and atrocious practices were the result. The gratuitous bloodlettings and cruel killings hardly bear thinking about. It would be enough to put anyone off religion for good.

Moreover, even if other religions are more benign, could Feuerbach not be right in that not all of them suffer from the same basic problem: of being mere projections of human experiences onto an fictitious divine world?

The human eye of perception

Reducing the whole of religion to a pure world of fancy might seem tempting at first; especially when confronted with aberrations such as the Aztec sacrificial killings. Further reflection, however, shows that such a drastic rejection of religion cannot be correct.

It is wrong to jump from the inevitably human traits of religion to the conclusion that God and religion are no more than an illusion. First, I shall endeavour to show that the reality of God outside the mind and independent of the mind can be proved beyond doubt. But also, there lies an evident fallacy in denying the reality of God simply because we think of God in human terms.

The reason is simple. *All* our knowledge is human, by definition. There is nothing that we perceive that is not coloured by the humanness of our perception. Yet we know that reality exists and that we can attain reliable information about real things. In the same way, knowing God in a human way does not mean he is not real.

Read also ch.12 to ch.15

For instance, our eyes only see visible light, that is: photons with a wavelength between 4000 and 7000 angstroms.[1] On our retina we have cones that fall within roughly three ranges of sensitivity: blue (from 4000 angstroms), yellow and red (to 7000 angstroms). From this we construct in our mind the colours of the rainbow and many intermediate hues. Now it is true that the colours we see are a mental reconstruction. Colour is the way *we* interpret waves of light, and most waves, those outside our range – such as gamma-rays, X-rays, ultraviolet, infra-red and radio waves, we do not see at all.

But this does not mean that what we see does not correspond to a reality outside the brain. In that sense colours *are* real. And it is important they are, because we often have to base crucial decisions on their difference. In fact, the whole logic of evolution demands that our powers of perception re-

---

1 One angstrom is 0.00000001 cm.

flect reality. Like many animals before us, we learnt to see colour contrast because this helps us to relate better to the real world.

In other words: the fact that a perception is *human* does not mean that it is an illusion. To relate this again to our example of the sun: our spiritual ancestors were awed by the 'wonder' of the sun. In that wonder they perceived, rightly, that there is a real mystery about existence. In this way the sun became part of their *religious* experience. The experience is valid, even if the form in which it was expressed is entirely human.

Read also ch.46

Religions concern the ultimate questions of life. They try to voice the unspeakable. They attempt to respond to unfathomable mysteries. It is natural that they do so in human images and concepts. But why exclude the intuition that, underneath layers of human notions, they touch something real?

3.

Religions respond to human psychological needs – this does not invalidate their basic claim.

Many years ago I visited Jâdigirigutta, a small shrine in the Indian State of Andhra Pradesh. I joined hundreds of pilgrims who climbed to the temple on top of the hill and who waited patiently to be admitted in small groups to the cave where the local god resided.

He was known as *Narasimha*, the lion god with a human head. A woman, close to me in the queu, held a coconut wrapped in a linen cloth. She told me that she was infertile and had come to ask for a child. When we entered the sanctuary cave, she bowed down before the stone idol and said a prayer. Then she handed the coconut to the attending Brahmin priest, who took it and tied it to the ceiling of the cave. I was told that the woman had thus made a vow. She would come back, once her child was born, to bring gifts for a sacrifice.[1]

In this everyday incident, we can find ingredients common to all religions: the experience of a human need; the turning to God for help; the belief that correct religious practice can enhance prosperity and happiness. But does this not also reveal the Achilles heel of religions? Could religions be just that: a palliative for insecure emotional needs?

Sigmund Freud (1856-1939), the founder of psychoanalysis, thought as much. He maintained that the origin and basis of religion could be explained away entirely in psychological terms. Since we often meet unpleasant realities in life, he said, we use our human capacity of dreaming to create imaginary solutions. We create an unseen world in which we can ultimately obtain what we want.

Read also ch.24

---

1 A similarity with the story of Hannah in *2 Samuel 1,1 - 28* is striking.

The personified representation of our ultimate happiness is located in our loving mother and our *heaven* is envisaged as our restoration to her sheltering arms and comforting breasts. Likewise, we accept an omnipotent Law, which supports us but also rules us, out of awe for our powerful father. Thus *God* is born as a surrogate parent.

For Freud, the whole of religion, both in the past and the present, arises from human fear and from the wish-fulfilling potential of our brain. It is all one big illusion!

> *"The religious person calls back from his memory the image of his father, of such exaggerated importance to him in his childhood days. He raises this image to divinity, and establishes it mentally as something present and real."*[1]

> *"Being confronted with dangerous, uncontrollable and un-intelligible forces within and outside of himself, he remembers, as it were, and regresses to an experience which he had as a child, when he felt protected by a father whom he thought to be of superior wisdom and strength, and whose love and protection he could win by obeying his commands and avoiding transgression of his prohibitions."*[2]

Is God a virus?

Recent years have seen even more aggressive studies on our conscious and sub-conscious identity. Daniel Dennett contends that our own "self" is an illusion. It is like a software programme in the hardware of our brain. Our "self," the "I" we believe we are, does not really exist. It is a web of words and memories that guides our body and that makes it somehow a unity. It is the 'narrative centre of our body.' And religion is a short segment of the programme, a "meme," which infects the programme as any software virus would.

---

1 S. Freud, *The Complete Psychological Works*, ed. J. Strachey, London 1974.
2 E. Fromm, *Psychoanalysis and Religion*, Yale 1950, p.11.

"The Self is an imaginary construction by Homo Sapiens, an element of the internal, virtual machine of consciousness that keeps him going."[1]

"Religion is no more than corrupted software of the mind. God sits in people's brains like a virus."[2]

In assessing these views we should, first of all, observe that they contain a lot of truth. All our religious notions are shaped by the limitations of our human mind. Our religious experiences bear the imprint of human psychology. Even when God reveals himself to us, as I believe he/she/it does, we can only relate to God through human knowledge and human love. All our religious acts are subject to the rules of human psychology.

But does this invalidate religion? Is *everything* we do not conditioned by our psychological needs?

All our relationships are psychological events and are steeped in human emotions. But this does not mean that we do not have real relationships. Our partners are real people; and we are generally not mistaken about the negative or positive value of our friendship with them. In the same way, our relationship to the divine mystery, to God, however psychological and emotional, is thereby not less real. *Read also ch.39*

When we grow up, we relate to our mother and father. These parent figures are real, and so are the love and security we experience in them, even if some of our early experiences can also be painful and traumatic. Just as our initial bond with our parents enables us to relate to other people – who are real people, it can also enable us to relate to God, if God exists. The traces of our parental bond in such a relationship do not prove that God is not real.

---

1 D. C. Dennett and D. R. Hofstadter, *The Mind's I: Fantasies and Reflections on Self and Soul*, New York 1981; D. C. Dennett, *Consciousness Explained*, London 1992, esp. pp. 412-430.

2 R. Dawkins, 'Is God a computer virus?', *New Statesman & Society*, 1 January 1993, pp. 42-45.

It is true that we can deceive ourselves by hallucinations,
illusions, fantasies and fallacies. What saves us from them is
critical perception: common sense and the powers of rational
inquiry and sound judgment.

Read also ch.46

The inescapable dimension

Read ch.12-15

Later we will consider the evidence, inherent in our
world itself, that point to the existence of God. For the moment
it may suffice to reflect on the undeniable fact that the majority
of human beings, to whatever nation they belonged or belong,
have from the earliest times onwards spontaneously perceived
a religious dimension.

Read ch.8

However varied people's interpretations have been, they
are remarkably united in their verdict: the spiritual dimension
of the world is real. A leading modern psychologist acknowledges this fact.

> *"Philosophers and theologians have spoken of the
> 'nunc stans,' the abiding now, the instant that knows
> no temporal articulation, where distinctions between
> now, earlier and later have fallen away or have not
> arisen. All of us know, I believe, poignant moments
> that have this timeless quality: unique and matchless,
> complete in themselves and somehow containing all
> there is in experience."*[1]

Other psychologists and psychotherapists have written in
similar vein, expressing their judgement, based on dealing
with innumerable case stories, that the religious dimension is
real.[2]

---

1 H. Loewald, 'Comments on Religious Experience,' in *Psychoanalysis and the History of the Individual,* New Haven 1978, p. 65.

2 Many psychotherapists affirm the importance of the spiritual dimension for human wholeness. Among them: V. E. Frankl, *The Unconscious God,* New York (1945) 1975; *The Will to Meaning,* New York 1970; R. May, *Man's Search for Himself,* New York 1953; *Love and Will,* New York 1969; W. W. Meissner, *Psychoanalysis and Religious Experience,* New Haven 1984; A. Grunbaum, 'Psychoanalysis and Theism,' *Monist* 70 (1987) 152-192; S. Leavy, *In the Image of God. A Psychoanalyst's View,* New Haven 1988.

Such a universal and lasting assessment by the human race can only point to an overwhelming reality that cannot be dismissed lightly. It is an assessment which, as likely as not, resonates in our own intuitive insight. What is needed is to test the universal perception further.

If God and religion were mere illusions, then morality *Read* would have to be reduced to self interest. Freud acknowledged *ch.33* this, calling the Christian law of unselfish love "unreasonable, *& 37* unpsychological and impossible to fulfil."[1] But in a letter to the neurologist James Putnam, on July 8, 1915, he confessed:

> *"When I ask myself why I have always behaved hon-ourably, ready to spare others and to be kind wherever possible, and why I did not give up being so when I observed that in that way one harms oneself and be-comes an anvil because other people are brutal and untrustworthy, then, it is true, I have no answer."*[2]

Even Freud, therefore, witnessed in himself the response to a deeply spiritual value.

The truth of the matter is that our experience of religious values is personal, and therefore subjective and psychological. But this does not prove that there is no objective basis to relig-ion. William James argues this point convincingly in his clas-sic treatise on the psychology of religion.[3]

Just open your eyes

F.B.Pratt has countered the objection of psychologists in a parable:

"On a planet not far from a brilliant sun lived thousands of intelligent beings. But, although they all moved about in perpetual sunlight, few were aware of this because most were

---

1 S. Freud, *Civilization and its Discontents,* Standard Edition, vol.21, p.143.
2 E. Jones, *Sigmund Freud. Life and Work,* London 1953-57, vol.2, p. 465.
3 William James argues this point convincingly in his classic *The Varieties of Religious Experiences,* Fontana edition, New York 1960, pp. 475- 477.

"No need for psychotherapy after this, love!"

blind. Only a few of these beings could actually see, only very few.

One day one of these chosen few opened his eyes and received light sensations. He reported that he could see the sun. One psychologist among those beings, who was blind himself, came to examine the phenomenon.

"Aha," he said. "You claim you saw the sun after opening your eyes? Well, the matter is clear. Your seeing light sensations is not due to there being a sun outside, but only to the opening of your eyes. By opening your eyes you have projected your wish to see a sun. The sun you see is imaginary and a product of your mind."

But the man who could see insisted: "I do see the sun!"

"Is that so?" said the psychologist. "Well, try if you still see it with your eyes shut. No? It doesn't work? You only see the sun with your eyes open? Well, then show me a single point in your experience not consistent with my psychological explanation. You can't? Well, then it is clear that it's the opening of your eyes that makes you see the sun! The sun does not exist."[1]

The universal perception of God and of religion that we have inherited entails a totality of beliefs and feelings, a coherent perspective on life, an imaginative grasp on our world. May we assert, from psychology alone, that all this rests on an illusion? Is it not more likely that religious belief responds to something real, that it reflects a true aspect of the mysterious reality of which we are part?

---

1 F. B. Pratt, *Religious Consciousness*, New York 1920; also in *Readings in the Psychology of Religion*, Nashville 1959, p. 77.

4.

All human concepts of God are limited and flawed.

In temples and shrines throughout mainland China a host of gods and goddesses are worshipped by the Taoist faithful. But chief among them is Grandfather Heaven, who is also known as the Jade Emperor. He is invariably portrayed as a wise, middle-aged king, dressed in splendid robes and wearing signs of authority.

The ancient Mayas of Latin America (100 - 900 AD) also believed in a range of gods and goddesses. They called their ruling god *Itzamná* and represented him as a victorious warrior or as a snake. He was the creator-god, as well as lord of the fire and of the hearth.

The tribes of Guinea, on the west coast of Africa, believe in a supreme god who is very powerful, but hidden, and many smaller gods and goddesses. The supreme god is the god of life and fertility. In the clandestine rites of secret societies, his power is invoked to further personal aims.

If we study the religions of the world, we cannot but be struck by the almost infinite variety of images people have made of divine realities. And, almost without exception, they have cast God (or the gods) as replicas of themselves.

Anthropomorphism, i.e. speaking of God as if he/she/it were a human being, is also found in the Judeo-Christian tradition. When we call God "our father who is in heaven," we are describing him/her/it in human terms. We may say, "God hears my prayer. God protects me wherever I go. God rejoices when I do good, he is angry with me when I do evil." In all such cases we are ascribing human actions and human feelings to God.

Read also ch.17

There is nothing wrong in itself in using human images and words; as long as we are aware of the distortion they necessarily imply. In fact, when we speak or think about realities outside our immediate human experience, we have no choice. We can only speak or think about them in a human way.

Allow me to use a down-to-earth comparison to explain what I mean.

Seeing in a dark glass dimly

Have you ever tried seeing yourself through your dog's eyes? As your best friend it can share your moods and a measure of your life. But there is much it will never grasp. How will

"He says he can make God send rain from a blue sky!"

it understand your preference for Labour or the Tories? Or the meaning of your child's first birthday? Or why you enjoy watching *Coronation Street* on television? Dogs think in categories such as play, meat, territory, who-is-boss? and going for a walk.

We are somewhat in the same boat when trying to understand God. Obviously we live on a higher plane than dogs do, but in other ways the comparison holds good. If God exists, he/she/it towers infinitely above and beyond us and we can only make sense of God by using our limited human ways of thinking.

The human image we have of God also shows up in more subtle forms. Many people who reject God do not really reject the transcending reality of God, but a distorted image of God.

There is the *Super-Manager God* of some evangelicals and charismatics. He is the God you turn to in all emergencies. What is your problem? Your wife has got cancer? You are preparing for an important job interview? You are wondering whether you will beat the traffic and make a crucial meeting in time? Don't worry! Talk to God. He will fix it! If you are his friend, he will sort things out. He will even give you rain from a blue sky!

For some 'cultural' Christians who have for all practical purposes stopped going to Church, God is a vague *Father Christmas* figure. He wears a long, white beard and watches *Read ch.17* everything on earth from his throne in heaven. He is kind, but pathetic, the heavenly counterpart of his stereotype minister on earth: the rambling, bumbling, effeminate and useless parish vicar as often portrayed on TV.[1]

And what about the *Tyrant God* who makes life so miserable for a number of people? They imagine him as a difficult-to-please Disciplinarian, the all-seeing Eye, the strict Master who expects perfection from everyone. He sends suf- *Read* fering, they think, to test us. He demands severe penances for *ch.29* the smallest transgressions. He is opposed to sex and pleasure and enjoyment. He is only mollified when he sees we abjectly confess our sins.

The litany could go on. Who can blame sensible persons for rejecting such gods, gods who bear no resemblance to what we can know about the real God?

On the other hand, limitations in our concept of God do not disprove God's Truth. Our being acutely aware of the humanness of religious thinking and practice can only be an advantage to us. It will help us focus all the more on the underlying Reality all religions worship.

---

1   P. Hanley, *Finding Faith Today*, London 1992, pp. 75-78.

5.

Science does not supply answers to the ultimate questions of meaning.

A few years ago I had to give a series of lectures in Kampala, the capital of Uganda. As I was making the preparations for the journey, it struck me how much we depend on science and technology to smooth our path. I was vaccinated (*medicine*). I bought maps and books on the country (*geography* and *history*). I ordered my ticket (*computer science*) and travelled by plane (*aviation*).

I commented on this to a fellow passenger who was sitting next to me during the last leg of the flight between Nairobi and Entebbe. He was a biologist himself, a native Ugandan, who had been forced to flee the country during President Amin's reign of terror.

"You're right," he said to me. "And Uganda needs the help of science right now. We have to find a way to stop AIDS. In Kampala alone more than 30% of people are HIV positive. We also have to find new pesticides that are safe and that can effectively protect our maize and coffee. But science can't do everything."

"Like what?" I asked him.

"One of the main problems in Africa, and even world wide, is the inferior status ascribed to blacks everywhere. I live in England and often see discrimination at work."

"But surely science can do something," I said.

Read also ch.26 "It can, or rather, scientists can. In 1772, in Liverpool, a negro slave called James Somerset was given his freedom when a scientist declared in court that the black man was a human being. But scientists have also made terrible mistakes. Joseph Arthur Comte de Gobineau, Houston Stuart Chamberlain and Alfred Rosenberg, for instance, promoted as a scientific theory that blacks come from inferior races from which the white race should be kept separate."[1]

"That's awful," I said.

"Exactly. And it was not *science* that was at fault, but *the scientists* as persons. For science can only answer limited questions, according to the nature of each discipline. It can compare blood groups, or genetic data, or languages, or cultural customs. But it cannot answer questions about the value of things, or their ultimate purpose. If we ask why we should respect all human beings equally, science has no answer. The question will only be answered because of one's philosophy of life, or one's religion."

Read also ch.27

Limited focus

The spectacular advance of science is an achievement of our own age of which we can rightly be proud. When the knowledge of science joined the power of technology, our world was truly revolutionized; and on the whole for the better.[2] Through science we are able to make the most of our available resources.

Science is a method of studying things systematically. Suppose my area of interest is tulips. I proceed in a scientific way if I make detailed observations, and note them down; if I compare my findings with those of other botanists; if I advance a hypothesis and test the hypothesis by controlled experiments; if I publish the results and listen to peer criticism. In the end I help build up a reliable set of data and theories that will advance our scientific knowledge of tulips.

But by the rigorous limits science rightly imposes on its methodical study, other aspects of human life are excluded from its view. Think of beauty and art.

---

1 Joseph-Arthur Comte de Gobineau, *Essay on the Inequality of the Human Races*, Paris 1853-1854, new ed. 1967; H. S. Chamberlain, *The Foundations of the Nineteenth Century*, 2 vols. 1911; *Race and Personality*, 1925.

2 C. P. Snow, *The Two Cultures and the Scientific Revolution*, New York 1959.

*"Bloggs, you're here to study them,
not to enjoy them!"*

A riot of crimson, purple and yellow tulips can enliven my garden and fill me with excitement whenever I see them. A bouquet of tulips can convey a message of esteem and affection. Arranging tulips Japanese style can be my form of *Ikebana* meditation. In other words: tulips mean much more to me than botany can ever disclose. Of course, as a sociologist I can study the value of flowers in human interaction, but *describing* such values is one thing, *experiencing* beauty, art, purpose, love and joy quite another.

Unfortunately, people are often unaware of the limitations of science. They believe that science and technology cover all aspects of life and that the meaning and purpose of existence can also be established through scientific study.

Science as such is neither for nor against religion. It is merely an instrument. It is we, human beings including scientists, who have to discover the wider, religious, dimension of life, beyond science.

"Yes, the unspeakable exists. It manifests itself; it is mystical reality. . . . Even if all possible scientific questions had found their answer, the real problems of life still remain untouched. . . . The solution for the riddle of life in time and space, lies outside time and space."[1]

Ultimate questions transcend the limits of science, as also leading atheists admit.

"Questions about the nature of existence and the destiny of man, how things began and how they will end, why there is something rather than nothing, and why it is as it is, are not questions which any of the sciences asks and are not questions which any of the sciences could attempt to answer."[2]

The author goes on to show that it is not a matter of hoping that science will eventually be able to supply the answers. Ultimate questions "lie outside the terms of reference of the positive sciences."

In other words: for the answers to ultimate questions we need philosophy, ethics and especially religion.

I am not speaking of external, organized religion here, in the way we can speak of more 'religions' in the plural, each having a specific sets of doctrines, traditions, rites and practices; that is: 'religions' in a derived sense. I am speaking here of religion as such, of spirituality, of ultimate search, of openness to all dimensions of reality.

---

1 L. Wittgenstein, *Tractatus Logico-Philosophicus*, New York 1951, pp. 185-189.
2 H. J. Blackman, *Humanism*, Harmondsworth 1968, p. 41.

Religion, not science, tackles questions such as: Is there a purpose to our existence? What is the meaning of my life? To whom am I ultimately responsible for my actions? Science cannot provide an answer because these questions lie outside its scope.

6.

The kind of science that rejects God amounts to a dogmatic creed that contradicts true scientific principles.

A number of people harbour the mistaken notion that our scientific world view has, once for all, made religion out of date. One reason for this belief is the claim, put forward by some scientists, that all reality is ultimately *material*. If that were the case, there would be no place for God, a spiritual soul, immortality, afterlife or whatever.

The materialist trend of thought started centuries ago. One of its components, known as *positivism*, was formulated persuasively by the French philosopher Auguste Comte (1795-1857). Comte maintained that human beings pass through three stages of understanding: the theological one (in which God features), the philosophical one (when we still talk of Absolutes like Truth) and the positive one (when we only consider the facts as we see them).

> *"In the positive phase the mind has given up the useless search for Absolute notions, for the origin and destination of the universe, and the causes of phenomena, and applies itself to the study of their factual laws. . . . Reasoning and observation, duly combined, are the means of this knowledge. What is now understood when we speak of an explanation of facts is simply the establishment of a connection between single phenomena and some general facts."*[1]

Another element is known as *materialism*, that is: the tenet that everything in the universe, including intelligence,

---

1 *The Positive Philosophy of Auguste Comte*, translated by H. Martineau, London 1852, vol I, p. 2.

*"Now I know I'm descended from you,
I've solved all the mysteries of my existence!"*

'spirit' or whatever, can be reduced to physical and chemical processes. One of its pioneers was Ludwig Büchner who declared that nothing exists outside matter.

> *"Science gradually establishes the fact that macrocosmic and microcosmic existence obeys, in its origin, life and decay, mechanical laws inherent in the things themselves, discarding every kind of supernaturalism and idealism in the explanation of events."*[1]

Now it is quite natural for scientists to proceed within their scientific studies as if only matter existed; it is quite an-

---

1 L. Büchner, *Force and Matter*, London 1855; other classical works were: E. Haeckel, *The Riddle of the Universe*, London 1899; H. Feigl, *The "Mental" and the "Physical"*, New York 1967; J. J. C. Smart, *Philosophy and Scientific Realism*, New York 1963.

other to maintain that matter *is* the only reality. The next steps then follow logically. A spiritual dimension to one's life is denied. Human intelligence and freedom are reduced to blind forces. The whole universe is explained in terms of chance and materialistic evolution. With this, we are told, the problem of the universe has been solved.

> *"It would be brash, indeed, to claim complete understanding of the extraordinarily intricate process, but it does seem that the problem is now essentially solved and that the mechanism of adaptation is known. It turns out to be basically materialistic "*[1]

> *"This book is written in the conviction that our own existence once presented the greatest of all mysteries, but that it is a mystery no longer because it is solved. Darwin and Wallace solved it, though we shall continue to add footnotes to their solution for a while yet."*[2]

What are we to make of such claims?

A trap to avoid

Science advances theories which are 'models of the world' seen from a particular point of view. Science cannot supply an over-arching system of meaning. The materialist theory too is no more than a theory.

From being a mere hypothesis, materialism has recently become for some scientists a dogma, a truth accepted as true beyond proof. But as the zoologist Alister Hardy reminds us, such a dogma contradicts the essence of science. "Science by its very nature cannot be dogmatic; its views are always changing as new discoveries by observation or experiment are continually made. There is today almost no scientific theory which was held when, say, the Industrial Revolution began about 1760. Most often today's theories flatly contradict those

---

1   G. G. Simpson, *The Meaning of Evolution*, Yale Univ. 1950, p. 230.
2   R. Dawkins, *The Blind Watchmaker*, Harmondsworth 1991, p. xiii.

of 1760; many contradict those of 1900. In cosmology, in quantum mechanics, in genetics, in the social sciences, who now holds the beliefs that seemed firm sixty years ago?"[1]

Science formulates theories which by their very nature are temporary and relative. The historian of science, James Burke, points out the boundaries that limit any scientific view.

"In spite of its claims, science offers no method or universal explanation of reality adequate for all time. The fact that over time science has provided a more complex picture of nature is not in itself final proof that we live by the best, most accurate model so far.

Scientific knowledge is the artifact of the mental structure of a particular time, and its tool."[2]

Scientists are quite correct when they affirm that their scientific research as such does not prove or disprove religious beliefs. Religion lies outside the purview of science. But scientists who claim that science proves God does not exist or that religious realities are false, contradict the openness to truth and the limited scope which are principles of scientific study itself.

---

1 A. Hardy, *Science, Religion and World Unity*, Oxford 1979, p.8; his examples are quoted from J. Bronowski, *Science and Human Values*, New York 1964.

2 J. Burke, *The Day the Universe Changed*, London 1985, p. 337.

7.

Scientists too derive their *values* from outside the realm of science.

Values are the principles according to which we guide our decisions and actions.

These are some of the common values that underlie the accepted methodology of science:

• Observations, conclusions and reports should be based on a rigorous respect for factual truth. Not only cheating and lying, but exaggerations and slanted presentations go counter to correct science.

• Scientific discoveries should be submitted to peer review and should be available to colleagues working on related problems. Favouritism arising from racial prejudice, jealousy or personal bias damage the progress of international science.

Such principles do not derive their validity from science itself. They are laid down and accepted by human beings, who impose them on the scientific process. These principles are like an infra-structure of well paved highways on which the vehicles of the various sciences can run smoothly and effectively.

Scientists depend no less on outside values when considering the use that will be made of their scientific discoveries.

This is obvious from our everyday experience of how science operates. Nuclear power unleashes enormous energy. Nuclear physics by itself is entirely neutral to its use; the same energy can be employed for selfish purposes, for destruction of other human beings or for industry. The application of a scientific invention depends on the values scientists, and their masters, believe in. And, in the past, conscientious scientists have taken courageous decisions as human beings.

"I know its a stupid question – but which did come first – science or religion?"

Scientists carry responsibility

Leonardo da Vinci (1452-1519) kept the submarine he had designed a secret "on account of the evil nature of people who would practise assassination at the bottom of the seas," as he tells us in his *Notebooks*.

Richard Boyle (1627-1691) withheld the formula of a poison he had worked out. John Napier (1550-1617) hid his blueprint for a new weapon. And Michael Faraday (1791-1867) refused to work on a poison gas to be used in the Crimean War.

Scientists know that the question they need to ask is not just: "Does this work?," but, "Am I allowed to use it? Am I doing the right thing?" This is a question of conscience, a

Read also ch.30

question of religious values, which they need to answer as free, responsible human beings.[1]

The philosopher of science Karl Popper came to the conclusion: "There can be no scientific basis to morality, but science needs a moral foundation."[2]

It is obvious to all thinking people that we can use our new scientific tools to better the condition of innumerable men and women who still live in utter poverty. Many are undernourished, or ill, or condemned to a ceaseless struggle for bare existence. They are imprisoned in ignorance and superstition. But why should we bother to spend time and resources on them?

In his plea for a universal, humanitarian campaign the agnostic Julian Huxley admitted that he had to appeal to religious values.

> *"The highest and most sacred duty of man is seen as the proper utilization of the untapped resources of human beings. I find myself inevitably driven to use the language of religion. For the fact is that all this does add up to something in the nature of a religion.*
>
> *. . . . I am using the word 'religion' in a broader sense, to denote an overall relation between man and his destiny, and one involving his deepest feelings, including his sense of what is sacred."*[3]

The principles of truth, fairness, service to the community and respect for other human beings are *religious* values. Also scientists cannot fulfil their task responsibly without them. *Read also ch.34*

---

1 R. J. Forbes, *The Conquest of Nature. Technology and its Consequences,* Harmondsworth 1971, p. 138.
2 K. Popper, *Conjectures and Refutations,* London 1959.
3 J. Huxley, *Evolution in Action,* Harmondsworth 1963, pp. 157-158.

8.

We must return to our roots by recapturing what is mysterious and sacred.

Space invaders from another galaxy landing on planet earth would in their study of human beings soon stumble on the phenomenon *religion.* In cities, towns and villages they would identify temples, churches, synagogues, mosques and shrines. They would observe religious festivals and rites. If they were thorough in their search, they would even discover that religion was found with all races of human beings from the earliest known history. Probably this would not surprise them. They would understand; for the odds are that our extra-terrestrials themselves would hold their own religious beliefs and practices.

It is sometimes said that human beings are 'incurably religious.' This rather facetious statement hides an undeniable fact: the impressive, wide and all-pervasive influence of religion on human life. 'All through human history and all through present-day societies, there appears some systematic reaching out to what is regarded as sacred.'[1]

Even the onslaught of modern technology and secular living have not eradicated religion. In our world of urban conglomerates, offices, underground trains, television, computers and mobile telephones, much of our life has changed. We do new jobs. We have modernised our homes. We have acquired fresh tastes and eat different food. Health care, schools, politics and social awareness, all have undergone radical changes. But, apart from some pockets of people who are totally alienated from religion, belief in a meaning that goes beyond everyday life persists.

---

1 *The New Encyclopedia Britannica*, 1986 edition, vol. 26, p. 569, 1b.

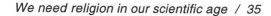

"I understand it's the custom to put a button in it!"

For what else is religion but a conviction, borne out by deeds, that there exists a dimension that reaches higher, further and deeper than we are normally aware of?

There is more to human life than meets the eye.

More to oneself;

more to one's neighbour;

more to the world that surrounds us.

There is more to the past out of which we come;

and especially, it would seem, more to the present

moment, maybe even infinitely more.

There is more to the interrelationships that bind us

together as persons.

And the further we probe as human beings, the deeper

the mystery we find, or the reward, or the involvement.

It is this "more" that provides at least one of the bases for human religion.[1]

We human beings have seldom been content to be "superficial," to remain on the surface, to imagine that reality does not transcend our finite grasp; and throughout most of our history on this planet we have attempted to order our lives, both personal and cultural, in terms of that transcendence.

At the heart of religion lies belief in the Divine, in *God*. There have been wide variations in the way God has been conceived of and in the way he/she/it has been worshipped. But there is no doubt that the conviction that the Divine exists has inspired, and still inspires, thousands of millions of individuals all over the world. God is also the focus that unites countless religious groupings, making people share celebrations, institutions and value systems. Belief in God has driven some people to excesses, but it also has often brought out the best in people.

The highest, deepest and most comprehensive that human beings have been capable of has, more often than not, been motivated, nurtured and guided by openness to God.

Present-day beliefs

The European Values System Study of 1991 covered Western Europe. The figures show that 70% believe in God. 20% say they are not sure what to believe and only 10% deny the existence of God. The proportion of women who believe is slightly higher than men. Even among those who never go to Church (that is about half the population), 56% say they believe in God and 24% that occasionally they set aside time for prayer.[2]

The question remains: what kind of God do people believe in?

---

1 W. C. Smith, *The Meaning and End of Religion*, New American Library, New York 1964; here in the Propaedia Volume of *the New Encyclopedia Britannica*, 1986, p. 299 1b.

2 The figures for Britain vary only slightly from the European averages. See N. Timms, *Family and Citizenship. Values in Contemporary Britain*, Dartmouth, Aldershot 1992, pp. 67-78; S. Ashford and N. Timms, *What Europe Thinks. A Study of Western European Values*, Dartmouth, Aldershot 1992, pp. 33-47.

If we combine information gleaned from many items in the survey, the following picture emerges. About half the population believe in *a personal God*, a God who can know and love, and to whom one can direct prayers.[1] Another two out of every ten consider God *a Supreme Spirit* or *Life Force*. Many of these people also pray, but their prayer is not directed to God, it takes the form of meditation or contemplation.[2] Since God transcends all human concepts, different approaches are not mutually exclusive, anyway.

Read ch.38 to ch.41

Obviously, the facts also reveal a great deal of confusion about God in people's minds; and things may get worse. Since, in the West, religion is treated as a strictly private matter, the topic of God is often taboo, not only among friends, but even in families. Moreover, a thousand and one occupations tend to crowd thoughts about God from people's minds: demands at school, pressures at work, TV, music, games, you-name-it.

It is striking that people with more opportunity to think, like farmers and housewives, score higher on personal prayer (66% and 75%), whereas the younger age group – between 18 and 24 years – score low on 'praying to God' (37%) or 'taking moments of prayer or contemplation' (51%). Is this because, in spite of having more leisure time, they fill it with distraction and noise?

Many people in our scientific age try to re-discover religion. This need not be a return to naive religious practices of one's childhood, but a new personal conquest of deeper truth.

Our life on earth is shrouded in mystery. Questions like: Why do we exist? What do we live for? stare us in the

---

1   When asked whether they believe in a 'personal' God, only 38% say Yes. However, the meaning of 'personal' is ambiguous. People's true belief shows in the fact that 48% say they 'pray to God' outside of religious services (23.4% often; 24.7% sometimes).

2   The total proportion of people who say they take 'moments of prayer, meditation or contemplation' is 62%.

face. Science cannot provide the answers to such ultimate questions. Religion can, at least to some extent.

9.

"Religion is useful for social functions. That's all."

"In my experience, religion functions best at key social events in our life: at weddings, christenings, funerals and memorial services. The Church supplies beautiful ceremonies for such occasions. I don't see how it can help me succeed as a person."

It is true, religion provides beautiful services for social events. They are only meaningful if what they express externally, corresponds to internal realities. All ceremonies ultimately revolve round our *self*, our person. Baptism means: we belong to God and to God's community. A wedding unites two individuals in a special bond of love. The funeral affirms the person's continued existence in God's embrace.

Our most precious possession in life is our own self. Money, power, success and pleasure can never fully satisfy us. They cannot guarantee happiness. True human happiness arises from a sense of well-being deep within us, from being happy to be ourselves. What we *possess* is not the same as who we *are*.

Jesus Christ is recorded as having said:
What will a man gain by winning the whole world
at the cost of his true self?
Or what can a man give that will buy that self
back?[1]

It may be that Jesus referred here to the example of Alexander the Great who had been, for a few years, the most powerful man on earth. He had conquered Persia, Egypt and part of India. But he died, after a prolonged drinking bout, young and unhappy. According to a legend

1   *Matthew* 16,26.

known to Jesus' contemporaries, Alexander had been buried with his hands dangling, empty, outside his coffin.

Notice that for Jesus, Alexander was a failure not because he died, but because he betrayed his true self. Death is not the worst thing that can happen. Missing out on our true self is.

What is our true self?

It is easy to grasp that our self is not the same as what we own. It is more difficult to grasp that our self is more than our social identity. That is because we often confuse the two.

We can all imagine a rich and successful woman losing everything she owns because of, let us say, a war. She still is herself. Or is she? Of course, she still possesses her social identity. But that is not what we mean when we say that she is still herself. We can affirm that she still is herself if she has managed to maintain her dignity and self esteem in spite of losing all she owned.

Our social *identity* is the sum total of all the external circumstances that make a person unique. They include: our nationality, our place and date of birth, the identity of our parents, male or female gender, the appearance of our face, marks on our body, our fingerprints, our name. They are the kind of things immigration officials put on our passport. "This is so-and-so. You can recognise him or her by these signs."

Read also ch.28 & ch.39

Our *self* is the sum total of all our our personal searchings, our convictions, our decisions, our habits, the character traits we have developed, the trials we have faced up to, our experiences of growth: in short, everything inside us that makes us who we are.

We cannot change our identity, but we have to *make* our own self. Even though we do this with the help of

*"Prejudice to good order and military discipline.
Private Nobody did think for himself – Sah!"*

others, the quality of our self depends on how much we have
invested in terms of risk, commitment and even suffering.

Meet ME

There are people whose selves remain underdeveloped.
They do not think for themselves. They copy convention in
everything they do. They are afraid to face up to uncertainty,
doubts, problems. They have never had the courage to live up
to their real convictions; as Sydney Carter expressed it in this
cynical song:

I wore the mask of a baby.
Teddy bear and curly hair.

Wore the mask of a baby
for everyone to see.

He then goes on to describe how he wears successively the mask of a school boy, of a soldier, of a man in love and of a married man. It all ends in a correct social funeral.

Go ring the bell for a dead man!
Go bury the mask! That's all I ask!
Bury the mask of a dead man.
You'll never bury ME. . . .

There are many reasons why we may not have cultivated our own selves. In some families, creativity and personal growth are not encouraged. Some cultural traditions stress blind belief and unquestioning obedience rather than our own search and forming our own conscience. Peer groups at school, in college and at work try to impose ideologies, customs and conventions.

Read also ch.50 & ch.57

For our self to survive and to grow into a unique distinctive personality, we often have to fight, to hurt, to seek our own way, to face up to threat and to risk adventure. There is no shortcut to becoming ourselves. It is part of our social birth as a mature person.

Facing our true self, with all its potential and its weaknesses, is the highest challenge of religion. For we can survive our social encounters by wearing a mask; we cannot become a *self* without, consciously or unconsciously, coming face to face with Ultimate Reality.

10.

"The history of all religions, including that of Christianity, is a litany of injustices and failings."

"No one doubts that it was religion that shaped the Christian Middle Ages in Europe. But they are rightly known as the dark ages. There was so much superstition, repression of freedom and religious warfare. If we go by the historical record, mankind is better off without religion!"

I believe that an objective study of history does not present such a one-sided picture. To obtain a more balanced view, we have to consider the reasons for the negative side and to acknowledge also the positive achievements. Let me give examples taken from the Middle Ages.

Yes, religious zeal often led to excesses. One example is the crusades against the Muslims who had occupied the Christian places of pilgrimage in the Holy Land. From 1095 to 1270 AD wave after wave of Christian armies rode east to face the Turks.

A typical event illustrates how things could go wrong. On June 7, 1099, a Christian army of 1200 cavalry and 10,000 foot soldiers arrived at Jerusalem. Since Jerusalem was heavily fortified and well supplied with provisions, the Muslim forces were confident they could hold the city almost indefinitely.

The crusaders, however, felt committed to a divine mission. After a year of perilous travel and heavy fighting, they had now arrived at the Holy City. It was their duty to liberate the sacred places: the hill where Christ died, his tomb, the room of the Last Supper, the Temple area. On July 8 they observed a strict fast. And, under the scoffs of the the Muslims who were watching from the walls, they walked round the city in solemn procession, praying and singing religious hymns.

The attack began on the 13th of July. Siege towers were brought near to the walls. Some knights jumped on to a section of the wall. Others scaled the walls by ladders. After fierce and heroic man-to-man combat, a gate was taken. The Christian army flooded in and the Muslim force surrendered.

One of the Christian commanders, Tancred of Normandy, had promised protection to civilians in the Aqsa Mosque. This promise was ignored by the fanatic knights. Everyone was mercilessly slaughtered: Muslim men, women and children, as well as Jews. The 'soldiers for God' thus became murderers.

The massacre was inexcusable, of course. No amount of religious enthusiasm can justify the taking of innocent lives.

The persecution of dissenters

The fanatic zeal of the Middle Ages raged also against *heretics*. 'Heretics' were people who proclaimed a doctrine that was perceived to contradict Christian belief. Heretics were considered very dangerous persons. They upset the established social order. Worse, they rebelled against God who, it was believed, had guaranteed revealed truths. Heretics might also "infect" other people with their false ideas. For all these reasons, the religious logic went, they deserved death if they persevered in their heresy; and they might be saved if the punishment brought them to their senses.

The punishments inflicted on heretics were humiliating and painful. Men and women accused of heresy were tortured to make them change their mind. If they refused to recant, they were burnt at the stake. In 1252 AD Pope Innocent IV publicly endorsed the practice in his bull *To Extirpate Pernicious Errors*.

In 1600 AD Pope Clement VIII ordered that Giordano Bruno, an astronomer and occultist, be condemned to the stake 'as an impenitent and pertinacious heretic.' Bruno addressed his judges with the words: "Your fear in passing judgment on me is greater than mine in receiving it." The system was already collapsing by then.

Brother Joachim shows exemplary zeal – even in the debate on how to grow marrows!"

On the 7 December 1965 the Catholic Church, assembled in a session of its Second Vatican Council, solemnly declared that every person has the right to religious freedom, and that no one may be coerced into thinking or acting against one's personal conscience. *"The human person has a right to religious freedom. Freedom of this kind means that all people should be immune from coercion on the part of individuals, soicial groups and every human power so that, within due limits, nobody is forced to act against his or her convictions in religious matters in private or in public, alone or in association with others."*[1]

---

1   *Dignitatis Humanae*, no 2; *Vatican Council II*, ed. A. Flannery, Dublin 1975, p. 800.

The medieval practice of torturing and killing 'heretics' was thereby acknowledged to have been a grave injustice and a serious mistake.

Cost and pay-off

All right, people who lived during the Middle Ages were forced to endure such religious excesses. The point can be made that they also reaped the benefit of Christian belief and practice. Tens of thousands of monasteries and convents provided the infrastructure that changed rural jungles into civilised communities. The monks brought education and improved methods of agriculture. Nuns looked after the sick and the poor.

The Christian Middle Ages laid the foundation for life as we know it now. The importance of the individual was cultivated. The study of nature, even if still mixed up with alchemy and superstition, prepared the way for our present-day sciences. The principles of democracy: equal voting for leaders, legislation by common consent, responsibility to an assembly of representatives, were all principles first practised by religious orders and congregations.

In no way should we discount Europe's debt to the Greeks and the Arabs. But it was the positive Christian world view that released the potential of lasting international change. The scientific, social and political values that underpin the present world order have their roots in Christian Europe.[1]

The same can be said about religious traditions in other countries, their institutions and their leaders. Because they are human in members and organization, all religions show failings and shortcomings. But all of them also contributed to the welfare of the societies to which they belonged.

Read also ch.35 & 36

Human religions, like other organized social forces, show achievements and failings. I agree that the achievements

---

1   J. Burke, *The Triumph of the West*, London 1985.

by themselves do not suffice to prove a divine origin. But neither do the inevitable errors and lapses disprove it.

The human aspect of religion, though it is a trait we always have to keep in mind so that we can protect ourselves against mistakes and excesses, does not prove that religion should be abandoned altogether.

Religion is an inalienable part of us as human beings. Like other areas of our existence: family, work, leisure and health, religion carries human features. It is something we have to live with.

11.

"Religion makes us hate ourselves."

"From what I have seen and read, religion is actually telling us to hate ourselves. We are presumed to be sinners. We are told to do penance and covert. We are expected to give up lots of things which normal people take for granted. If I am in trouble, I would rather talk to a psychotherapist than to a priest or minister!"

Read also ch.3 & ch.9

There are certain problems for which I too would consult a psychotherapist. But in what you say there seem to be two assertions with which I cannot agree. The first one is the assumption that psychotherapy can do without religion – which I am convinced is wrong. The second one is the statement that religion teaches us to hate ourselves.

Jesus taught us to love our neighbour *as we love ourselves* (Mark 12,31-33). How can we be good to others, if we are not good to ourselves? We have to begin with the desire to really love ourselves. never mind what some misguided preachers may tell us.[1]

Self love should not be confused with selfishness. Self love means that we like ourselves – in spite of our shortcomings, that we wish ourselves well and that we are committed to be good to ourselves. To love ourselves is healthy.

Read also ch.58 & ch.64

Being good to ourselves does not mean pampering ourselves, pitying ourselves, plying ourselves with shortlived pleasures at the risk of becoming hooked to them. Loving always demands discipline, the willingness to forgo things for the sake of the person loved. This is also required when we love ourselves.

As we will see later, self love paradoxically reaches its peak when we deny self for a really worthwhile cause. We only

---

1 *Mark* 12,31-33

find life if we are prepared to lose life.[1] This amazing truth only dawns on us as we gain more experience. We obtain more from giving than from receiving.[2] Our greatest happiness comes from making others happy. However, while keeping these paradoxes in mind, we should give time consciously to love and foster our self. And this requires paying attention to basics.

Progress in developing our self will not come from learning a few tricks. Do-it-yourself psychology books suggest dozens of techniques that are supposed to polish our self image, to help us make friends or survive embarassing situations. Such books may contain a few useful tips on practical behaviour. They decidedly pass over the main issue at stake: our deeper personality structure.

To liberate our real self, to change it, to help it assume its truly unique character, we have to uncover the deepest layers of our personality.

Digging Deep

For the sake of simplicity, we may think of ourself as operating constantly on four levels as psychologists tell us:

1. The top layer: *the surface level.*

Let us assume that I am having a cup of tea with a colleague in a canteen. As usual, she has a brilliant plan. She has noticed that Indian neighbours in her street looked rather lost at Christmas. She will invite them in for tea on Boxing Day.

2. The layer second from the top: *the relational level.*

To continue our example: by having our tea break together and by sharing confidences, the two of us express a degree of mutual acceptance.

3. Third from the top: *the level of one's basic attitude to life.*

---

1   *Mark* 8,35.
2   *Acts* 20,35.

"Who are you?"
"The same person who signed the cheque
you gave me I hope!"

My colleague obviously has a positive approach to people in general. Her Boxing Day project reveals a deep confidence in others. I'M OK, YOU'RE OK. Her friendliness springs from a basic attitude towards other people and towards life in general.

4. Fourth from the top: *the level of religion.*

Remember, when I talk about 'religion' in this context, I do not refer to it as to a denomination (as in 'the Jewish, Christian, Muslim religion'), but as the ultimate interpretation of life. Even secular humanists who deny adhering to 'a religion,' actually have a kind of religion in that they seek to adhere to truth, justice, human equality and other fundamental values.

On the other hand, Christians who claim to believe in the God of love, may in the reality of their religious level well be slaves to a God of tyranny and fear.

Even in the simple example given, my colleague's religious interpretation of life plays a part.She has resolved questions that lie at the foundation of her judgement about other people, her overall approach to life and to her motivations. What is the purpose of life? Who is my friend? Does anybody really love me?

All four layers are active at the same time, even though we are usually only conscious of the top ones. On the other hand, the deeper the level, the more our true self is affected. The roots of our personality lie on the religious level. It is there that our most fundamental self is formed.[1]

Read also ch.39

Appearances may deceive. It is one thing to agitate for or against religion on level one; quite another to understand one's true religious values deep down.

Most of our fallacies of judgment and inhibitions of action lie on level three, the layer of our basic stand. Our mind is made in such a way that the contents of any layer can be changed by modifications on a deeper level.

To find our true self, we need to uncover the religion we hold, consciously or unconsciously. To develop our true self, we need to affirm the religious values we want to live up to. We have to come face to face with the 'God' who lurks in the deepest recesses of our personality.

---

1 P. Watzlawick, J. H. Beavin and D. D. Jackson, *Pragmatics of Human Communications*, New York 1967, Chapter 8.1 - 8.5.

Part Two

Creation

12.

The universe in which we live demands an explanation outside itself.

One of the oldest arguments for the existence of God rests on the fact that the universe itself, like any of its component parts, requires an adequate explanation.

"Look around you," Greek philosophers would say. "The world displays astounding order. The sun, the moon, the stars, plant life, the animals and human beings: all belong together in an intricate pattern of co-existence. It could not be there without a Maker. Neither would it be what it is without a plan."

Who of us, when we look at a statue or picture, does not at once think of the sculptor or painter?

When we see a new dress, ship or house, don't we at once reflect on the designer, the shipbuilder, the architect?

On entering a well ordered city, in which everything is well arranged and regulated, will we not recognise at once that it is controlled by wise and efficient authorities?

When we then look around us at what is surely the greatest of cities, namely the world;

and when we see all the land, both mountains and valleys full of vegetation and animal life;

and the rivers and streams, overflowing at times, and then depending on the supplies of the rainy season;

and the steady tides of the ocean;

and the marvellous temperature of the air;

and the regular cycle of the seasons of the year;

and then too the sun and the moon and the regular courses run by the planets and the fixed stars

– would any one of us who sees all this not naturally, or I should rather say, of necessity,

conceive the notion of the Father and Creator and Governor of all this system?

For there is no artificial product that can exist of its own accord, and the world is the most artificial and skilfully made of all things.[1]

This spontaneous argument based on order in the world still has its appeal, even for sophisticated thinkers. Some years ago I heard Fred Hoyle, the famous astronomer, give an interview on BBC radio. At the time, Hoyle had retired to the countryside. "I know a Creator exists," he said, "because the world bears the marks of one. When I walk through country lanes here, I see stone walls round the fields. I know the walls did not make themselves. They were constructed by farmers. All the more so when I meet a tractor on the road: it could never assemble itself. In the same way the universe bears the stamp of a Mind."

Read also ch.13

Both Philo and Hoyle were using two-tier world language here. Today we realise that the image of a Supernatural Architect does not really fit the bill. But they point they were making remains valid. The universe requires a Cause.

Read ch.17

Adequate explanation?

Now you might object that evolution explains everything. The point is, it doesn't. *Evolution explains connections within the universe, not the universe itself.*

Read also ch.21

Suppose an uneducated tribal head hunter of darkest Papua New Guinea finds himself suddenly in an aeroplane. He might, of course, restrict his attention to individual items he has never seen before: his passenger seat, the overhead lamp,

---

1   Philo of Alexandria (20 BC - 54 AD), in *Works of Philo Judaeus*, London 1890, vol. 3, pp. 182-183 (I have modernised the translation).

"I'll have him – medium rare!"

the music-playing earphones, the windows of the cabin, other passengers. He may also, if he is intelligent, begin to ask wider questions – and discover that everything, including himself, is part of one extraordinary artificial bird: the aeroplane. The inner connections inside the plane do not explain how the whole plane came about, or why it can fly in the air.

The same applies to our universe. It is its totality that requires an explanation. The physicist Paul Davies expresses the situation in these words:

> *Look around you. See the complex structure and elaborate organization of the universe. Puzzle over the mathematical formulations of the laws of physics. Stand perplexed before the arrangement of matter, from the whirling galaxies to the beehive activity*

of the atom. Ask why these things are the way they are. Why this universe, this set of laws, this arrangement of matter and energy? Indeed, why anything at all?

Every thing and every event in the physical universe must depend for its explanation on something outside itself. When a phenomenon is explained, it is explained in terms of something else. But if that phenomenon is all of existence – the entire physical universe – then clearly there is nothing physical outside the universe (by definition) to explain it. So any ex-planation must be in terms of something non-physical and supernatural. That something is God.[1]

Even with all our latest scientific insights, the main question remains.[2]

Why a universe at all?

Read also ch.23 **The same applies to our inter-connected, evolving universe: it requires an explanation for its totality. Even if we know all causality *within* the world, we still do not know why all of it exists to begin with. It requires an explanation from *beyond* the universe.**

---

1 P. Davies, *God and the New Physics*, Pelican 1984, pp. 46-47.

2 P. Davies also highlights specific features of the universe that demand an explanation: the *anthropic principle*, for instance, the fact that a universe producing conscious life requires physical laws that do not deviate from ours by an extremely fine balance (to a precision of trillions times trillions times trillions of a degree), ib. p. 171; see also his books *The Edge of Infinity*, and recently *The Mind of God* (London 1980, 1994) in which he says: "From a study of the universe we can see that 'we are truly meant to be here.' "

13.

We meet God's creative 'mind' in the ocean of truth that surrounds us.

When Bertrand Russell published his *Principia Mathematica* in 1913, a close friend wrote him a letter pointing out a telling mistake. Russell checked his calculations, and found that his friend was right. What should he do? The book had taken him long to complete. He surmised that the mistake would pass unnoticed by the vast majority of readers. Could he let it go? He agonised about it for an entire night.

By the next morning he had reached his decision. He re-called all printed copies and revised the relevant sections. It was a matter of principle, he tells us. Since he knew that what he had written was wrong, it was his duty to correct it. He owed this obligation to Truth.

Read also ch.30

During his life, Bertrand Russell declared himself an atheist many times over. But was he?[1] One of Russell's daughters is said to have remarked that her father was a deeply religious man, with Truth as his God. I think she assessed him correctly. But a better way of putting it, might be to say that Russell touched God in Truth, even though he did not realise it.

Read also ch.34

Human knowledge advances by our attempts to find out the truth about things. It is the basis of our every day common-sense interaction with the world. It is also the fundamental principle of science. Scientific research tries to establish facts, to study things as they are. Truth is its "God."

Now, it is necessary here to reflect on the nature of Truth. Truth to be truth, must reflect reality. And we cannot *make*

---

1 Bertrand Russell grew up in stifling Puritan surroundings, as he describes in The Conquest of Happiness, *London 1940. Was he fighting the severe patriarchal God of his childhood?*

*"Floating on the ocean of truth, eh?
Well, heave anchor. You're nicked!"*

reality. We can only *discover it.* We cannot change the facts.
We have to take them as they are, whether we like them or not.
Even if we try to deny them or present them differently for
whatever purpose, we know, at the same time, that what we
say does not correspond to *the truth.*

We grasp the truth in our mind. For instance, I grasp that
the earth is round, even though it looks flat. But the roundness
of the earth is not a construction of my mind. The earth was a
globe for millions of years before human beings *discovered* it
was round. Our mind does not make something true or false.
Our mind recognises it *is* true or false.

Truth is so fundamental that it encompasses even the universe as such. Time and space are elements *of* our universe.
But truth goes *beyond* our universe. For what we think about
the whole universe is also either true or not; and was true or
not even before we knew of it.

Moreover, our mind itself, and its ability to grasp truth are an important reality in the universe. Why should we favour an explanation of the universe through a 'bottom-up,' i.e., purely physicalist causality? Does our own mental experience not point to a valid 'top-down' causality?[1]

The answer seems inescapable. We float on an ocean of truth. Truth is an absolute aspect of reality and of being. And as such truth points to God, both as the Ultimate Reality that validates truth and the 'mind' that makes everything knowable.

In a nutshell, the argument from truth to God is this: our deep-rooted conviction that truth is a matter of discovery and not invention is best accounted for – especially in its fullest scope, that is to say, including the truths of mind as well as of matter – on the supposition of an infinite creative Mind that makes things what they are and preserves them as what they are for us to discover.[2]

Read ch.38 & ch.40

Truth, therefore, links us to God. It is from God that truth derives its immutable nature and its knowability. Sir Isaac Newton, who formulated the laws of gravity and who also was a deeply religious man, stated:

"I do not know what I appear to the world, but to myself I seem to have been only a boy playing on the seashore, and diverting myself in now and then finding a smoother pebble or a prettier shell than ordinary, whilst the great ocean of truth lay all undiscovered before me."[3]

---

1 J. R. Searle, Minds, Brains and Science, London 1984.

2 B. Hebblethwaite, *The Ocean of Truth,* Cambridge 1988, p. 110; see also M. L. Diamond, "A Modern Theistic Argument," Modern Theology 6 (1990) pp. 287-293.

3 D. Brewster, *Memoirs of the Life, Writings and Discoveries of Sir Isaac Newton,* vol 2, London 1855, re-issued 1974, ch. 27.

14.

We feel in our bones
our total dependence *in being*.

The concept of dependence *in being* at first seems complex and abstruse. Allow me to elucidate it and to explain some related philosophical terms.

Think of our various degrees of dependence. We depend on our boss for job security and financial income. We depend on our parents for the genes we have inherited. We depend on farmers to grow our food and on the police to protect us from criminals. All these are partial forms of dependence. Dependence *in being* refers to a more basic dependence: dependence in the very fact of our existence and in being what we are.

We also need to reflect on different degrees of 'being.' We need to distinguish imaginary, contingent and necessary being.

You may have read the stories of Superman, the champion who was born from an alien father and mother, and who flies through the air from one part of the globe to another to rescue people in need. For many teenagers he is a hero whose character they imagine in great detail. Yet, he does not actually exist. He is only *a fictitious being*.

Now think of Winston Churchill. He was not fictitious. He actually existed. But on reflection we realise that his existence was not of itself necessary. He was born of a fortuitous meeting of his parents. He studied, fought as a soldier, engaged in diplomacy and politics, wrote books. Thousands of random events made him eventually the great leader he was. Nothing of this happened of necessity, including his very existence. We express this by saying that Curchill was only *a contingent being*.

"Your contingency plan had better be good, Winnie — or they'll make you contingent!"

Every object or person within our universe is contingent. Everything we know needs an explanation, not only for its particular properties (which are explained by physical causes), but for its *being*. Our vision of this is obscured because we usually focus attention on how something depends on another thing in immediate causality. So we move from one link to another link in a long chain. What we overlook is that not only each link, but the whole chain needs support. Somewhere there must be a peg that supports the whole of its weight, otherwise it would drop to the floor. The peg supports the whole chain and every one of its links.

The same is true of the universe. Everything in it is contingent. Even an infinite series of contingent beings cannot hold the whole chain of the universe in being. For that we need

Read also ch.23

a reality that possesses being of its own, a *necessary being*. That necessary being is God.

The origin of *being*

The strength of this argument is increased by the fact that it has been independently developed by philosophers and mystics in many separate parts of the world. The terminology may differ. The substance of the argument remains the same.

This how Chuang Tzu, of Ch'i-Yuan in China during the 4th century BC, describes it.

"If no one else exists, I don't exist.
If I didn't exist, I could not perceive.
I am close to the truth, but I don't know why.
There must be some primal force, but I cannot find any
evidence.
I believe it acts, but I cannot see it.
I can feel it, but it remains intangible."[1]

"Tao possesses reality and substance.
It can be given; not received.
It can be obtained; not seen.
It is its own source and origin.
It existed before heaven and earth;
yes from all eternity.
It makes spirits and gods divine;
makes heaven and earth to be born."[2]

Though he is using other words, Chuang Tzu's thought is plain. The universe needs an explanation because it is contingent. It could exist or not exist. It is dependent in being. However, the reality it ultimately depends on, must be a necessary being, namely divinity, the Tao.

---

1   Chuang Tzu, *Sayings*, 2,3.
2   Chuang Tzu, ib. 6,1.

Agnostics often state that proving that a Creator exists because the universe cannot make itself, does not help us. For then the question airses: who made the Creator? The objection shows a complete lack of understanding the argument. The universe requires a Creator because it is *contingent.* If the Reality that created it, is also contingent, the argument repeats itself. But ultimately it will require *a necessary being,* a being that is not made, that exists in its own right, that is: Being itself.

Fifteen hundred years ago Indian philosophers had also come to the same insight.

In the beginning, my dear, there was Being alone, and nothing else besides.

Some people say: "In the beginning there was non-being alone, with nothing else besides. From that non-being, being was produced."

But how, indeed, my dear, could it be thus? says the teacher.

How could being be produced from non-being?

On the contrary, my dear, in the beginning there was Being alone, with nothing else besides.

All creatures, my dear, have their root in Being.

They have Being as their foundation, Being as their support.[1]

In other words: God as the necessary Being, the foundation of being, the ground of being, is the source of being for all that exists.

The great philosophers of the Middle Ages spent much time and energy refining the argument. Its classical formulation may sound abstract. Basically it remains as valid as ever:

We find things in nature that are possible to be and not to be, since we find they are generated and cor-

---

1 *Chandogya Upanishad* VI, 2,2; 8,6.

rupted, and consequently, it is possible for them to be or not to be.

But it is impossible for such (contingent) things always to exist; for that which can not-be, sometimes is not.

Therefore if everything can not-be, then at one time there was nothing in existence, because that which does not exist begins to exist only through something already existing.

*Therefore, if at one time nothing was in existence, it would have been impossible for **anything** to have begun to exist; and thus even now nothing would be inexistence – which is absurd.*

Therefore, not all things are merely possible.

There must exist something the existence of which is necessary – This all people speak of as God.[1]

Few of us can be professional philosophers. The question thus arises: is the argument of dependence *in being* no more than an academic exercise, reserved for the privileged few?

Awareness that life is a gift

The answer is: no. In a more direct form we know the truth of it in our bones. At crucial points in our life, all of us become aware of our smallness and brittleness. As human beings, we are severely *dependent*.[2] Basically, we have not made ourselves. We could not choose to be black or white, a woman or a man, to be intelligent or just middle of the road. Our situation of dependence shows itself in unhappy as well as happy circumstances.

---

1   Thomas Aquinas (1224- 1274 AD), *Summa Contra Gentiles*, I, ch. 12-12; III, ch.29; see also the modern discussion in J. Macquarrie, *Principles of Christian Theology*, London 1977, pp. 117-122.

2   H. Richter points out that Western society tends to argue away and smother our basic human limitation, including the possibility of suffering. Our boasts of greatness, which are contradicted by our experience, introduce neurosis into our culture. This leads to psychological break down of individuals and social dictatorships; *Der Gotteskomplex*, Hamburg 1979, pp. 29, 40-41, 63.

Our intrinsic human limitedness may make itself felt when a close relationship breaks down; or a loved person dies, or illness strikes us, or we fail badly in spite of our tireless struggles. Perhaps, we find ourselves in a personal crisis. On such occasions it is not just the particular problem that hits us, but a sudden realization that we are, after all, *just human.* There is only so much we can do, and no more.

Read also ch.49

The same realization may dawn on us in just the opposite kind of experience. We may feel extremely happy because of a wonderful partner, or the birth of a child. We may be elated by a breath taking view, a magnificent painting, an enchanting piece of music. We may feel the thrill of having done some creative work. And we suddenly are conscious of the fact that, in spite of our own involvement, in all this we have received *a gift.* We feel that, in spite of our smallness, we are privileged to have been given the experience.

Read also ch.56

Read also ch.60

Awareness of our radical dependence is another way in which our contingency of being manifests itself. It unmistakably points to a higher power on which we ultimately depend. Both our fragility and the 'gifts' we receive, come from God. And love is one such gift.

15.

We touch God in love,
and in whatever concerns us most.

However necessary abstract reasoning can be at times, it often fails to convince. It is as if part of the evidence is lacking. It reminds me of the story of an American scientist who took part in the development of the first atomic bomb.

Read also ch.7 & ch.30 When the ethics of designing such a destructive device were discussed, he saw no problem. It was just a question of clear reasoning, he said. If we make bombs, it makes no difference in principle whether they kill a hundred people in one go, or a million. But then he learnt that his own brother, who had fought in the Philippines, had been transferred to Japan as a prisoner of war. Suddenly the whole perspective changed. The decision now became personal.

Our argument about *being* takes on a new dimension when we grasp that we are talking about something very personal. The mystery is our existence. And our existence includes all the people and things that are meaningful to us: our close family and friends, our life's work, our desires and fears, our most cherished ambitions.

To understand what God means, ask yourself: What do I really care about? What matters most in my life? What am I really concerned about? What do I take with absolute seriousness? What would I be ready to suffer or even die for? *Whatever stirs you deeply – in that reality you are touching the reality of God.*

I will work this out through a powerful example: our admiration for tenderness and love.

Our present secular society is deeply torn by contradictory values. On the one hand, we subscribe to principles of human rights and of respect for the environment. On the other hand, many people adopt a mechanistic view of the universe, in which all is dominated by purely physical forces.

The end result is bare, merciless co-existence. Soldiers are trained in ruthless combat, involving even nuclear and chemical weapons. Politicians ruthlessly disregard the needs of Third World nations. Police officers brutally impose law and order. Banks and businesses pursue a heartless economy in which human beings are just pawns, and in which scarce resources are savagely depleted for short-term gains. Where is mercy, love, respect for what is precious, though delicate?

The answer is that, in a mechanistic universe governed by survival of what is fittest, there is no convincing justification for values such as kindness, love and self sacrifice. What is left are such flimsy motives as: instinctive behaviour, the mutual benefit of cooperation, emotional ties, and so on. There is no compelling *rational* reason for keeping a cantankerous parent alive, for nursing a mentally handicapped child or for supporting Brazilian natives whose primitive ways of life are threatened.

Read ch.34 & ch.37

If mercy and love are real values in the universe, we thereby acknowledge other priorities, and another primacy of being. Love only becomes meaningful if love was meant to be there. Love finds its justification in principles that transcend our narrow existence. Love, too, is an absolute and so it points to God.

Read also ch.56, ch.57, ch.58 & ch.59

The thoughts of God

The Hindu scholar S.Radhakrishnan, who served as President of India (1962 to 1967), recalls the ancient saying in the *Bhavagadgita*: "Whatsoever being in our world is endowed with glory and grace and vigour, know that to have sprung as a fragment of God's splendour." He adds:

> *Truth, beauty and goodness are absolute values. They point to God. They are the thoughts of God and we think after him.*

Truth, beauty and goodness are not existent objects like the things that are true, beautiful and good, and yet they are more real than the persons, things and relations to which they are ascribed.

Truth, beauty and goodness, though not known by the senses or reason, are apprehended by intuition, or faith as believers would put it.

They are grasped as being a reflection of the being and essence of God.[1]

The important thing is not to make God small, not to picture him to ourselves as a Santa Claus sitting high up on a cloud. He/she/it is overwhelmingly greater and all-pervasive than anything we can imagine, and the best way to *sense* this presence is to probe it in depth.

Read ch.17

The name of the infinite and inexhaustible depth and ground of all being is *God*. That depth is what the word *God* means. And if that word has not much meaning for you, translate it, and speak of the depths of your life, or the source of your being, of your ultimate concern, of what you take seriously without any reservation.

Read also ch.29

Perhaps, in order to do so, you must forget everything traditional that you have learned about God, perhaps even the word itself. For if you know that God means depth, you know much about him.

You cannot then call yourself an atheist or unbeliever. For you cannot think or say: "Life has no depth! Life is shallow. Being itself is surface only." If you would say this in complete earnestness, you would be an atheist; but otherwise you are not.[2]

1 S. Radhakrishnan, *Recovery of Faith*, Delhi 1955, pp. 82-83; *An Idealist View of Life*, London 1961, pp. 157-158.
2 P. Tillich, *The New Being*, London 1964, pp. 152-160.

16.

Believing that the world is 'created' is not an abdication of common sense or sound reason.

From time immemorial our ancestors have believed that the world we live in finds its ultimate explanation in a divine reality. Whatever religion they belonged to, in whichever part of the globe they lived, human beings were convinced that the visible world they saw was under the control of divine power They believed our world was *created*.

There are sound reasons to show that their insight was basically correct, as we have seen. Our monumental scientific discoveries do not resolve the riddle of our universe. Rather, they heighten its mystery. We did not make ourselves, either as individuals, as a human race, or even as an evolving cosmos. We are *created,* in the sense that for our existence we owe everything to an overriding outside power which, for the moment, we will call God.

Read ch.12 to ch.15

Believing in our being created is not the same as being a "creationist." Creationists are a small group of fundamentalist Christians who maintain that the creation story of Genesis 1,1 - 2,4 should be taken literally. They state that the universe was created by God in six days and that all living beings were directly created by God as they are now. American creationists earned notoriety by succeeding in having the teaching of evolution banned from schools in certain North American states; till in 1968 the United States Supreme Court ruled that anti-evolution laws are unconstitutional.

Creationists refuse to accept the findings of modern science. They also misunderstand, and misrepresent, the teaching of the Bible. In reality, whether the world came to its present state in 4000 years or 15 billion years, whether life existed from the beginning or evolved gradually, makes no difference to the need of a Creator. On the contrary, the longer the uni-

Read ch.22

verse has existed and the more complex it is, the more it requires a Creator to keep it in existence.

Awareness of creation

Read ch.12 to ch.15

Not only are there convincing arguments that prove that our world did not bring forth itself, that it depends on a creative divine reality; what is more, this dependence on God is a dimension of our life that is not difficult to become deeply aware of, once we have discovered it.

Allow me to use a comparison. Many people go through life without paying much attention to gravity. They learned about gravity in school. They also meet its reality in everyday life: when carrying objects, when walking up a slope, when balancing cups on a tray, and so on. They just take it for granted.

What they do not realise is that their everyday gravity is not just determined by the bulk of the earth on which we live, but by an immensely heavy iron ball in the centre of the earth.

The outer layers of the earth, the so-called upper and lower mantle, are made of stone. The iron core starts from a depth of 3000 kilometers and goes down all the way to 6500 kilometers. Its composition is 90% iron and 10% nickel. In addition to its natural weight, the metal is highly compressed. The average pressure in the core is 300 gigapascals, which equals 3 million atmospheres. It is this clump of iron in the earth that makes gravity on its surface 81 times greater than on the moon, and its density three times greater than that of the Sun.

But realise this: no one has actually *seen* the iron core. Even with our most powerful drilling towers, we have not bored down to depths exceeding 12 kilometers. We know of the iron core through many complex calculations. Seismic waves recorded after earthquakes bounce off the border of the core in a characteristic way. The mass of the earth can be measured astronomically, and its excessive weight requires a heavy component. The existence of the iron core can thus be demonstrated, even though no one has *seen* it.[1]

Not many people will study the scientific arguments that prove the core's existence. Most leave this to geologists. But all of us feel the pull of gravity. Gravity is there, whether we advert to it or not. When we become aware of the iron core, we discover a new dimension. We begin to realise that we relate to the centre of the earth in a far more continuous and dramatic way than we had thought.

The same applies to our dependence on a Creative Reality. We are constantly under his/her/its pull, whether we advert to it or not.

We must say that God is present in all things, not, indeed, as part of their nature, but as an agent who acts on it and touches it with his power. . . .

God causes being in things, and he does so not only when they begin to exist but as long as they are conserved in being.

As long then as a thing has existence, so long must God be present to it. But being, that is the act of existence, is the reality which is most intimate in each thing and which is most profoundly in each thing, since it is the absolute basis for everything that is in a thing.

Hence God is continuously present in everything – and intimately so.[2]

Accepting creation should result in a new awareness, a recognition of God's pull in our daily life, a realization that God supports us in the core of our being.

---

1 R. Jeanloz, "The Nature of the Earth's Core," *Annual Review of Earth and Planetary Sciences* 18 (1990) pp. 357 - 386; J. A. Jacobs, *The Deep Interior of the Earth,* Chapman & Hall 1992.

2 Thomas Aquinas, *Summa Theologica* I, q.7, a.1, c.; see R. J. Henle, "The Presence of God," *Spiritual Life* 29 (1983) pp. 208 -217.

17.

We should drop the awkward image of a supernatural Creator, not the reality of creation.

For primitive tribespeople the whole of nature was pervaded by unearthly power. Gods and goddesses, elves, demons, gnomes, fairies, and sprites inhabited every nook and cranny of their forest. Keeping these ethereal beings happy was their main concern, especially the chief God or Goddess who was often believed to live on a high mountain.

With the rise of urbanised civilisations, religion too became more refined and sophisticated.

Starting from around 800 BC, thinkers in many countries revised their concept of God. Abandoning the crude "magical" ideas of the past, they formulated theories which recognised the absolute *transcendence*, i.e., the otherness, of the Supreme God. We find roughly parallel definitions of this transcendence in ancient China, India, Persia, Mesopotamia, Egypt, Palestine and Greece.

This new approach led to what I will call *the two-tier world view*. In brief it comes to this: above our own, earthly world lies heaven, the world of God. God is imagined as sitting on his throne in his palace, high above the blue sky, surrounded by angels and heavenly beings who form his court. God is the architect who designed and created the earthly world. As its immediate ruler, he frequently leaves his mark on our earthly world by revealing messages and by dispensing blessings and curses, to help his friends and punish his enemies.

The God of the two-tier world is often referred to as the "supernatural God," since he inhabits the heavenly realm, the "super nature" that lies above ordinary nature. He is also known as the "interventionist God" on account of his frequent

interventions in our world order — by revelations, miracles, providential care and so on.

Traditional Christian language presents God as such a supernatural God in a two-tier world. Both the Hebrew Scriptures and the New Testament use this language. It is also the vocabulary handled in worship. God is addressed as the Almighty Father, Creator of heaven and earth, whom we beg to cast his eyes on us, his earthly children. God is thought to protect us from evil and shower us with blessings. He cares for us from his exalted position, above.

Now the use of such language is quite legitimate as long as we remember that it only expresses *an image* of God, not the actual reality. But until the beginning of this century most believers, including Christians, took the two-tier world and its presiding God literally, as if they expressed factual entities. The super world of heaven was assumed to be a real place outside and above earthly space. God was accepted to be a real supernatural Person, like us except that he was infinitely greater than us in every respect.

It is the image of this supernatural, interventionist God that is largely responsible for our generation's reluctance to accept God.[1]

For we know now that the world progresses by evolution, without interventions by a supernatural Creator. Nor do we need an interventionist Manager God in our day-to-day lives. When farmland is dry we do not pray for rain, we install irrigation. When we run up a fever, we do not expect a miraculous cure, we call on a doctor. The supernatural, interventionist God is dead in our technological age.

Read also ch.40 & ch.58

But does that mean there is no God at all? Rejecting *an image* of God is one thing, rejecting the reality of God is quite another. If the two-tier world view is proving untenable, why should this disprove God?

The inadequacy of the supernatural God image shows that in the past we have underrated God. If God exists, he/she/it is totally different from our world. The new images that are emerging in contemporary understanding point in this direction. God is *the God Beyond*, i.e., beyond the supernatural God. God is the Ground of our Being, our deepest Self, the underlying Life Force that supports and embraces all.

Read also ch.4 & ch.42

Whenever we think or speak about God, we should always remember the limitations of the images implied.

---

1   Read A. Freeman, *God in Us*, London 1993.

Images are just images!

The well-known artist Réné Magritte painted a smoking pipe, with underneath the caption *Ceci n'est pas une pipe – This is not a pipe!* When questioned about this, he replied: "You can't stuff tobacco in this pipe, so it isn't really a pipe at all. The image is not the thing it represents."

We should think of God as *the creative force* **behind and in everything, rather than as a supernatural Architect or an interventionist Maintenance Man.**

Read also ch.28 & ch.44

18.

If it is true that we are being created in God's image, we have found the deepest source of our self-worth.

A friend of mine who returned from volunteer work abroad, joined a London-based Charity. For a fraction of the salary her qualifications would entitle her to, she agreed to counsel people who are in trouble. Since she needed a place to live, she approached a bank for a mortgage.

"What are you worth?," the bank manager wanted to know.

She soon realised this meant the sum total of her assets, savings and regular earnings. These amounted to little. Her request for a mortgage was refused: she wasn't *worth* it. "I hope I'm worth a little more in God's eyes," she said to me.

Now we all may feel a measure of sympathy with the banker who, after all, was only doing his job. The question the incident raises, however, is real. What *are* we worth?

Few of us are silly enough to imagine that the real value of our life is written on bank notes. The marketing consultant who demands £500 + VAT for half a day's service, puts a price on his time. But the same man will probably gladly spend an entire night nursing his sick baby daughter, changing her nappies and carrying her in his arms, without even thinking of payment. There is more to life than money.

Psychologists tell us that the dominant drive in our lives is the need of self esteem. Yes, physical security, food and sex are basic cravings. But our survival as a human being, as a knowing, searching, conscious individual, depends on something else: on finding our own value. The most important thing for all of us is to know that we are worth something, that we mean something to other people, that our existence makes a

"What am I worth? – Let's see – a cardboard semi-detached – three cigarette butts – a bottle of meths – and unbounded optimism!"

difference, that we, as individuals, are worth knowing and loving. The supreme law of life, as Alfred Adler put it, can be summed up in one commandment: "Thou shalt not diminish the sense of worth of thyself."[1]

People want to fulfil their fullest self, to realise their potential, leave an impact on the world, make something worthwhile of their life. Extensive research on European values systems bears this out in two principal spheres of activity: the family and work.

---

1 H. Ansbacher, *The Individual Psychology of Alfred Adler*, Basic Books 1946, p. 358.

What do we ask from life?

In marriage, for instance, though an adequate income (37%) and good housing (34%) are welcomed, most people attach a higher priority to values that affirm the self: to having a partner who is faithful (84%), who shows respect (84%) and tolerance (79%), and with whom one enjoys a healthy sexual relationship (63%). It is as if people say: As long as I am recognised as a person, as long as I am loved and can give love, my marriage is a success.

The same approach can be observed in people's attitude to work. Good pay (69%) and job security (57%) rank high as priorities, for obvious reasons. But generous holidays (25%), absence of pressure (25%) and even favourable working hours (40%) are considered as of less importance. People prefer a job that stretches their potential:

"an exciting job" (62%);

"a job that meets my abilities" (53%);

"a job in which I feel I can achieve something" (53%);

"a job which gives me opportunities to use my initiative" (47%);

"a responsible job, that is useful to society" (44%).

In other words: people want meaningful jobs.[1]

Read also ch.9 & ch.11 Self worth and meaning are closely related. When people measure their worth by their family and their job, they are saying to themselves: "I mean a lot to my husband and my children," or "What I do is meaningful to my colleagues, my pupils, my customers, society at large, and so on."

In fact, we spend a lot of time throughout the day reviewing and assessing the daily events that give us, or deny us, self esteem, that make us feel approved or rejected. We are so en-

---

1 S. Ashford and N. Timms, *What Europe Thinks. A Study of Western European Values*, Aldershot 1992, pp. 50-54, 74-77.

"Shift your feet, Mr. Coward. You're not the only important one 'round here!"

grossed with this that psychologists call it the 'inner newsreel,' the endless testing and rehearsing of what is going on between us and other people. "Yes, I'm worth something. No, I'm not."

But what if relationships at home turn sour and if my job collapses? Do I have any worth *in myself*? The playwright Noel Coward stated: "My sense of my own importance to myself is tremendous. I am all I have: to work with, to play with, to suffer and to enjoy. In the final analysis it's not the eyes of others that I'm wary of, but my own." What am I worth in my own eyes?

Underneath the immediate relationships that give meaning to our life lurk deeper questions.

Who gives me my worth?

The constant harangue that we address to one another: "notice me," "love me," "esteem me," "value me," may seem debasing and ignoble. But when we tally the sum of these efforts, the excruciating earnestness of them, the eternal grinding out of the inner newsreel, we can see that something really big is going on – really vital.

When you pose the question: "Who am I? What is the value of my life?," you are really asking something more pointed: that you be recognised as an object of primary value in the universe. Nothing less."[1]

Am I an object of primary value in the universe? This is the real issue that is at stake. It evokes the question of *ultimate* meaning, and thus of religion.

Read also ch.39 Seen through the eyes of religion, we derive our ultimate worth from our occupying a unique position in a created universe. The Bible teaches that God made man and woman in his own image. *God created the human being in his image, in his own likeness he created them, male and female he created them.*[2]

Read also ch.58 **In other words, we carry in us the imprint of an infinite, mysterious, timeless Reality. We reflect 'God.' Surviving in demanding circumstances, through our consciousness and free will, we are like gods and goddesses ourselves. And we enjoy the love and friendship of the mysterious Origin of all that exists.**

---

1   E. Becker, *The Birth and Death of Meaning*, Penguin 1971, p. 84.

2   *Genesis* 1,27.

19.

Creation presents us
with a larger frame of meaning.

Reacting against the shortcomings of traditional religion, some thinkers in our own time have formulated a radical alternative. Professing themselves *atheists* or *agnostics*,[1] they adhere to a philosophy of life which is usually referred to as *humanism.*

Humanists start from the assumption that human beings are on their own. God does not exist. Also, there is no sequel to life on earth. "The life we live now is all there is." We have to take responsibility for our own life and for that of other people. Human values stand central. That is all we live for.[2]

Read also ch.34

Humanists are willing to accept that life is meaningless, futile and absurd when seen on a wider level. We are told to accept this fact manfully, to acknowledge it rather than lapse again into the childish comforts of religion. Bertrand Russell, a great mathematician and philosopher, as well as an avowed atheist, urges us to disown the gods of savages; to reject the slavery of those who are doomed to worship Time, Fate, Death and the other forces of nature; to shake off all cowardice and face our final destruction with courage.

Here are some extracts from his famous essay *A Free Man's Worship*:

- *"The world which science presents to us is purposeless and void of meaning."*

- *"Man is the product of causes that had no prevision of the end they were achieving; his origin, his*

---

1 *Atheists* are people who state unequivocally that no God exists; *agnostics* declare that they have insufficient evidence for either the existence or non-existence of divinity.

2 V. Gordon Childe, *Man Makes Himself*, New York 1951; H. J. Blackman, *Humanism*, Harmondsworth 1968.

> *growth, his hopes and fears, his loves and his be-*
> *liefs, are but the outcome of accidental collocations*
> *of atoms; no fire, no heroism, no intensity of thought*
> *and feeling, can preserve an individual life beyond*
> *the grave; all the labours of the ages, all the devo-*
> *tion, all the inspiration, all the noonday brightness*
> *of human genius, are destined to extinction."*

> • *"Brief and powerless is man's life; on him and on*
> *his race the slow, sure doom falls pitiless and dark.*
> *Blind to good and evil, reckless of destruction, om-*
> *nipotent matter rolls on its relentless way."*[1]

Cliffhanger tension

Another atheist, Edward Klemke, also advocates that "we make the best of a bad job." He sees his experience of life reflected in the story of a Syrian merchant. The man led his camel through the desert dreaming of water, date palms and shade. The man and his animal arrived at a dark abyss. The man leant over to look into the gaping ravine. Suddenly the camel lurched forward, with teeth showing and protruding eyes, and pushed him over the edge.

Fortunately for the Syrian, his clothes were caught in a rosebush. He hung suspended over the ravine. When he looked down he saw at the bottom a panther waiting to devour him. Over his head he heard two mice chewing away at the roots of the bush so that it began to sag more and more. "In spite of this desperate situation, the Syrian was thralled to the point of utmost contentment by a rose which adorned the bush and wafted its fragrance into his face."[2]

Edward Klemke finds that this story expresses both the agony and thrill of human existence. All of us hang by the thread of a few vanishing years over the bottomless pit of death, destruction and nothingness, he says. We cannot deny

---

1 B. Russell, 'A Free Man's Worship' in *Mysticism and Logic*, New York 1951, pp.44-54.
2 R. Hertz, *Chance and Symbol*, Chicago 1948, pp.142-143.

those stark facts. What we can do is to make the best of the fleeting moments of enjoyment that come our way: *"What your situation is, I cannot say. But I know that I am that Syrian, and that I am hanging over the pit. My doom is inevitable and swiftly approaching. If, in these few moments that are yet mine, I can find no rose to respond to, or rather, if I have lost the ability to respond, then I shall moan and curse my fate with a howl of bitter agony.*

But if I can, in these last moments, respond to a rose – or to a philosophical argument or theory of physics, or to a Scarlatti sonata, or to the touch of a human hand – I say, if I can so respond and can thereby transform an external and fatal event into a moment of conscious insight and significance, then I shall go down without hope or appeal yet passionately triumphant and with joy."[1]

This may sound like the brave talk of a man condemned to death, but it does offer meaning. It substitutes the *ultimate meaning* proposed by religion, with *immediate meaning* here and now. The *large meaning* is denied; a *small meaning* retained: the joy of a significant fleeting moment. *Read also ch.11 & ch.59*

There is nothing 'small' about immediate meaning in itself. It makes good sense. The ancient Romans coined the expression *Carpe Diem*, "make the most of every day," to instil a positive attitude in people facing personal loss or financial disaster.[2] But then as now it may hide a deep pessimism. And the question remains: are we really hanging over a bottomless pit? Could it be that Klemke's 'rose' reveals the wider dimensions of ultimate reality uncovered by religion?

Let us listen carefully to what Klemke says. *"If I can respond to a rose – or to a philosophical argument or theory*

---

1 E. D. Klemke, "Living without appeal," in E. D. Klemke, *Reflections and Perspectives,* The Hague 1974, p. 109; see also E. D. Klemke (ed), *The Meaning of Life,* Oxford 1981.
2 "Pluck the day. Rely on tomorrow as little as you can"; Horace (65-8 BC), *Odes* I,2,8.

"Carpe diem, chaps! Carpe diem!"

of physics, or to a Scarlatti sonata, or to the touch of a human hand. . . ."

Is it not striking that Klemke mentions precisely those human experiences that disclose deeper realities?

A philosophical argument or theory of physics can, indeed, thrill us precisely because they concern factual truth. Truth is fascinating. Truth draws its power from the nature of creation and compels us to assent. The unchangeability of Truth derives from God.

Read ch.13

The same applies to the other examples mentioned by Klemke. He is transported by a Scarlatti sonata, or the intimacy of love. Again, these are experiences which carry meaning because they take us outside ourselves to the level of transcendence and timelessness. What else are people saying when they tell us that music lifts them to the highest heaven, that music opens a vista on the universe, that music is the human incarnation of the divine force of creation? The same, and more, can be said about genuine human intimacy.

Read ch.15

In other words, Klemke's 'rose' is either just a drug, a momentary escape, a pain killer – and then it demeans rather than ennobles. Or it puts him in contact with 'ultimate meaning' and that would explain why it makes him come out triumphant in spite of suffering and death.

Read ch.52

On what grounds do I exclude a universal, ultimate context of meaning? Am I sure that all that exists is the physical world I see? Do I do justice to myself by reducing my self worth to success in coping with day-to-day events? Will death put an irrevocable end to all I am? Precisely because human life is so precious, we should explore the fundamental questions carefully.

Read ch.58 & ch.59

20.

Being aware of the creative dimension of life improves life's 'wholeness.'

With psychologists, we may distinguish four levels of meaning, roughly corresponding to our basic needs. We can see them as an ever widening horizon of our world.

The first, most intimate and basic level, is our **personal core.** It is the level of what one is oneself, one's *true* self, one's special gifts and talents, what one feels oneself to be deep down inside, the person one talks to when alone, the secret hero of one's inner sanctuary.

The second or next deepest level is our **social range of friendships**. It represents the most immediate extension of one's self to a select few intimate others: one's husband or wife, one's children, friends, relatives, perhaps even one's pets.

The third and next deepest level we may call our **secular role**. It consists of commitments we undertake at a greater personal distance and of wider implication: the company we work for, the party, the nation, science, social welfare, humanity.

The fourth and deepest level of meaning is our **link to the Sacred**. It is the invisible and mysterious level of power, the inside of nature, our being part of creation, our relationship to God.[1]

Now it is obvious that people live on all these levels at once, but each one of us assigns importance to one source of meaning rather than to another.

In the extreme individualism of our western culture, there are those that remain stuck at the surface level. They involve

---

1 E. Becker, *The Birth and Death of Meaning,* Harmondsworth 1971, pp. 184 - 192.

themselves with the pursuit of pleasure and physical health to such a degree that it culminates in a self-centered narcissism. "I must pamper myself in such a way that I do not need anyone else to make me happy." This will inevitably lead to an agonising intellectual and emotional void, but for the moment it satisfies animal nature. What is lacking is a truly *human* quality of living.[1]

Read ch.11

Others concentrate on their family, deriving almost all satisfaction from close and intimate relationships. Again others devote themselves entirely to a cause, at great personal cost and to the exclusion of practically every other concern. A final group attach such great value to the sacred dimension that they sacrifice everything else in its pursuit.

Well-integrated personalities derive their self-worth from a healthy mix of all sources of meaning. At least, that is how it used to be. The erosion of the religious dimension has left many people trapped within small horizons, and therefore vulnerable and confused.

The question therefore arises: what is the actual source of our self-worth? Is it nothing more than a moment of bravery in a battle against sure destruction, no more than a snatching of small, immediate meaning? Or does it lie in our integration into a larger frame of timeless and transcendent values?

Read also ch.59

This is not a superfluous question. It is a question of life or death. Seven out of every thousand deaths in Britain are suicides, mostly by people who give up. Many more quietly despair, sinking ever deeper into a quagmire of loneliness, frustration, absurdity, a sense of waste, an abyss of nothingness.

Family and friends can let us down. The cause we live for can crumble, or turn against us. The religious dimension can

---

1   C. Lasch, *The Culture of Narcissism*, New York 1979; G. Lipovetsky, *L'ère du Vide*, Paris 1983; M. Gauchet, *Le désenchantement du monde, une histoire politique de la réligion*, Paris 1985.

liberate us to see things in a wider perspective, and to face overwhelming odds with a sense of hope.

Read also ch.10

I know that the wrong kind of religion can also be a hindrance. It can fill people's minds with superstition and cripple their progress through imposing nonsensical taboos and rules, just as the wrong kind of medicine can worsen the illness. But the existence of bad medicine does not disqualify medicine as such. Moreover, religion is much more than a cure against ills.

Read also ch.58 & ch.64

Good religion enhances enormously the quality of our life It underpins and enlarges the value of our family relationships and secular commitments. It provides real meaning to self sacrifice and love. It makes us aware of the immense mystery surrounding our cosmos and brings us face to face with ultimate Reality. In this way it establishes our real worth on a cosmic level.

Jumping out of our well

The Chinese philosopher Chuang Tzu (4th cent. BC) tells the parable of the Yellow River. Like most people, he tells us, it begins its life being ignorant and presumptuous. Thousands of wild torrents pour their water into it, so that it swells into a mighty stream. The river laughs, proud of its achievement. Boastful and haughty it gushes its way downstream to the coast. There he sees the ocean and his face falls. He tries to measure its vast expanse and fails. He offers his apologies. And with good reason.

Of all the waters in the world
the Ocean is the greatest.
Though all rivers pour into it, day and night,
it never fills up.
Though it returns its water day and night,
it never runs empty.
Its level does not drop in summer.

It does not rise at the time of floods.
No other water can match it.[1]

When like the Yellow River we become aware of the *Tao*, of the divine dimension,[2] we are overwhelmed by its mystery and magnitude.

Perhaps, it will frighten us at the beginning. Then the realization will dawn on us that the *Tao* is not hostile. It is the infinite, universal, creative force that carries us, and that fills us from within. It has always been there, though we were not aware of it. We did not know it because we were trapped in a kitchen-and-garden horizon.

Chuang Tzu concludes by saying: "Can you talk about the ocean to a frog in a well?"

---

1 Chuang Tzu, *Sayings*, 17,1.
2 This is how Chuang Tzu defines the Tao: "A mysterious reality, complete before heaven and earth, silent and void, standing on its own and unchanging, ever present, never surpassed, the mother of the ten thousand things. I do not know its name; therefore I call it *Tao*" (25,1).

21.

"Has evolution not disproved creation?"

It may look as if the universe was organised by an outside Mind. We know now that all of it can be explained through evolution. Physical evolution produced galaxies and stars from the initial explosion, the Big Bang. Biological evolution produced complicated forms of life through chemical processes and the struggle for survival. There is no need of a Creator.[1]

The objector has a point. In the past, the hand of God was seen in specific examples of plant or animal design which we now recognise to have been shaped by evolution. Birds do not fly because God sketched wings on an imaginary drawing board in heaven. It was aerodynamics that helped animals jump from trees, and this paved the way, very gradually, through a process of genetic mutation and elimination of the unfit, to all the marvellous features of flight: the shape of the wings, the superfine structure of strong, flexible feathers, the correct balancing of body weight.

I want to state this very clearly. Modern believers accept wholeheartedly all the physical, chemical and natural processes that moulded our galaxies and that drove the evolution of life. Our own emergence as human beings was part of those processes. But that does not diminish the necessity of postulating creation.

Everything *inside* the universe is subject to the laws of nature. However, these laws do not explain the existence of the *Read ch.12* universe itself, nor why it follows *these* laws and not other ones.

Formerly people imagined that God designed each plant and animal separately and that he created them one by one. We know better now. We understand now how the whole universe

---

1 R. Dawkins, *The Blind Watchmaker,* Harmondsworth 1988.

"I told him he wasn't evolutionwise aerodynamically ready yet, but he wouldn't listen!"

is interrelated, how new species of life are formed in response to pressures and opportunities.

But we still have no explanation for the existence of our marvelously integrated, steadily evolving universe. In fact, the mystery has deepened. Without a creative force present in the process, evolution could not happen.

22.

"Does the Bible not contradict evolution?"

It is easy for you to say that evolution and creation go together. But Scripture teaches another kind of creation. According to the book of Genesis, God created the world in six days, making the sun, the moon, the plants, the animals, the fishes and human beings on separate days. You cannot be both a believer and admit evolution.

Wrong! The creation story in Genesis 1,1 - 2,3 does not teach *how* God created the world. In fact, it **never** intended to teach this, in spite of later generations of believers reading it that way. The story has a spiritual and theological purpose, not a scientific one. Spreading creation over a week was a literary device to highlight the meaning of the sabbath worship. On the seventh day people were expected to take time off to acknowledge their Creator.

Here are the first verses in a literal translation:

In the beginning God created
the heavens and the earth.
The earth was formless and void,
and darkness lay upon the face of the deep.
And God's mighty wind swept
over the face of the waters.

And God said: "Let there be light!"
and there was light.
God saw that the light was good

and God separated the light from the darkness.
God called the light Day,
but the darkness he called Night.

Evening came and morning.

That was the first day. . . .

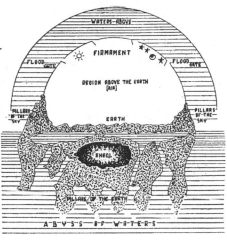

This is not a scientific account, it is poetry!

The structure of the story is clear. The world is created as a house for its human occupants. The sky is the ceiling, the firm ground the floor. The sun and moon are lights. The plants and animals are furniture and food supplies. Human beings are at the centre of the world: they are created in God's image, because they have intelligence and free will.[1]

In presenting this picture Scripture obviously follows the popular imagination of the time, as Galileo Galilei already pointed out. Scripture's purpose is spiritual, not scientific. It is interested in how we go to heaven, not how the heavens go.[2]

The purpose of the story is to teach the fact of our being created, of our depending on God; not *how* it was done. Fundamentalist Christians who still defend a six-day creation are not only scientifically out of date; they also misinterpret Scripture.

---

1   Sketch of Hebrew universe as in *Origins*, ed. L. Pereira, Poona 1964, p. 245.

2   Galileo Galilei in a letter to the Duchess of Lotharingen, 1613 AD. *Briefe zur Weltgeschichte*, ed. K. H. Peter, Munich 1964, pp. 80-82.

23.

"You may not apply the laws of causality to the whole universe!"

The principle of causality works within the universe. Yes, within the universe everything requires a causal explanation. However, the principle does not apply to the universe as such, to its totality. From the fact that every human being has a mother, it does not follow that the whole human race has a mother. Even if every soldier wears a helmet, the whole army does not wear one. The whole universe belongs to a different logical sphere.[1]

Yes, the universe does belong to another logical sphere. You are right in pointing out that causality within the universe is physical. This same kind of causality cannot cause the universe as a whole. Otherwise its physical cause would itself be part of the universe.

But, from another point of view, the objection as it stands is preposterous. It would imply that we are allowed to explore 'the reasons why' for things within the universe, but not for the universe as such. But this is precisely the most important question of all!

Moreover, this 'ultimate' question we are asking, concerns a different kind of causality, the causality of existence, of *being*. This is not the physical causality we know from our experience within the universe. Whatever is produced physically, emerges from previous energy, matter or space. We assert that the whole universe receives its *being* from a creative power, that it has been created out of nothing.[2]

---

1 B. Russell, "Debate on the Existence of God," in *Why I Am Not A Christian*, London 1957, pp. 144-168.

2 Physicists sometimes talk of fundamental particles being created out of nothing. This is improper use of language. The particles, usually in opposite positive and negative pairs, are in a different state of energy of the space-time continuum. Even a vacuum in space-time is not nothing.

"Glad tidings, Dear – Our search for contingent balls is ended!"

There you go again! Talking about the whole universe. How do we know whether what applies to objects within the universe, applies to the totality as well? Can't the universe have its own type of being?

No, it can't. Remember that we are talking about existence and reality. Why do we **exist**? This question applies equally, if not more, to the totality of the universe.

Richard Taylor explains this in a thought experiment. Imagine, he says, that you find a large strange ball in the middle of a forest. You will not doubt that it needs an explanation for its existence. For, looking at it, you see that is not a necessary thing, it is *contingent,* which means that it is there but could also not be there: it needs an explanation.

Now suppose you annihilate the forest in your imagination; or even the entire world that surrounds the ball. Suppose the ball is the only thing that is left, that it constitutes the entire physical universe. It would still remain contingent. It would still require an explanation. Its existence has not suddenly been rendered self-explanatory.

Even if it is the only thing that has ever existed in all imaginary time, it would still require an explanation.

Read also ch.12 & ch.14

Again, it matters little whether the ball is large or small, complex or simple. It would still require an explanation. What is more, it would be absurd to say that it requires an explanation for its existence if it is six feet in diameter, but that if it were as vast and complex as our universe, it would not require an explanation for its existence. Chocolate remains chocolate whether you have just one bar, or galaxies full of it.[1]

In other words: the universe requires an explanation beyond itself for its existence.

---

1 R. Taylor, *Metaphysics,* Englewood Cliffs 1983, pp. 93-94.

24.

"You accept the so-called 'proofs' for God because you *want* to believe in a God!"

I am convinced that believers have already made up their minds. They want to believe in God. That is why they will accept any 'proof,' however far-fetched or flimsy it may be!

To some extent, what you say is true; not in the sense that the proofs are not valid, but in the sense that 'God' and the proofs relate to each other in an unusual way.

Our mental map of the world carries God as a key referent. God is not just the conclusion of an argument. He is a linchpin in our thinking, a hub that holds our thoughts and feelings together in a coherent structure.

In many publications about God, by both believers and non-believers, God is presented as the end of an argument. In reality, he/she/it is the beginning of the argument.

Yes, we need to *prove* the existence of God; but we should understand this proof in the correct way.

It is necessary to demonstrate that belief in God is rationally justified. We owe this to our own intellectual make up. We are forced to it by the need to defend our beliefs. Some of our contemporaries assume that "science has disproved religion." Believers need to counter open attacks by militant atheists. Throughout this book I attempt to show that faith can be justified on excellent grounds.

However, it is crucial that we understand how we acquire religious knowledge and how arguments for its truthfulness function. For silly mistakes have been made.

Believers and atheists have been arguing about God's existence for thousands of years. But since most people were deeply religious in the past, the academic arguments were restricted to theologians and philosophers. This changed with the upsurge of modern science in the seventeenth and eighteenth centuries.

The new scientific methodology was based on *induction,* on observing facts and drawing conclusions. Philosophers demanded a similar approach regarding proofs for the existence of God. They postulated the principle that God, like any other object, should be proved by observation and deduction. Christians rose to the challenge and began to construct such proofs.

The so-called *theistic proofs* produced in the debate, though scoring valuable points, were bound to fail. They had unwittingly copied unproven assumptions of their opponents. The greatest error lay in thinking that belief in God rests on a foundation of layer upon layer of separate arguments. The imagined structure was: general principles at the bottom, then evidence, then God lying on top.

The whole argument then looks like a ramshackle stack of shelves with God, as a fragile vase, perched on top.

Not only does this incorporate the misguided idea that God is a separate entity like other objects in the world; it also makes belief in God very insecure: he can then easily be 'toppled' by any counter proof.

The approach is wrong for the simple reason that our knowledge is structured in a different way and that God holds a far more basic position in it.[1]

---

1 This erroneous procedure is often referred to as foundationalism. Its shortcomings have been especially exposed by the Calvinist theologians Alvin Plantinga and Nicolas Wolterstorff; see A. Plantinga, *God and Other Minds,* Ithaca 1967; *God, Freedom and Evil,* Grand Rapids 1974; A. Plantinga and N. Wolterstorff (Ed.), *Faith and Rationality,* Notre Dame 1983; R. Audi and W. J. Wainwright, *Rationality, Religious Belief and Moral Commitment,* Ithaca 1986. A brief, but excellent account of the issues involved is given by K. J. Clark, *Return to Reason,* Grand Rapids 1990.

Most of us learn about God from our family, from society around us, from literature and culture, from the language we learn to speak. Our ideas of God are confirmed in our mind by our own intuitive perception and by religious and spiritual experiences that come our way. We start with an outlook on the world in which God, however we define him, already has a place. Before we begin to reflect and reason logically, we have a hypothesis in which God is included.

Read also ch.15

God in the structure of our thinking

Secondly, since God represents the Absolute in this integrated world view, God occupies a central position, much more like the hub in a wheel. The meaning of life, our origin and destiny, the norms for good and evil, everything is held together by God.

As I said before, this does not mean that we do not need to justify belief in God through rational argument.[1] We do. But the process is different. We do not arrive at God as at one object among many. Our arguments affirm God as the central reality: the source of all being, the basis of all truth, beauty and love, the *depth* of our existence, the overarching frame of meaning.

---

1   The Calvinist theologians went too far in their opposition to Foundationalism by claiming that knowledge of God is 'properly basic'; which means that it is so self evident that it does not need proofs. See G. I. Mavrodes, 'Jerusalem and Athens Revisited,' in *Faith and Rationality*, l.c. pp. 192-218; W. L. Sessions, 'Coherence, Proper Basicality and Moral Arguments for Theism,' *International Journal for the Philosophy of Religion* 22 (1987) 119-137; B. Langtry, 'Properly Unargued Belief in God,' *International Journal for the Philosophy of Religion* 26 (1989) 129-154; P. Draper, 'Evil and the Proper Basicality of Belief in God,' *Faith and Philosophy* 8 (1991) 135-147; M. Hester, 'Foundationalism and Peter's Confession,' *Religious Studies* 26 (1990) 403-413.

"I've just grasped that God is part of my complete phenomenological gestalt!"

Most people already begin with a hypothesis in which God holds a central position. The proofs they consider will either affirm or weaken their whole mental construction of the world.

Here are some different ways in which authors have expressed the way we come to know about God:

• *"Belief in God begins like any other reality we learn. It is impossible to learn a language or function in society if one does not from infancy believe most of what one is told. Yet most of what one hears, in so far as it is evidential at all about the world, is not systematic, controlled, or replicable evidence; and a person will never have an opportunity to ver-*

ify more than a tiny fraction of it through more reliable means."[1]

• *"God's nature is something one has to grasp as well as one can in one's imagination; and only then can one try to justify one's imaginative grasp by various arguments or logical illustrations."*[2]

• *Belief in God is part of **a natural and coherent perspective.** It is a coherent and natural way of accommodating all the factors that incline us towards accepting our view of the world*[3]

• *Belief in God is part of **a complete phenomenological gestalt,** that is: a unified perception of reality within which we live.*[4]

It is not a question of our wanting to believe in a God, and therefore accepting any arguments. It is rather that various reasonings, insights and experiences combine to confirm a world view in which God holds a central position.

Read also ch.47

1   J. Hobbs, 'Religious and Scientific Uses of Anecdotal Evidence,' *Logos* 12 (1991) 105-121, here p.115. See also: D. R. Anderson, 'Three Appeals in Peirce's Neglected Argument,' *Trans Peirce Society* 20 (1990) 349-362, here p.349; 'An American Argument for Belief in the Reality of God,' *International Journal for the Philosophy of Religion* 26 (1989) 109-118.

2   A. B. Palma, 'Notes Towards God,' *Sophia* 25 (1986) 4-17; here p.14.

3   W. H. Davis, 'Evidence and belief,' *Sophia* 30 (1991) 1-22, here p. 5.

4   S. Prasinos, 'Spiritual Aspects of Psychotheraphy,' *Journal of Religion and Health* 31 (1992) 41-52, here p. 50.

25.

"Why do the same arguments that convince some people leave others cold?"

If evidence is valid, we would expect that it makes a similar impression on any observer. However, as far as belief in God is concerned, there is a marked difference. Believers accept certain evidence, non-believers something else. It shows that the reasoning here is totally subjective.

The reason is that the change over from unbelief to belief, and the other way about, involves a major reversal of structural thought. It brings about a new perspective. It requires a paradigm shift, a re-ordering of one's mental constructs.

Atheists have their own, integrated construction of reality in which God has no place.

Those atheists who still cling to the old wheel, by simply replacing God with an absolute value such as Truth, may have an implicit belief in God, as we have seen. Bertrand Russell summed up the meaning of his own life in three overriding passions: his longing for love, his search for knowledge and his pity for the suffering of other human beings.[1] Are Truth and Beauty and Love not precisely aspects of the transcendent reality expressed in the notion of God?

Read also ch.34

But there are real atheists, people who deliberately and consistently exclude the existence of any reality apart from the observable universe.[2]

The interesting thing about this is that to prove atheism, that is: to prove the *non-existence* of God, turns out to be an impossible task. It is like proving that there are no other universes beside our own.[3]

---

1 B. Russell, *The Autobiography of Bertrand Russell*, London 1967, Prologue.

2 See e.g. M. Martin, *Atheism. A Philosophical Justification*, Philadelphia 1990.

3 S. A. Shalkowski, "Atheological Apologetics," *American Philosophical Quarterly* 26 (1989) pp. 1-17.

"Come in – I'm an atheist and I've got all the time in the world!"

Likewise, the change over from atheism to belief is the turning upside-down of a world view. It is a structural reversal, a paradigm shift. That is how those who experience it describe it. The final event is usually a sudden adjustment of one's complex belief structure.

Graham Greene who found faith only as an adult, experienced this shift. In *The End of the Affair*, he makes the adulteress-heroine Sarah Miles write to her lover Bendrix: "I've caught belief like a disease. I've fallen into belief like I fell in love."

G.K.Chesterton testified to it being like many jagged and unconnected pieces suddenly joining up in a snug fit. "No one will be convinced about the reality of God if we find that

Read also ch.47

something proves it," he said. "What really convinces us is when we find that *everything* proves it."

One consequence of this situation is that both atheists and believers argue from within their own framework of convictions. As William James shrewdly observed, "the truth is that in the metaphysical and religious sphere, articulate reasons are cogent for us only when our inarticulate feelings of reality have already been impressed in favor of the same conclusion."[1]

A single argument will not easily dislodge one's complex network of beliefs. Rather we will have to focus on the totality itself.[2]

Read also ch.64

For those who have experienced religion, it is not difficult to recognise that it does not concern detail but the whole, that it involves the totality of life and universal meaning.

---

1 W. James, *The Varieties of Religious Experience*, Edinburgh 1902; London 1960, p. 88.

2 See also P. Lee, "Reasons and Religious Belief," *Faith and Philosophy* 6 (1989) 19-34; J. L. Golding, "Toward a Pragmatic Concept of Religious Faith," *Faith and Philosophy* 7 (1990) 486-503.

Part Three

Conscience

26.

Our inherent dignity as a human being derives from a higher principle.

We should treasure our freedom as one of our most precious possessions. The *Universal Declaration of Human Rights*, which has now been accepted as law by almost every country in the world, establishes the right of every human person to be free from all forms of slavery.

All human beings are born free and equal in dignity and rights. . . . (art. 1).

Everyone is entitled to all the rights and freedoms set forth in this Declaration, without distinction of any kind, such as race, colour, sex, language, religion, political or other opinion, national or social origin, property, birth or other status. . . . (art. 2).

Everyone has the right to life, liberty and the security of person (art. 3).

No one shall be held in slavery or servitude. Slavery and the slave trade shall be prohibited in all their forms (art. 4).

We are so used to enjoying such freedoms that we forget the thousands of years it has taken us as a human race to acquire them. Around 1800, for instance, most governments could still arrest and imprison subjects indefinitely without proven charges. Women had few public rights. Workers were totally at the mercy of their employers. Slavery thrived in all Muslim States. And European slave traders captured around 80,000 slaves a year in Africa, transported them to America under appalling conditions and sold them there into a life of total servitude and dependence.

Alexander Falconbridge, a surgeon who served on slave ships, has left us a contemporary record (1790 AD) of how

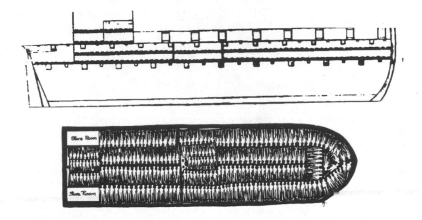

This old drawing shows how slaves were stowed on the Brookes, a ship from Liverpool. The ship measured 100ft by 25ft, and had a capacity of 320 tons. Packed in this way it carried 300 slaves, but on occasion extra platforms were added along the side walls, doubling the load to 609 slaves! Eyewitnesses report that during the journey the decks were covered with blood, excrement and vomit.

slaves were treated. During the day they were chained, stark naked, to the railing of the deck. At night hundreds were packed in small spaces, manacled to each other, with no ventilation and no proper toilets. They were mercilessly scourged at the least protest. Many died from suffocation, dysentry and exhaustion.[1]

Among the forces which eventually put a halt to these inhuman practices was the growing sense of responsibility among European leaders. The slave traders excused their actions on all kinds of grounds: some races were inferior by nature and suited for slave work, they said, slavery was an economic necessity, and so on. But William Wilberforce tire-

---

1 Ch. and D. Plummer, *Slavery: the Anglo-American Involvement*, Newton Abbot 1973, pp. 66- 67.

lessly campaigned for the abolition of the slave trade. In 1789 he put its atrocities before the British House of Commons and added:

> *There are principles that go beyond politics. When I reflect on the command which says: 'Thou shalt do no murder,' believing the authority to be divine, how can I dare to set up any reasoning against it?*
>
> *And when we think of eternity, and of the future consequences of all human conduct, what is there in this life that should make any man contradict the dictates of his conscience, the principles of justice, the laws of religion, and of God.*
>
> *The nature of this trade and all its circumstances are now open to us. We can no longer plead ignorance. We cannot evade it. It is now an object placed before us. We cannot pass it. We may spurn it. We may kick it out of our way, but we cannot turn aside so as to avoid seeing it; for it is brought now so directly before our eyes that this House must decide, and must justify to all the world, and to their own consciences, the rectitude of the grounds and principles of their decisions.*[1]

Read also ch.30

It was only in 1807 that the Bill forbidding slavery in all British Dominions was finally adopted. It was a victory of conscience, that would be duplicated by similar victories in other parts of the world.

Slavery was abolished in French colonies in 1848 and in the USA in 1865. Legal slavery continued to exist in Saudi Arabia till 1964; among the Tuareg Berbers of the Sahara until 1973.

The source of human dignity

Today slavery persists in modern forms. Girls are sold into prostitution. Domestic slaves are kept in some Muslim

---

1 H. Pederson (Ed), *The World's Great Speeches*, New York 1965, pp. 212 - 219.

countries. Bonded labourers are so tied to their masters that they enjoy virtually no freedom at all. But these aberrations are prosecuted as real crimes. Slavery is no longer tolerated by the world community. The *Universal Declaration* indicates the reason: it bases human freedom on the inherent dignity and inalienable rights of all members of the human family. Human dignity is its ultimate principle.

It could be argued that we are free because other people *give* us our freedom. It would then be just a question of everybody doing everybody else a favour. We would receive our freedom by common agreement. But that is obviously not how the *Universal Declaration* sees it. It speaks of 'inherent dignity' and 'inalienable rights.'

> *"Recognition of the inherent dignity and of the equal and inalienable rights of all members of the human family is the foundation of freedom, justice and peace in the world."*

The International Law that protects human rights clearly bases human freedom on some worth we possess in ourselves, as human beings. What is that worth?

The *Declaration* also refers to our human conscience. "Disregard and contempt for human rights have resulted in *Read also ch.30* barbarous acts which have outraged the conscience of humankind," it says. By what norms does our conscience judge? They are norms that transcend the capricious rules laid down by individuals, communities, nations and religious denominations.

The *Declaration* states that "everyone has duties to the community in which alone the free and full development of his personality is possible." Again, are these duties just imposed on us by other people? Are they not of necessity duties that derive from higher principles?

Suppose for a moment that the United Nations is the highest human authority on earth. It could then be argued that our human freedom and basic human rights are *given* to us by the United Nations. This in turn would then imply that the United Nations might, at some future date, exclude these rights from a particular race, for instance from the Aboriginals in Australia or the Bushmen in South Africa.

Read also ch.37

A higher principle

This is not so difficult to imagine. In 1921, the senior-most archaeologist in the United States, Henry Fairfield Osborn, presided over the Second International Eugenics Congress in New York. Eugenics was a widely popular movement at the time. It held that some races are genetically superior to others. The interests of humanity are served best by breeding superior people and by preventing those who are inferior or unfit, from reproducing.

Osborn also opposed immigration into the United States of Asians, Italians, Greeks or Slavs from Eastern Europe. Racial purity should be promoted to halt the degeneration that would inevitably result in national decline, genetic suicide and extinction.

> *"In the United States we are slowly waking to the consciousness that education and environment do not fundamentally alter racial values. We are engaged in a serious struggle to maintain our historic republican institutions through barring the entrance of those who are unfit to share the duties and responsibilities of our well-founded government. The true spirit of American democracy that all men are born with equal rights and duties has been confused with the political sophistry that all men are born with equal character and ability to govern themselves and others, and with the educational sophistry that education and environment will offset the handicap of heredity."*

Osborn, who was the director of the Museum of Natural History in New York, arranged the exhibits of human evolution in such a way that it became a story of human decline by

"*What d'ye mean we don't take tips?
– You dull-witted Neanderthal!*"

the intermarriage of such superior races as the Cro-Magnon with the dull-witted Neanderthals. The lessons for eugenics were explicitly pointed out in many exhibits.[1]

Read also ch.5 & ch.7   Suppose that in the future the United Nations would be dominated by leaders who think as Osborn did. They might believe it to be their duty to strengthen the human family by a judicious ethnic isolation of 'inferior' races or by prescribing birth control for all those deemed unfit. Would they have the authority to do so, if the majority of the members of the United Nations were to support them?

The present *Universal Declaration of Human Rights* clearly says **No**. Human beings have an *inherent* dignity. Peo-

---

1 R. Rainger, *An Agenda for Antiquity*, Alabama 1994.

ple have *inalienable* rights, rights which can not be taken away by other human beings, of whatever authority they are.

The *Universal Declaration* therefore unequivocally admits that human dignity and human freedom derive from a higher principle – which, by implication, can only be God.

27.

Every individual possesses inalienable rights which no human power may disrespect.

The attempt by the Nazis in Germany during World War II to extirpate the Jewish race shocked the world community. Awareness grew in all free countries that nations, as well as individuals, are subject to a superior law that they may not transgress without punishment.

In the Nüremberg trials of 1945-1946, the top German leaders were brought to trial, not only for crimes against peace, but also for crimes 'against humanity.' And they were held responsible for atrocities committed against any civil population even if their crimes had been in accordance with the laws of the country where those crimes had been perpetrated. In other words, the world community did not accept excuses such as: "I only implemented national laws," or "I just did as I was told." The world community held that there are basic human rights of which individuals cannot be deprived by states or by political leaders.

Since World War II, everyone accepts the principle of such fundamental human rights, at least in theory. But many people have forgotten that, from its very beginning, the principle was legitimated on religious grounds.

The question first came up in the Graeco-Roman civilisation. May dominant nations treat subservient nations as they like? May masters use their slaves in any way they fancy? The answer of many philosophers was: they may not. For all nations and all individuals have to obey a higher law, the law of the gods, a law which protects all human beings.

In a famous stage play of 440 BC at Athens, Sophocles highlighted the problem. When the rebel Polynices died in an attack on the city Thebes, King Creon forbade that anyone should bury him on pain of death. But his sister, Antigone, ignored the prohibition. She collected her brother's corpse from the place where he had died and buried him. When Creon challenged Antigone, asking why she had dared to transgress his decree, she replied:

> *"For it was not Zeus, the father of the gods, that published me that decree. I did not attribute such authority to your decrees, as if you, a mortal being, could override the unwritten and unfailing statutes of heaven. For the laws of heaven date not of today or yesterday, but from all time, and no one knows when they were first put forth."*

In other words, even at that time Sophocles proclaimed that there are human rights, such as the right to a decent burial, which no human ruler can deprive an individual of, because they are rights granted by 'the laws of heaven.'

Read also ch.33

The law of nature

The same conviction was expressed by the Roman senator Marcus Tullius Cicero (106 - 43 BC). Even though at the time Rome was the most powerful state in the western world, he admitted a universal law, more lasting than the Roman code, that imposes on all human beings their basic rights and duties. He said that this law can be known by the use of our mind.

> *"Sound reason reflects a true law, a law that agrees with nature, a constant, eternal law found among all human beings. This law issues commands – to make us do our duty; forbids – to hold us back from mischief. However, it never orders good people to do the impossible, nor does it coerce evildoers against their will.*
>
> *No one may abrogate any part of this law, nor deny its binding force in any way. Neither the senate nor the people's assembly can absolve us from it. We cannot have recourse to another lawyer or inter-*

*preter against it. The law does not differ in Rome
from what it is in Athens, does not differ now from
what it will be in the future. No, this one and immutable law holds all nations in its grasp.*

*For there is one common teacher and emperor of all
nations: God. He invented this law. He formulated
its contents. He promulgated it.*

*Whoever does not obey this law will be alienated
from his own self. For, having shown contempt for
human nature, he will bring down upon himself the
severest punishments, even if he believes he can escape other penalties."*[1]

Jewish and Christian writers acknowledged the same reality. Genesis 1,26-27 taught that every human being was created in God's image, and thus had to be respected as a
reflection of God. Isaiah 51,7 had spoken of God's law that
lives in people's hearts. Paul works this out further, purposely
contrasting the external law, such as the Jewish *Torah* with the
inner law in people's hearts.

*"When Gentiles who do not have the external law,
do by nature what the law requires, they themselves
become their own law, even though they do not have
the external law. They show that what the external
law requires is written on their hearts."*[2]

The theologians of later centuries elaborated the idea further. Through the power of our intellect we can perceive what
things are like and what they are meant to be. They called this
the law of nature or *natural law*. "The light of our human reason by which we distinguish good from evil and by which we
discern natural law, reflects God's light shining in us. Natural
law is nothing else but a rational creature discovering God's
purpose in creation."[3]

---

1 Quoted by Lactantius (240 - 320 AD), *Divine Institutions* 6,8.
2 *Romans* 2,13-15).
3 Thomas Aquinas (1224 - 1275), *Summa Theologica*, 1,2, q.91, a.2; freely
   translated.

Also natural law *evolved*

Now there are different ways in which such a 'natural law' can be understood. No doubt there are fundamentalist Christians who think of this law as something that a supernatural God added to creation as an extra. They imagine God creating the world first, and then imposing some rules and obligations on the created world. For instance, God created men and women for procreation. And, to guide human marriage, he then imposed prohibitions against fornication, adultery, polygamy, and so on.

But this is not the correct or classical understanding of *natural law*. Natural law is nothing else than nature itself. It is the natural consequence of things being the way they are. If men and women evolved to bring forth new life through their union, there are certain consequences. Both the father and the mother, for instance, have obligations regarding their offspring, especially since human offspring requires a long period of nurturing and education. But natural law by itself does not determine whether this purpose is best achieved by polygamy or monogamy, nor what would constitute adultery. Such details are laid down by cultural or religious laws, and can differ from one community to the next.

Read also ch.31

Natural law derives from God, not in the sense that God promulgated a set of special decrees, but in the sense that God as the Creative Reality is the ultimate authority on which nature rests. As we know now, everything in the universe, though upheld in being by God's creative power, evolves from lower to higher forms of being. Natural law is part of all that. As creatures endowed with reason, we carry more responsibility to respect nature and the way things should be. By showing that respect, we implicitly show respect to the Ultimate Reality that creates the universe.

This is where human rights find their legitimation. The right of every human person to freedom, to a share in the world's resources and to respect flows directly from our sharing life, as creatures who receive everything we have from the same God. It is only because of the existence of *natural law* and its religious foundation that human rights can be upheld.

One of the first modern, political documents that explicitly mentions human rights, bases these rights unequivocally on belief in a Creator. It was the Declaration of Independence of the first Thirteen American States in 1776.

> *"We hold these truths to be self-evident:*
> *that all human beings are created equal,*
> *that they are endowed by their Creator with certain inalienable rights,*
> *that among those are life, liberty and the pursuit of happiness."*

Read also ch.35

The liberal institutions which the modern world has brought into being spring ultimately from religious, and, more specifically, from Christian roots. The conviction of the unconditional value of the individual human person is an heirloom of the Judaeo-Christian tradition. It has its origins in the biblical notion that the human person is the image of God, in other words that something of the dignity and glory of God is reflected in every person who bears a human face.[1]

---

1   W. Kaspar, "Is God Obsolete?," *Irish Theological Quarterly* 55 (1989) pp. 85 - 98.

28.

We can be free and autonomous people because God *makes* us free and autonomous.

We only become fully and truly ourselves by taking free and autonomous decisions. A parrot cannot think its own thoughts. A robot does what it is programmed to do. Mature human beings make up their own minds, and assert their own self-worth by taking responsibility for their own decisions

The question is: does God stand in the way of such mature human freedom?

A friend of mine, a fifty years old bachelor, whom I will call Richard, faced a rather vexing problem that involved his ageing mother. When Richard's father had died and his mother began to need daily care, Richard obtained a place for her in a first class nursing home.

Richard used to visit his mother once a week, an event which became extremely important to her. Richard was her only child. As the years passed, she grew ever more emotionally attached to him. Richard was genuinely pleased that he could make her happy in this way. On account of it he even put up with the minor irritations she caused him: by fussing about him, by attempts to interfere in his private life, by occasionally smothering him with well meant maternal advice.

The problem arose when Richard, who was a senior partner in a law firm, was headhunted for an exciting new job that would entail a transfer from London to Glasgow. It would mean being far away from his mother, fewer visits, leaving her heartbroken and lonely. He genuinely did not know what to do. Was she not more important than his job? But would he get a similar chance again?

"The Bible says:'Love your father and your mother'," Richard said to me. "In a way I've always lived up to that. But now I don't feel free. When I was a teenager I had to fight my mother to get my own independence. Now I still feel bound to her – in a more subtle manner. Why can't I be just myself, absolutely free?!"

The question of inner human freedom was the key question of life for the existential thinker, Jean-Paul Sartre. We only become a truly free person, Sartre maintained, by taking our own free, authentic decisions. And these decisions should not be dictated by an outside moral order, by a scheme telling us what is good or bad. We make things good or bad by our decisions. Total liberty for any person means that the person acknowledges himself or herself as the absolutely creative source and goal of the sense of life.

Sartre saw belief in God as one of the chief obstacles to genuine human freedom. If we are *created*, he said, someone else, the Creator, determines our nature and our purpose. If a smith makes a spade, that spade is an object whose aim and function are fixed beforehand. If God were to create a human being, he would fix that human being according to a conception in his divine understanding. The human being would have to conform to God's idea of herself or himself, and thus be an object and not genuinely free.

Even if God were to exist, Sartre affirmed, and if we are created, we would need to rebel against God. To become truly free, we would have to assert ourselves against God in radical independence.[1]

Is God our rival?

Sartre has presented his ideas in many of his plays. In his masterpiece *The Flies*, Sartre tells the story of Orestes, the abandoned child of Agamemnon, the King of Argos. When Orestes returns to Argos as a young man, he finds that Aegistheus has killed his father Agamemnon, married his mother and usurped the throne of Argos. Moreover, he finds that the

---

1 J-P. Sartre, *Existentialism and Humanism*, London 1948; *Being and Nothingness*, New York 1966.

population is held in submission by a feeling of collective guilt, exemplified by the flies which plague people everywhere.

When Orestes decides to avenge his father by killing the usurper, the king of the gods *Zeus* is worried. Zeus is worried because Orestes is a truly free man. He feels no remorse. He will do exactly what he wants to do. In a conversation with Aegistheus, Zeus reveals the deepest source of his anxiety:

Zeus: *"I don't mind if people commit crimes. . . . In fact, it serves my purpose If they feel guilty, they will be subject to me all the more. . . . But this Orestes is different. He does not feel any pangs of conscience. He is preparing to kill you efficiently, with great coolness and detachment. He will kill you like a young chicken, and then leave you, with bloody hands and a clear conscience. . . ."*

Aegistheus: *"Can't you stop him? Can't you do something about it?"*

Zeus: *"No, I can't. . . . I must tell you a terrible secret which gods and kings are careful to keep under cover. Human beings are really free. They are free, Aegistheus! They can do what they like, but they don't realise it. They don't know it. Once they do, our power is broken. We're lost!"*[1]

Since Sartre denies any over-arching frame of meaning, he sees every human attempt at authentic freedom as ultimately doomed to failure. We are utterly alone in our decisions. Reality is fleeting, contingent and unpredictable. By taking our absolutely free choices, we are emulating being equal to God, but this desire is actually unrealisable and leads to frustration.[2] In *The Flies* Orestes says to Zeus: "What have I to do with you, or you with me? We shall glide past each other like ships in a river, without touching." But Orestes does not leave as a happy man. He leaves the city in a hurry and

Read also ch.19

---

1   J.P. Sartre, *The Flies*, New York 1947, Act 2,2; scene 5.

2   J.P. Sartre, *Being and Nothingness*, New York 1966, pp. 724- 725.

*"Let others blame the gods –
We'll make a fortune!"*

alone, because people want to kill him. The flies that plagued Argos follow him, buzzing and stinging with frenzy. . . .

I think this is the advice Sartre would give Richard:[1] "Grow up. Don't feel bound to the ten commandments imposed by a fictitious God. Don't feel guilty about leaving your mother. If you want to leave her, do so. Assert your freedom by responsibly determining your own life instead of having other people, or a fictitious God, do so for you!"

What to think of all this?

I believe that Sartre's concern about human freedom and autonomy has to be taken seriously. We do become adults by taking our own, free decisions. When we grow up, we usually have to liberate ourselves from parents, or parental substitutes, who try to determine our life for us. We become ourselves by

Read also ch.9

---

1 Compare the parallel of Matthieu who leaves his pregnant girl friend in Sartre's novel, *Age of Reason*, London 1947.

consciously facing the choices that lie before us and by choosing what we ourselves want to do and want to be.

Is God an obstacle in this process? Yes, he can be. Many people look on God the way Sartre did: as a Super Parent who has already laid down what is good for us and what is not, long before we were born. Such a God stunts our maturity and our freedom. Sartre has a valid point in saying that we need to rebel against such a Parent God to establish our true independence.

Read also ch.39

Created in the image of Freedom

The truth of the matter is, however, that this is not the right picture of God. God is the Creative Reality, but not a toolmaker in a two-tier world. God supports our personal freedom precisely because, through evolution, he/she/it supported the development by which we received our own power of reason and our sense of autonomy. In other words, God creates us as *free* people, responsible for our own decisions.

Read also ch.17

The Bible is emphatic about this. Human beings are said to have been created *in God's image* (Genesis 1,16-28), precisely because they possess this divine-like freedom of will and independence of action. To see God as minimising or curtailing that basic freedom is missing the whole point of the special dignity of human beings. What we do then, in reality, is to project onto God the immaturity of parents who stop their children from becoming adults.

Read also ch.9 & ch.39

The truth lies in the opposite direction. It is only because we believe in a God who is the source of freedom and autonomy, that our human freedom becomes meaningful. If we are just reasoning animals who have evolved in a mechanistic universe, our freedom is very limited, and ultimately doomed to failure. It is then just an exercise in self assertion, without lasting value. Sartre's pessimism is then completely justified. "Things are entirely what they appear to be and behind them there is nothing. . . . I have learnt that I always lose. Only bastards think they win." But if God exists and if he/she/it *enables* us to be free, our actions have value in themselves.

Read also ch.58 & ch.64

Then it makes sense to choose what is true, honourable, just and loving. Then it is worth making sacrifices for other people. Not in the sense of 'laying up a reward in heaven,' but in the sense that truth, honour, justice and love have meaning in the universe.

God is the all-encompassing personal Freedom that makes human freedom possible. When we make a free choice, God creates that freedom in us. Even if we choose the wrong thing, God still supports us in the act of choosing. In this sense God is like the air that surrounds us and that we breathe; or like the water in which fish swim and from which they draw their oxygen. God enables us to be autonomous and free in the same way as air enables birds to be alive and to fly.

Partners, not servants

Read also ch.47

According to our Christian belief, God never coerces us into a response. He offers his friendship to us: in the Old Testament through the covenant, in the New Testament through our becoming God's adopted children in Jesus Christ. We are invited to respond to his offer freely. No one else can give this response on our behalf. Even if we were baptised as children, our parents and godparents only gave a preliminary response. We ourselves have to ratify the commitment later, for it to become an adult relationship with God.

Now to return to Richard's problem. Yes, God wants him to be really free. The commandment: "Honour your father and your mother" is not to be looked upon as a decision imposed on Richard by God; rather as a value found in human relationships which Richard would surely have realised even without its mention in the decalogue. God has not made up his mind as to which option Richard should take. Since Richard's situation is unique, like every human situation, God leaves it to Richard to weigh up the pros and the cons of accepting the new job.

Whatever decision Richard takes affects Richard himself as a person. If he decides that the job has greater priority – perhaps, he can do much more good in Glasgow? or it opens many new doors? – well and good. Richard might then take action to keep the link with his mother as close as possible. Perhaps, she too could move to Glasgow? Or perhaps, he could have a special phone-for-the-elderly installed in her room, so that he can talk to her once every two or three days.

On the other hand, Richard might decide to give preference to his mother's needs, and stay close to London.

Richard felt enormously relieved to know that he was truly free and that God wanted him to take the decision as a responsible, free person. After a period of discernment, he declined the new job in order to remain close to his mother. She died three years afterwards.

Richard said it had been one of the most difficult choices in his life, but he was happy with what he had done. He felt it had been as important to him as it had been to his mother.

29.

God does not interfere with the responsible use of our human freedom.

In October 1972 a plane from Uruguay strayed far from its flight path and crashed high in the Andes. Attempts to locate it failed. Only two months afterwards the wreckage was spotted from the air, and a group of 16 survivors was found. They had a horrendous tale to tell.

The plane had crashlanded on a high mountain slope in dense fog. Most of the crew and the passengers survived the landing. After the initial shock they found they were completely isolated in snowbound, barren terrain. As well as they could, they encamped themselves in the wrecked plane and some makeshift huts, waiting for the rescue parties which, they were sure, must be on their way. No one came.

In the beginning they ate the packed dinners lying ready in the plane's pantry. Then supplies ran out. They went outside to look for food, but found nothing except snow, which they melted to have water. They sent pairs of scouts to look for a way down the slopes. Some came back exhausted and frustrated, others did not return at all. Meanwhile temperatures were freezing and the first passengers began to die of starvation.

It was in those desperate circumstances that the leaders of the group took a grisly decision. To stay alive, they had no choice but to eat the flesh of those that had died. And that is what they did. There is no need for us to dwell on the gruesome details. The fact is that it is certainly because of that decision that as many as sixteen stayed alive for so long.

I am starting with this unusual and rather shocking episode for two reasons. (1) When I heard the story first I was teaching students in Hyderabad, India, and one of them said:

"I thought people in Latin America were Christians! How could they do a thing like that!." (2) The incident depicts our human situation so well. Our daily life may not be as dramatic as a crash in the Andes, but it does often confront us with unusual situations. Rarely can we base our key decisions on a simple application of rules and conventions. In almost all cases we have to assess the circumstances and their implications, and then choose what *we* consider right and proper.

Read also ch.49

Yet there are many people, including Christians, who think that, if you believe in God, all you do when you are confronted with choices is to study the rule book. God has laid down laws and regulations which you are supposed to follow. Virtue consists in obeying his commandments, sin in transgressing them. God is for them the supreme Lawgiver who judges us from his throne high up in the two-tier world.

Read ch.17

It is necessary, therefore, to have a good look at socalled religious laws and see what we can make of them. I will do so from a Christian perspective, though I am confident the same would apply to many other religions.[1]

It is customary for Christians to distinguish the following kinds of laws:

1. Natural law.

This comprises the rights and obligations that flow from our being what we are. The Ten Commandments are reckoned to belong to this category, in as far as they express general human duties, such as worshipping God, respecting other people's life, property, and so on.

Read also ch.27

2. Revealed law.

For Jews, this would include the 613 commandments (*mitzvos*) contained in *the Torah*, i.e., in the first five books of the Bible. Christians consider these as provisional laws, meant

---

1 Since it is especially Catholics who are often suspected of being mere blind and passive 'followers of the law,' I will, moreover, explain the matter from a Catholic perspective.

"Ah, if God would play by the rules,
I'd win every time, Father!"

for Old Testament times. Though they may still contain some guidance, as laws they have been abrogated.

Both the Gospels and Letters of the New Testament contain commandments which are sometimes referred to as 'revealed law.' However, they are not 'laws' in the strict sense of the term, but principles and examples.

For instance, Jesus teaches us not to swear any oaths,[1] but when challenged during his own court-case to speak on oath, he did so.[2] Again, Jesus upheld the life-long bond of marriage and forbade divorce in principle.[3] But both Matthew and Paul[4] introduce exceptions, showing that it is not an absolute law. Many of Paul's guidelines to the Churches are out of date, and have been superseded long ago.

---

1   *Matthew* 5,33-37
2   *Matthew* 26,63-64.
3   *Mark* 10,11-12.
4   *Matthew* 5,32; 19,9; 1 *Corinthians* 7,12-16.

3. Church law.

Catholics would reckon here both general practices such as fasting in Lent and attending the Eucharist on Sundays. They would also put here the practical guidelines which the Church issues from time to time. Cremation, for instance, was discouraged at one time, now it is allowed. Periodic abstention in family planning was frowned upon by Church authorities at first, now it is the preferred method.

Freed from slavery to 'law'

Now, while the terminology of 'law' is still being used in the sense explained above, the important thing to note is that Christians believe that Christ has truly liberated us from all external obstacles to freedom including laws. *Christians believe they are free from any law. The only law that they acknowledge is the Holy Spirit in their hearts.*

When Christ taught that love of God and love of our neighbour is the highest commandment, he instigated a religious revolution. It is not the external laws that matter, whatever they are. It is *love*, the interior principle of responsible action, that supersedes any law.[1] This does not need to surprise us. For Jesus revealed that God himself is love, and that all morality can be summed up in a living up to the principle of love.[2]

Read also ch.56 to ch.58

Paul is equally emphatic. We cannot be saved by fulfilling external laws. We are saved by a new law which God has written in our heart: the law of the Spirit of life. This law is the love which has been poured into our hearts by the Spirit of God.[3] St. Thomas Aquinas, who is seen by conservative Catholics as the norm of orthodoxy explains it as follows:

> *"It was necessary for Christ to give us a law of the Spirit, who by producing love within us, could give us life."*[4]

1 *Luke* 10,25-37.
2 *1 John* 4,7-12.
3 Read *Romans* and *Galatians;* esp. *Rom* 8,1-2; 5,5; *Gal* 5,1-6.
4 Thomas Aquinas, *Commentary on 2 Corinthians*, ch.3, lect.2.

"That which predominates after Christ's coming is the grace of the Holy Spirit which is given through faith in Christ. Consequently, the New Law is chiefly the grace itself of the Holy Spirit, which is given to those who believe in Christ."[1]

To put it in the words of Cardinal Seripando, who presided over the Council of Trent (1545 - 1563 AD): "We have received the Spirit of God in our mind, to take the place of external law."[2]

External laws, which tell us what to do and what not to do, will not really change *us*. But God's Spirit can. God's Spirit enables us to act responsibly and in harmony with selfless love. People who act like that are not under any law. They live by grace and not by the law.[3] As Paul so aptly says: "The letter (of external laws) kills, the Spirit (who works in our hearts) makes alive."[4] Even the commandments found in the Gospel, in as far as they would be external 'laws,' would fall under the letter which kills:

"The letter that kills denotes any writing that is external to a human being, even the moral precepts such as are contained in the Gospel. Therefore the letter, even of the Gospel, would kill, unless there is the inward presence of the healing grace of faith."[5]

Signposts on the way

Why then do Christians still have 'laws,' such as Church laws? The answer is that such 'laws' can serve a useful function as suggestions, guidelines and warnings. Paul compares the external law to a tutor who guides a teenager and gives him lessons. The laws are like traffic signs and notices which point

Read also ch.64

1 Thomas Aquinas, *Summa Theologica* I-II, q.106, a.1, c.
2 H. Jedin, *Papal Legate at the Council of Trent,* London 1974, p. 562.
3 *Gal* 5,18; *Rom* 6,14.
4 *2 Corinthians* 3,6.
5 Thomas Aquinas, *Summa Theologica* I-II, q.106, a.2, c. St. Augustine taught the same in *The Spirit and the Letter,* ch. 14, 17, 19, etc.; see also S. Lyonnet, "Liberty and Law," in *The Bridge* 4 (1962) pp. 229-251.

out danger: they are for the unjust, not for the just. Since all of us are shortsighted and weak, we need such help. But it is we ourselves who take the final decision on the strength of our inner conviction.[1]

Christians who face a difficult decision, like the Uruguayans in the crash, will therefore ask themselves the following questions:

• What does our *human reason* tell us to do in the circumstances?

• Are there aspects we should remember in the light of Christian sensitivity to *love and other Gospel principles?*

• Are there things we can learn from *previous experience,* i.e., from Church regulations or recommendations, etc.?

These are the kind of questions they should *always* ask themselves when considering a moral option. For ultimately, the decision will be theirs. They may not hide themselves behind 'a lawgiver.' They will be judged by their own conscience: by their inner reasonings, by the intentions and motives of their heart, by their courage in doing what they believe is right.

The survivors of the crash went, I am sure, through such a process of discernment and decided that their own survival outweighed the natural respect we should have for the bodies of other human beings, even if they have died. We who know their predicament only from a distance and who are not part of all that went through their minds and hearts, may not stand in judgment. But in my own mind I feel that they took a responsible decision which did not offend human dignity.

Decisions of life or death

Would the same have been true if they had *killed* one of the passengers to serve as food?

---

1   *Galatians 4,1-7; 5,1; 5,18; Romans 6,14; 1 Timothy 1,8-11.*

This is not just a theoretical question. It has happened. In June 1988 a boat with Vietnamese refugees was picked up by Philippine fishermen in the China Sea. They too had suffered starvation, and in order to stay alive, some passengers had been killed and eaten.

The boat had started out from Ben Tre in South Vietnam with 110 people on board. The ship lost its course and drifted aimlessly. The captain left. The refugees were soon without either water or food. After forty people had died of starvation, an ex-airforce officer named Phung Quang Minh, who was 33 years old, took charge.

In the stifling tropical heat, eating flesh from corpses seemed an added health risk. So he ordered that Dao Coung, a 30-year old man, be strangled, sliced up, boiled and fed to the travellers. Dao Coung was on the verge of dying from starvation and, Phung said, would have died any way.

Before the group was rescued, four others were killed and eaten in the same manner.

Here, of course, other principles are at stake. Since every human individual has an inalienable right to live, was Quang allowed to take one life to save others? "Thou shalt not murder!" is a recognised part of natural law. Yet, again, I do not want to be the judge. In exceptional circumstances, some people are sent to their death for the common good, such as soldiers into battle. And most Western countries tolerate a high level of abortion, even for the mere convenience of parents. . . . They may have much less justification than Quang had.

The point is that in all such circumstances, whether we are Christians or not, God does not interfere with our responsible decisions. Yes, we have to respect other people's rights as we find them in natural law. We have to listen to the promptings of the Spirit of love in our heart – If Phung Quang Minh had done so, he might have offered himself as food to others!

But, in all this, it is not God who decides for us, but we who make our own decision.

"For freedom Christ has made you free," Paul said. "Do not submit again to a yoke of slavery."[1] If people are the subservient slaves of laws and commands, it is not because God wants them to be like that.

"The prohibition to make idols," the famous Rabbi Kotsker said, "implies that we may not make idols of God's commands."[2] We owe allegiance to the living God, to his Spirit in us, to the freedom and autonomy God gives us; not to his external commands.

---

1 *Galatians* 5,1.
2 L.I. Newman, *The Hasidic Anthology*, New York 1868, p. 193.

30.

Conscience is a universal experience that points to objective morality and God.

During World War II the Japanese Navy transported Dutch prisoners-of-war in cargo ships from Indonesia to Thailand to make them work on a railway line that would connect Bangkok overland to India. Since the prisoners were usually kept below decks, Allied planes would attack the ships, and sink them with everybody on board.

Two Dutchmen, whom I will call Steve and Martin, were lucky enough to be scrubbing the upper deck during one such raid. It happened just before sunset. A bomber dived and released three bombs, one of which was a direct hit. It tore a huge hole in the ship's hull so that the vessel began to capsize almost immediately.

Steve and Martin dropped their scrubbing brushes, ran to the railing and jumped over board. Martin had the presence of mind to grab a life saver that hung from the railing, before making the jump. It gave him a great advantage.

The ship sank within minutes. Both men struggled to regain their breath after the deep dive. Swimming in the rough, high sea proved very difficult. The few Japanese crew who survived had managed to put out a small life boat. They picked up their own survivors and disappeared in the dusk.

Steve, who was becoming extremely tired, noticed that Martin was propped up by the life-saver. He swam closer, and Martin grabbed his stretched out hand. But it soon became clear that the life saver, which was a simple ring made of cork, would not support both men at the same time.

On impulse, Steve wrenched the life saver from Martin and pushed him under water. Martin let go of the ring, crying out in shock and anger. Steve swam away as fast as he could.

"Don't leave me!," Martin shouted after him, but Steve swam on. When he looked round he had a last view of Martin's anguished and pleading face. Then they were separated by the waves.

It took Steve a full twenty-four hours before he was washed ashore near Atjeh on the northern coast of Sumatra. With the help of the local population he managed to escape discovery by the local Japanese garrison. After an eventful journey through the jungle, he made his way to an Allied army base at the other side of the island. There he was given a hero's welcome.

After the war Steve received a medal for having shown courage and endurance in exceptionally difficult circumstances. Nobody knew what Steve had done to Martin, but he himself could never forget it.

Martin's death remained on his conscience as an act of cowardice for which he could find no forgiveness. As Steve grew older, images of those dreadful moments would come back to haunt him. He would see Martin's face and hear his anguished cry. Before he died, Steve made a full confession of what he had done. "I can fool the whole world, but I can't fool God," he said.

Read also ch.37 & ch.57

Steve's story illustrates a general human experience. Whether we like it or not, we are censured by an inner judge who praises us when we do good and criticises us when we do wrong. We have a conscience which reminds us of the moral implications of our actions. Is it the voice of God?

Yes, says traditional religion. Or to be more precise: conscience echoes the presence of God in us. Conscience is the voice of our own reason which is aware of God and which reflects his judgment.

When a mother has told her 10-year-old son who is left alone in the home, not to take biscuits from the tin, the child remains aware of this parental injunction. If he takes a cookie all the same, his mind keeps reminding him that mother disapproves. It makes the child feel fearful and guilty. His conscience reveals awareness of his parent's will.

Could conscience work in this way on a deeper level?

Could conscience mean a profound awareness of our being responsible not just to earthly parents, or to our fellow human beings, but to a superior authority, the source of all truth and life, to God?

The basis of morality

Immanuel Kant, one of the patriarchs of modern thinking (1724 - 1804), pointed out that, when we accept free will, there must be an objective morality to guide it and that this requires a religious basis. He called it 'the categorical imperative' and said it made him inevitably believe in the existence of God.

Kant's fundamental tenet was that all our thinking is limited to sense experience and the realm of thought itself. Since we think in *mental* categories, our knowledge concerns ideas rather than reality in itself. Kant admitted that we have an idea of God which is an *a basic concept* unifying our whole worldview, but this idea could neither be proved nor disproved by any normal scientific proof.

Read also ch.24
According to Kant, God is the central idea in our mind. God is that on which everything that exists, depends. The idea of God makes it possible for our reason to consider all events, both external and internal, to belong to a greater unity. The idea of God is not fiction. On the other hand, as *an idea* God is not necessarily *a reality*. As far as pure reason goes, we only know God as a transcending thought, a unifying concept, a binding principle, an ideal.

> *"God is a mere ideal, yet an ideal without a flaw, a concept which completes and crowns the whole of human knowledge. Its objective reality cannot indeed be proved, but also cannot be disproved, by merely speculative reason."*[1]

---

1 I. Kant, *Critique of Pure Reason*, London 1964, p. 531.

However, the reality of God can be proved in another way, Kant said. For next to pure reason, which concerns itself with scientific knowledge, we have *practical reason* which deals with how we need to act. After all, we have practical experience of how to survive in a complex world. This experience has its own logic. Practical reason, in fact, has priority over pure reason since our ultimate interests are always practical. Even knowledge has to find completion in practical realizations. Well, practical reason finds the fact of morality. *"And it is morally necessary to assume the existence of God."*[1]

Read also ch.15

Kant explains his reasoning as follows. Every human being has the undeniable experience of the voice of conscience. It demonstrates that we acknowledge an objective moral order of good and evil. For we find in ourselves a command to do good, which Kant called "the categorical imperative": a *Thou Shalt* (therefore an imperative) with no ifs and buts – therefore categorical, that is: absolute.

This objective moral order, with its absolute command to do good, does not make sense without the following three realities:

(1) We are truly free to choose good or evil.

(2) There must be some transcending meaning in life, implying the immortality of our spirit.

(3) God must exist as the supreme source of the moral order.

Kant maintained that the objective moral order *postulates* human freedom, a transcendent meaning and the existence of God. They are necessary requirements for our practical reason to function. They have to be true to make sense of the world in which we live. These postulated realities are to our practical reason what axioms are to geometry, mathematics and logic: they cannot be proved but *must be true* for geometry, mathematics and logic to work.

---

1 I. Kant, *Critique of Practical Reason*, London 1954, p. 222.

God's verdict spoken in us

Kant has analysed conscience, and its relation to God, in another text, which I will render freely to improve its readability in English:

> *"The consciousness of an internal tribunal in a human being (before which 'his thoughts accuse or excuse each other') is known as CONSCIENCE.*
>
> *Every person finds himself or herself observed by an inward judge who threatens and keeps that person in awe. Now this judge may be an actual or a merely ideal person, a person reason frames to itself. Such an idealised person, the authorised judge of conscience, must be one who knows the heart; for the tribunal is set up in the innermost part of a human being. At the same time, the judge must also have supreme authority. Yes, he must at the same time possess all power in heaven and on earth, since otherwise he could not back up his commands with proper sanctions, such as his office of judge necessarily implies. However, a moral being of that stature, with authority over all, is called GOD.*
>
> *Therefore, conscience must be considered as the subjective acknowledgement of a responsibility for one's deeds before God. In fact, the concept of God, however obscurely, is contained in every awareness of moral responsibility."*[1]

All Kant' theories have not been generally accepted, but his argument to prove God from objective morality stands. In our own days, it has been reformulated as a proof based on our living and considered experience of life.[2]

When I consider the whole of my life, which includes my moral awareness, I realise with a practical certainty that I myself, my human freedom and God are not illusions, but reali-

---

1 I. Kant, *Grundlegung zur Metaphysik der Sitten*, Berlin 1780, p. 64.
2 H. Küng, *Does God Exist?*, London 1984, pp. 536-551.

"I trust the internal tribunal of your conscience troubles you not, Mr Bloggs?!"

ties. It is an act of fundamental trust on the part of my whole person, an affirmation of who I am and my responsibilities. For the whole of my experience makes no sense without accepting these realities.

> *"Two things fill the mind with ever new and increasing admiration and awe, the oftener and more steadily we reflect on them: the starry heavens above and the moral law within!"*[1]

---

1 I. Kant, *Critique of Practical Reason,* New York 1954, p. 260.

31.

The fact that human conscience developed *in evolution* does not disprove its role as a sensor of Reality.

When our human descent from animals came to be established by science, it was to be expected that a similar origin would be ascribed to human morality. Charles Darwin himself sketched such a development in *The Descent of Man*.

Darwin saw a precursor for conscience in the social instincts of animals. Parent birds take great trouble to feed their young. Bees literally work themselves to death to gather honey and pollen for the hive. A pride of lions will hunt as a well coordinated team. Such inborn traits promote behaviour that is useful to the species.

Animals also learn rules of behaviour by the approval or disapproval of their kind. Young chimpanzees, for instance, undergo years of training in the troupe during which they learn to share food, to obey elders, to stand watch and warn others of danger. When a dog is well taught by its master, it will not touch forbidden food even if its master is absent. If it eats food all the same, it will show signs of a 'guilty conscience': it will expect punishment because it knows it has done wrong!

With the full flowering of reason in human beings, such beginnings of a moral sense were given further shape in culture. Expectations and duties were expressed in language. The clan sanctioned some forms of behaviour as right, others as wrong. In the individual this gave rise to a moral conscience: to an application to oneself of the common approval or disapproval.

According to Charles Darwin, the *voice of conscience* comes about by a combination of many factors: inborn instincts, learned behaviour, cultural indoctrination, religious traditions, the habits of a life time and one's own power of reason. There is no need to refer to God. Conscience has a perfectly natural explanation.

Where does this leave us with regard to the question as to how conscience relates to God?

Strange though it may seem at first, Darwin's and Kant's observations are not mutually exclusive. They are both true. They complement each other in a meaningful way.

The awakening of responsibility

Human conscience certainly derived from the social instinct of animals. Like other aspects of human reason, our moral sense developed gradually. The perception of the world which was so partial and tentative in animals was slowly refined till it reached the stage of our own reasoned critical perception. This applies also to our perception of right and wrong.

Take, for example, parental care for the young. I was struck some time ago by a nature film on the feeding habits of crocodiles in Northern India. After the eggs have hatched in the warm sands of the shore, the mother picks up her tiny brood, small and vulnerable as lizards, manoeuvres them between her giant teeth and holds them ever so gently as she swims towards a small island in the middle of the river where the fledglings can grow up safely. There is so much tenderness in what we rightly consider a dangerous predator.

Such motherly love in a crocodile is certainly determined by instinct. Natural selection favours this trait because it ensures the survival of the species. A line of crocodiles that neglects its young will soon die out. The beginnings of perception, learning and responsibility are clearly visible.

In however primitive a way, crocodiles begin to perceive differences in the world around them. Some creatures are rivals and enemies, others are potential food, others again are partners and offspring. Crocodiles learn to adopt appropriate behaviour towards each of these categories. And, in doing so,

"*Take note, Jones, you are watching the origins of your own conscience!*"

they develop both their (limited) freedom as crocodiles and their (limited) responsibility in the world.

As intelligence increased, so did perception, learning and responsibility. Chimpanzees, for instance, have a much more sophisticated grasp of reality than crocodiles. They exhibit a more refined sense of social responsibility. Again, a scene from a nature film comes to mind. A chimpanzee baby had lost its mother and was approaching a strange troupe. Forlorn and unsure it crept up to a totally strange female. The large chimp eyed the little intruder with suspicion. One could almost read on her face the thoughts and feelings going through her mind.

Suddenly the young baby stretched out its tiny hand. The large chimp responded. It stretched out its own hand and touched the baby's. The commentator said it was the first time that such an adoption by chimpanzees had been seen in the wild. The mother took responsibility for the new baby.

All blind instinct? Instinct yes, but not totally blind. The female chimp recognised a baby in need and responded generously. Without being able to argue it out, as we would, it felt that here was a young life that needed to be protected. It followed its 'conscience' and must have felt rewarded by seeing the child grow in its care.

All this is just as Darwin said, but with a difference. For what we observe is a gradual awakening of intelligence and of responsibility. The crocodile, the chimpanzee and the human mother all respond to the need of a child. In all three there is an instinctual basis, but also a clear perception, most pronounced in the human mother, that the child has rights of its own, rights it received not from its parents, but from the Ultimate Reality that gives it existence.

To put it differently, every form of conscience is a response, and all of it is ultimately a response to reality and truth, and therefore to the Creative Energy that is God. In animals, 'conscience' is almost entirely instinctual; in human beings it is much more aware and explicit. The recognition of an objective good and evil implies the recognition of God.

Read also ch.21 & ch.50

32.

In conscience we ultimately respond to a Reality that is *personal*, to God.

Our conscience has been compared by writers and poets to:

- a guard on our ramparts;

- the pilot on our ship, setting out a safe course;

- a Geiger counter that takes positive and negative readings;

- a watch dog that barks at every intruder;

- the antennae of a butterfly.

All agree that conscience acts like a sensor that detects good and evil. Conscience is our human reason receiving signals of a special kind.

Receiving a signal is one thing; interpreting its origin correctly quite another.

When, in 1967, Jocelyn Bell at Cambridge recorded radio pulses that proved exceptionally regular, no one knew what caused them. Only gradually the insight dawned that a new kind of object had been discovered: the pulsar. Pulsars are dense stars made up almost entirely of neutrons. Pulsars spin rapidly round their axis, sending out radio waves like a lighthouse that spins as a top. One of them, nicknamed the Millisecond Pulsar, rotates at the rate of 642 times per second; which is amazingly fast for an object four times heavier than the sun.

Everyone has heard claps of thunder, or the pattering of rain against a window pane. Most people have taken the time to lie down in the grass and listen to the hum of a bumble bee or the chirp of crickets. But before 1967 no one had heard the clicking of pulsars. Now, with the aid of radio telescopes, we can. We can, because our listening has become more sensitive. We have attuned our hearing. The same fine-tuning is required in the case of conscience.

Our conscience is an inner 'organ' with which we listen to reality. We listen and we respond. We listen, and respond to, an acquired sense of good and evil, our task within the community, our experience of right and wrong. Ultimately we respond to God who creates the whole of reality, and to whom we ourselves and everyone else owes their existence and all their rights.

If we learn to listen sensitively to our conscience, we will unmistakably discern that it is God, the origin of everything that is personal and the source of all freedom, to whom we respond.

The 'voice' in me

No one has worked out the logic of this position more convincingly than John Henry Newman, one of the greatest English thinkers in the nineteenth century. I can do no better than make him speak in his own words (slightly modernised to give them a contemporary feel):

> *Suppose a person has allowed himself to commit an immoral deed, a thing mean and wrong in itself. He will then feel a lively sense of responsibility and guilt, even though the act itself may have no immediate social consequences. He will feel anxious and fearful, even though the deed may have been useful at the same time. He will have a sense of sorrow and regret even though the deed saved him pain and embarrassment. He will feel deep shame and confusion, even though there may be no other human beings who know of it.*
>
> *These various disturbances of mind: self-accusation, deep shame, haunting remorse, anxiety about the future, are characteristic of our conscience after*

we have done wrong. Their opposites: self-approval, inward peace, lightness of heart, and so on, indicate a good conscience, a conscience telling us that we have acted rightly.

Such feelings of conscience differ very much from our other intellectual powers, such as our 'common sense,' our sense of efficiency, our own good taste, good manners, our sense of honour and balance of judgment. Conscience has the peculiar trait of being deeply rooted in our emotions. It is always emotional. This means that it involves the recognition of a living object towards which it is directed. Lifeless things cannot stir our affections. Affections respond to persons.

If, as is the case, we feel responsibility, are ashamed, are frightened at transgressing the voice of conscience, this implies that there is One to whom we are responsible, before whom we are ashamed, whose claims upon us we fear.

On doing wrong, do we not feel the same tearful, broken-hearted sorrow which overwhelms us when hurting a mother? On doing right, do we not enjoy the same sunny serenity of mind, the same soothing satisfactory delight which follows on our receiving praise from a father? If so, we certainly have within us the image of some Person to whom our love and veneration are directed; in whose smile we find our happiness; towards whom we direct our pleadings; because of whose anger we are troubled and sad.

These feelings are such as require for their exciting cause an intelligent being.

We are not affectionate towards a stone. Nor do we feel shame before a dog or a horse. We have no remorse or regret for breaking a mere human law.

The emotions of conscience manifest Someone who is Personal.

> *The wicked person flees, even if no one is pursuing him. Why? Who is it that he sees in solitude, when he is alone? Whom does he face in darkness, in the hidden chambers of his heart? If the cause of these emotions does not belong to the visible world, the Person to whom his view is directed must be supernatural and divine. Thus the phenomenon of conscience shows that in the imagination of human beings there lives a picture of a supreme governor, a judge, holy, just, powerful, all seeing, who punishes the wicked, but rewards the good.*[1]

It is true that this "Person" to whom we respond in our conscience, is very much a Parent figure, modelled on our father and mother. It is natural that it should take this form. It is also natural that our concept of God will be greatly influenced by the experience we have had of our parents. There is an undeniable, psychological influence on the image we have of God.

The Speaker behind the voice

However, everything in our mind is psychological. All our relationships are influenced by human needs and human experience. The fact that we model the Reality to which we respond in conscience as a Parent figure, does not disprove that Reality. Rather, it shows that that Reality is experienced by us *as personal* – which is the point Newman is trying to make.[2]

Read also ch.3

---

1   J. H. Newman, *Essay in Aid of a Grammar of Assent*, London 1891, pp. 106-111.
2   For a discussion on the psychological character of all religious experience, see chapter 2 above.

33.

Belief in a personal God
frees us from moral scepticism.

I want to put before you two contrasting moral pictures.

A *Panorama* programme broadcast on British TV in 1994 documented vividly how in India social prejudice against women leads every year to the killing of hundreds of thousands of baby girls at birth. Males outnumber females by 36 million in India, a 4% population excess that cannot be explained by a statistical fluctuation. Girls are an economic liability to families since the parents have to produce a 'dowry' to get them married. Interviews with parents in Tamilnadu disclosed that the third or the fourth baby girl would often, at birth, be buried alive in a rubbish dump or refused food till she died.

I was particularly horrified by a lengthy report on a doctor in Rajasthan whose clinic specialises in eliminating female foetuses. With the lastest scanning equipment, the doctor establishes the sex of a child in the womb. If the child is female, more often than not it is aborted, sometimes just weeks before natural childbirth. The child is killed and then shown to the parents to prove she was really a girl, and thus worth to getting rid off.

At the same time I saw a news report on the civil war between the Hutus and the Tutsis in Rwanda. Among the accounts of the atrocities and massacres in the capital Kigali, there was also a story of real heroism.

An African religious brother, teacher in a local school, was offered the opportunity to escape to neighbouring Burundi, as much of the population did. But he had heard of a group of families who were trapped in the middle of the town. He decided to go there, in spite of the fact that that part of the town was in the hands of the army's murder squads. He managed to slip through to the troubled area. When he tried to lead people out, he was stopped by a military search party. They identified him as a leader. He was ferociously beaten and tortured, and then shot.

The Indian doctor would seem to be a murderer. The African brother gave his life to save people. We rate some people in our world as plain criminals, others as heroes and most of us somewhere in between. We live in a *moral* world. It does matter to us that greed, cruelty, exploitation and cowardice be exposed as such, that honesty, kindness, sacrifice and courage be valued and rewarded.

The main point I shall develop in this chapter is that moral values are ultimately absurd in a God-less materialistic universe.

The right of the strongest?

Suppose for a moment that the universe did come about by chance. Suppose that the mere physical forces of nature built up an earth such as ours, and that by purely mechanical evolution life progressed to produce 'thinking animals' such as we are. In such a world our 'mind' would be purely an accident, an afterthought. Good and evil would have no value in themselves. All that would matter is the programming of individuals in such a way that the genes of the species continue.

In such a world, morality would be really absurd. It would be absurd for at least three reasons: individuals would be expected to live up to moral obligations that did not serve their own good. Moral values would be irrelevant to the deep structure of reality. And scepticism about the real use of sacrifice and virtue would rob people of all motivation. I will explain this in detail.

A mother who already has three daughters gives birth to a fourth child. It turns out to be a girl. Is the mother allowed to kill her? Universal human conviction says: no! But we have to allow for extreme circumstances of poverty and cultural differences. The moral consensus today is that killing her is not allowed. Even if it were a custom tolerated by local law –

which it is not in India! – killing a child at birth is recognised as a crime against human life. The child has the right to live, like any other human being.

Now, in a materialistic world the reason for this moral judgment might be just *a feeling*, a feeling of compassion with no substance. The feeling, moreover, is nothing more than a psychological trick played on us by our genes: it is to the advantage of the species that murder is curbed. For practical reasons society may also impose sanctions, to guard persons from being killed by others. But all this does not constitute a compelling reason, a real inner obligation, for an Indian mother to let her baby daughter live.

In a Godless world in which we are just accidental froth on the ocean of evolution, the individual would be right in always seeking his or her own personal interest. If parents are poor and the fourth baby is a girl, they would be right to take its life, if they can do so without incurring a prosecution. A doctor can then, with impunity, make huge profits on procuring abortions based on gender.

Read also ch.37 & ch.64

In a Godless world, the sacrifice of one's life would also be absurd. For what does the individual stand to gain from it? Perhaps he or she will *feel* good in having helped someone else. . . . But does that not make the hero or heroine a pathetic figure? For in reality they would have paid a high cost for the ridiculously small reward of 'a good feeling' before they died! They themselves, however, and we too, would rate their action as enormously valuable in itself, as doing some real good by saving someone else's life.

In a Godless world, therefore, morality as we know it would be odd and out of place. The law of the jungle would prevail; and worse. For human beings can be more cruel than animals.

No room for higher values?
In a totally material world, the blind forces of nature dominate everything. Even human beings are merely the

*"Quiet, Pluto! The law of the jungle
does not apply here!"*

chance outcome of unpredictable evolution. Morality is no
more than a *surface phenomenon* of human culture. Human
beings protect each other because it serves the strategy of their
genes: it promotes survival of the species. Actions are only
'good' or 'evil' because human culture marks them as such.
Morality is then totally accidental to the real physical forces
that make up the deep structure of the universe.

But this is totally against our own moral convictions. Human beings consider honesty, kindness, generosity and fairness as the highest achievements of life on earth. Of course,
there are cultural differences. But the international convergence underlying the moral code is impressive.[1] People reckon

1   A. C. MacIntyre, *A Short History of Ethics,* New York 1966; E. O. Wilson,

that heroic love, as demonstrated by the African brother, stands out as a peak in human existence. They attach the greatest value to such moral deeds; much more than to the nuclear, chemical and biological dynamics that support life.

In a Godless world, human achievements of art, education, science, social care, international integration and so on, are not, as we normally judge, the best of what we have on earth, but rather some accidental outgrowth of only peripheral importance.

Our unspoken human conviction is that our mental and moral successes express something about the deep structure of the universe, that they reveal what its highest values are really about. If they do not, the life we live is absurd. George Mavrodes, who calls a totally materialist world 'Russellian' after Bertrand Russell, draws the conclusion that it would be absurd:[1]

Read also ch.15 ch.19 & ch.56

> *"Any moral demand is superficial in a Russellian world. Something that reaches close to the heart of my own life, perhaps even demanding the sacrifice of that life, is not deep at all in the world in which, on a Russellian view, that life is lived. And that is absurd. . . .*
>
> *If you share my conviction that it cannot in the end be absurd in that way, then perhaps you will, like myself, be attracted to a religious view of the world. Perhaps you too will say that morality must have some deeper grip upon the world than a Russellian view allows. And, consequently, things like mind and purpose must also be deeper in the real world than they would be in a Russellian world. They must be more original, more controlling. The accidental collocation of atoms cannot be either primeval or final, nor can the grave be an end."*

Sociobiology: the New Synthesis, Cambridge MA 1975; C. Hibbert, *The Roots of Evil*, London 1978.

1 G. Mavrodes, "Religion and the Queerness of Morality," in *Rationality, Religious Belief and Moral Commitment*, ed. R. Audi, Ithaca 1986, pp. 213-226, here p.225.

Is life absurd?

If we lived in a totally materialist world, we would be driven to complete moral scepticism. If more and more people were to adopt the materialist view, the underlying moral obligations would lose their validity in people's lives. Through education people would begin to understand that their traditional view of morality, as implying real values of good and evil, belongs to the past. Morality would then amount to a combination of two factors: inner norms of behaviour with no more force than being 'in good taste,' and external sanctions imposed by society.

But, since real moral obligations would have disappeared, the principal rule of life would be to get as much out of it as we can, even at the expense of other people, provided we can get away with it. Everything would be measured in terms of our own advantage. Society would become utterly hypocritical, for it would punish people for crimes which, in actual fact, would not be wrong as long as they had not been detected.

This, however, would lead to one absurdity after another. It would lead to moral despair, for a thinking person would not know any more what is right or wrong, or how to judge the society of which he or she is a part.

Such total and unrelenting moral despair is an absurd state.

There may be people influenced by some aspects of existentialism who believe that life is absurd and simply accept it. My reasoning is not intended for those people. It is intended for those people who believe that if life is truly absurd, it ought not to be lived. Since it ought to be lived, it must not be absurd."[1]

---

[1] L. Zagzebski, "Does Ethics need God?," *Faith and Philosophy* 4 (1987) pp. 294-303, here p. 300.

34.

"I don't need God
in order to be a good and responsible person!"

"Atheists are of the opinion that morality is not something that necessarily comes from 'a higher authority.' Their morality comes from their experience of how the world 'ought' to work, not from someone else. . . .

Human beings are social animals who can only live fully when in co-operation with their fellows. This is a good enough reason to discourage most atheists from most forms of anti-social and 'immoral' behaviour, purely for the purpose of self-preservation. If there is a good reason independent of the existence of any deities, why invent one?

Many atheists behave in what might be described as a moral way because they feel a natural human tendency to empathize with other humans. You might ask why empathize with others — why care about things which cause others to suffer? One answer is that there is often no reason. Many atheists simply are that way."

These paragraphs were the answer of the American Humanist Association to the question: Do atheists have morals?

The same Association describes humanist morality in the following positive creed:

"When making decisions about what is right or wrong, I believe I should use my own intelligence to reason about the likely consequences of my actions. I believe that I should try to increase the happiness of everyone by caring for other people and findings ways to cooperate. Never should my actions discriminate against people simply because of their race, religion, sex, age, or national origin.

> *I believe that ideas of what is right and wrong will change with education, so I am prepared to continually question my ideas using evidence from experience and science.*
>
> *I believe there is no valid evidence to support claims for the existence of supernatural entities and deities.*
>
> *I will use these beliefs to guide my thinking and my actions until I find good reasons for revising them or replacing them with other beliefs that are more valid."*[1]

In assessing the Humanist view, we should first of all acknowledge that it *is* a moral view. Humanists who respect human dignity, who refuse to discriminate against people, who try to increase everyone's happiness and who use their own intelligence to determine a responsible course of action in all circumstances are good and honourable people. We have no quarrel with either their good intentions or their just behaviour.

We can also agree to the Humanist contention that "there are no supernatural entities or deities" if this is understood in a naive sense. Humanists frequently fight the imaginary Father-Christmas figure who sits on a cloud, watching the earth below. That is not, however, the truly transcending God Christians believe in. For God is the Ground of all Being, the source of Truth, Beauty and Love, the creative power that supports the whole universe without being part of it. *Supernatural entities or deities do not exist. God does.*

Read also ch. 17

We can even agree to the Humanist plea not to base morality on decrees issued by a supernatural entity on another plane. As I have explained in previous chapters, morality is based on human nature itself, on what we called *natural law*.

---

1   R. P. Carver, *Affirmation of a Humanist*, Amherst 1993.

This natural law, or the way things are, obviously owes its existence, like anything else, to the Ultimate Reality. But this should not be imagined as a series of arbitrary decrees issued by God and imposed on created things from above. Natural law, which we discover by the power of our human intelligence, springs from the inherent requirements from our human nature, "from our experience of how the world ought to work," to borrow the Humanist phrase.

Humanists also earn our sympathy for distrusting 'dogmatic' systems of thought. Fanatics, fundamentalists and authoritarian religious leaders have caused havoc on the moral scene, and have made many people suffer on account of it. Believers need to be humble and to be ready to learn from new insights and new experiences, to correct mistaken ideas and refine their moral sensitivity.

Read also ch.10

No ultimate norms?

We part company from atheistic Humanists in our conviction that atheist morality misses an ultimate foundation. Morality must be *absolute* in the sense that it cannot be just up to me to determine what is right or wrong. If I kill another person, it is not just an unfortunate accident, a slip from my gentlemanly resolve to respect others; it is a real injustice. For life is a gift to me. I do not own the world or the people who populate it. I am obliged to respect reality the way it is, and this means: other people, and ultimately the source of all Reality, God.

Read also ch.13

Our own intelligence, and the combined intellectual search of the human community, are certainly the main tools at our disposal for finding out what our obligations are. But these do not *establish* these obligations, our mind only discovers what they are. If we have to avoid causing suffering to others, it is not just to satisfy our own self image. Tolerance, kindness and human care are duties we owe, not just caresses and 'strokes' to please our own ego.

The Humanist reliance on human reason as the ultimate norm poses grave dangers. Many well-intentioned people will, indeed, come to the right decisions by the conscientious use of reason. But there are many others who both individually and as groups may come to appalling conclusions.

Read also ch.29

The fact that some individuals, or a lot of people, or even the majority of human beings find something reasonable, does not *by itself* determine that the conclusion is right. We need a higher norm, which we have to judge our arguments by: reality, the way things are created. Then we can show which arguments make sense, and which not.

Human reason is, indeed, the tool at our disposal to judge right and wrong. There we wholeheartedly agree with our Humanist friends. But reason cannot be the *ultimate* norm.

35.

"Religion hinders human progress."

When the banking system began in the 14th and 15th centuries, Church Councils tried to ban the practice, equating the taking of interest with the 'usury' condemned by the Bible. When Charles Darwin published his theory of evolution in *The Origin of Species* (1859), he attracted a wave of hostility from Christian believers. When Margaret Sanger launched her campaign for family planning and birth control in 1914, she encountered the fiercest opposition from Church circles. The litany goes on and on. Religious institutions, as the guardians of tradition, often block progress.

It is true that religious leaders and religious institutions have, at times, blocked progress. And, rightly or wrongly, it was mostly God who received the blame for it.

In their indignation against various 'innovations,' Christian enthusiasts have frequently overstated their case, alleging that *God* was against this or that. In recent years Christian leaders have become more circumspect, but the impression at times lingers on: God is displeased with people who think for themselves and who try to improve the world.

This is all the more regrettable as just the opposite should be the case. According to the Bible, God blessed the human race and told them to take charge of the world:

"Be fruitful, multiply and fill the earth and take charge of it.

Take responsibility for the fish of the sea, the birds of the air and every living thing that moves upon the earth."[1]

---

1   *Genesis* 1,28.

And when Jesus took leave from his disciples at the Last Supper, he spoke these remarkable words: *"Truly, I say to you, whoever believes in me will do the works that I do. Yes, greater things than I have done will that person do, because I go to the Father."*[1] Of course, Jesus was mostly speaking of spiritual leadership, but other achievements were also included. Jesus was very much concerned about such earthly realities as feeding the hungry, clothing the naked, housing the homeless, nursing the sick, and doing justice to prisoners.[2]

It is also fair to say that, contrary to the impression created by the few Christians who oppose progress, Christianity itself, with its stress on human responsibility, has been a major factor in bringing about the European scientific and technological upsurge. The point has been dramatically illustrated by James Burke in his television serial *The Triumph of the West*. It was the spiritual convictions underlying Western societies that gave them the key to explore the universe, advance the sciences, travel to other parts of the globe and establish a new vision of an international community.

Taking responsibility

It is risky to venture a guess at how future generations will judge our century. Perhaps they will criticise us for not preventing World Wars I and II, and for constructing and using nuclear bombs. They may also give us high marks, however, for the dynamism with which technological advances have been pressed into service, in order to raise the living standards of people all over the world.

We live in an incredibly expansive era. As human beings we have really taken charge of the earth. We have created a new world order of communication and international cooperation. We have given a new impetus to the responsible growing of food, to health care, to safe and efficient manufacture of

---

1 *John* 14,12.
2 *Matthew* 25,32-46.

"I wish I hadn't taken responsibility for those two ants!"

essential goods and to improving all the infra-structures of society.

Of course, grave areas of concern remain: the unrestrained depletion of the earth's resources, the neglect of the Third World poor, the danger of a take over of politics by commerce, the whole question of international justice. But even in these areas we appear to be making progress. Enormous changes are taking places, many – I am happy to say – for the good, and all these changes are carried forward by our human determination to make the best of this world we live in.

Read also ch.65

I believe we can be proud of our achievements as a human race. I am also strongly convinced that we carry an enormous responsibility for our planet. Its viability and health in future generations depend on us.

Religion may well retard progress in some instances. People who are unwilling to change, usually resist change through a mixture of personal, cultural, national as well as religious motivations. But this does not mean that religion as such is an obstacle to change.

On the contrary, most people who are religiously motivated, will find in their belief strong reasons for taking their responsibilities seriously. Because they believe in a Creator, they will have the courage to try new avenues and be creative in their own work. Because they treasure the primacy of love, they will be prepared to offer their services, even at a personal cost. *Read also ch.36 ch.64*

It is here that Christian faith comes into its own. However well-intentioned agnostics often are, their motivation for selfless love is inadequately supported by rational argument. If there is no transcendent dimension to life, if human beings came about by a blind process of evolution in which the strongest survive, why bother about the plight of the weak?

Just for the record!

It is noteworthy that Christian motivations do make a difference to the external manifestations of selfless service. The European Values Research study has shown that, though practising Christians form less than one quarter of the population of Europe, they provide about half of all unpaid, voluntary workers. This extends not only to religious charities (in which they account for 88% of volunteers), but to all other charitable services.

> "*In all fields of activity, the more intimately people are involved in the institutional church, the more likely they are to be actively engaged as volunteers. . . .*
>
> *Core Church members comprise less than one-quarter of the combined populations of Europe and North America, yet they are overrepresented in all fields of voluntary activity, accounting for between one-third and one-half of all volunteers in each ma-*

jor category if work (excluding religion where their share is even higher).

Even in fields such as conservation and animal rights or sport and recreation in which, on measures of religious disposition, religious orthodoxy and confidence in the church volunteers do not differ from the population at large, core church members remain the largest source of volunteers.[1]

---

1 D. Barker, "Values and Volunteering," in *Volunteering in Europe*, ed. J. Davis Smith, Berkhampsted 1993, pp. 26.

36.

"Religion erodes our sense of responsibility for others."

Religious people put the responsibility for what happens in this world on God. As Creator, he has made things the way they are. Religions therefore teach their followers to accept the status quo including differences in social status, suppression and injustice. Religions often promise rewards in afterlife, sweetening the pill of suffering and depriving people of the incentive to improve their present lives. For the sake of human progress, religion should be exposed as a dangerous opium that should be proscribed.

The claim that religion as such hinders the process of liberation cannot be factually sustained. Most reformers in the Western world have actually been motivated by their Christian faith; and in many other continents it was Christian missionaries who brought education, health care, social reform and human freedoms.

Let us look at India, for example. The Oxford History reports that it was the Christian missionaries who introduced such vital improvements as schools, hospitals, medical field work, famine relief and rural uplift. In particular, they spearheaded reforms that would liberate women. In Hindu society women were completely under male domination. Around 1800 the principal abuses included *suttee*, i.e., burning widows alive on the funeral pyres of their husbands, infanticide of baby girls, child marriage, social alienation of widows, *purdah*, i.e., seclusion from public society, polygamy and temple prostitution.

Christian missionaries galvanised the government to pass new legislation in order to curb the worst excesses. They also introduced schools for girls; overcoming an age-old prejudice by untiring diplomacy and "by providing living examples of a new kind of womanhood to India." Though sharing the faith was obviously a cherished objective for missionaries, it was neither a condition nor even the first aim in providing humanitarian services. Missionaries were concerned about the plight of the poor, the illiterate, the outcasts and women, whatever their religion. The first school for girls was founded in 1830. Schools were followed by colleges for women. On Independence Day in 1947, half the hospitals and colleges in India were missionary foundations. Less than three percent of the patients and students served in these institutions were Christians.

This is the assessment of a secular historian:[1]

"The efforts of the missionaries had a practical effect in giving women hope against the traditional monsters of ignorance, pain and disease. They brought with them a new conception of woman as a personality and of her place in society. The effects of these measures also appealed to the masculine mind and worked both by revealing possibilities not considered before and stirring uneasy feelings at continued acquiescence in the status quo now shown to be as unnecessary as undesirable.

In this way a women's reform movement within Indian society was born, which gradually wrested the initiative from external agency and made the movement truly Indian."

In 1966 I attended the opening of new Christian hospital in Hyderabad, India. The inaugural address was given by Prof. Dr. Pai, a Hindu who was the chief medical officer of the State of Andhra Pradesh. Talking about motivation for doctors and nurses in health care, he recounted the parable of the Good Samaritan. A Jew on a deserted stretch of road falls into the hands of robbers and is left half dead by the way side. A priest and a Levite also passed that way. They saw the man, but let

---

1 V. A. Smith, *Oxford History of India*, Oxford 1958, pp. 724-726.

him lie. Finally someone who belonged to a hostile nation, a Samaritan, also came by. *"When he saw the wounded man, his heart was filled with pity. He went over, poured oil and wine on his wounds and bandaged them. Then he lifted the man onto his own donkey and took him to an inn where he nursed him. Next day he took out two silver coins and gave them to the innkeeper. 'Take good care of him.' he said, 'and when I come back this way, I pay you whatever else you spend on him'."*[1]

Dr. Pai said that the parable of the Good Samaritan was the finest expression of the medical ideal of service he had ever come across.

Foot washing

Similar examples can be given for most other parts of the developing world, whether in Asia, the Pacific Islands, Africa, or Central and South America. Almost all the leading intellectuals in young independent countries received their education from missionaries who left comfortable lives and promising careers at home, to serve total strangers in far off and often dangerous countries. They were not colonizers or only concerned with 'winning souls,' as is often maliciously stated. In spite of undeniable human shortcomings, these Christian volunteers were genuinely motivated by the desire to implement the ideal of genuine *service of others* which Jesus Christ holds out in the Gospel.

"You know that the rulers of pagans like to boss over others and their leaders like to show their power. This is not the way it shall be among you. If any one of you wants to be great, he must be the servant of the rest. If one of you wants to be first, he must be your slave – like the Son of Man, who did not come to be served, but to serve and to give his life as a ransom for many people."[2]

---

1   *Luke* 10,30-35.
2   *Matthew* 20,25-28.

"Love your neighbour as yourself. . . . Love your enemies. Do good to those who hate you. Bless those who curse you. Pray for those who abuse you. . . . Treat others in the way you want to be treated yourself."[1]

"Did you feed the hungry? Give a drink to the thirsty? Did you welcome a stranger? Did you give clothes to someone who was naked? Did you visit a person in prison? . . . I tell you, whatever you have done to the least of these brothers and sisters, even if you did not think of me, you have done to me personally!"[2]

These have not remained empty words. During the last hundred years more than one and a half *million* Christian missionaries founded and staffed village schools, high schools, colleges, rural health units, hospitals, leprosy centres, social training centres, rural development projects, adult literacy programmes, women's emancipation projects you-name-it in the most inaccessible places on earth. Who then can seriously contend that religion erodes our sense of responsibility for human welfare?

---

1 *Mark* 12,31; *Luke* 6,27-28; *Matthew* 7,12.
2 *Matthew* 25,31-46; freely translated.

37.

"Morality is ultimately based on self-interest."

"Moralities are systems of principles whose acceptance by everyone as over-ruling the dictates of self-interest
is in the interest of everyone alike, though following the
rules of morality is not of course identical with following
self-interest. . . .

The answer to our question – 'Why should we be moral?' –
is therefore as follows. We should be moral because being
moral is following rules designed to over-rule self-interest
whenever it is in the interest of everyone alike that everyone
should set aside his interest."[1]

Kurt Baier, an avowed atheist, maintains that we do not
need religious belief to safeguard morality. His argument is
that morality is simply based on self-interest without reference
to religious values.

Now, it is obvious that self-interest does play a part in
morality. It is especially operative if we do admit religious
values. For acting morally also establishes our self-worth. The
costs of our morally good actions are offset by the gain in
inner, spiritual and religious value. That, of course, is in our
self-interest. For since the moral order constitutes the peak of
reality, our moral actions make us share in what is best, highest
and dearest from a human point of view.

But Kurt Baier excludes that kind of self-interest. He re-
stricts self-interest to earthly values. If I respect other people's
property, they will respect mine. If I don't harm people, they
won't harm me. In that sense, he says, it is in my interest for
everyone to act in the right way.

---

1   K. Baier, *The Moral Point of View,* Ithaca 1958, p. 314.

*"I've decided it's in everyone's interest
to vote for all of you!"*

Let us analyse his argument. It seems to consist of three
logically connected statements:

• It is in everyone's best interest for everyone to be moral
(where 'everyone' includes me).

• Therefore it is in my best interest for everyone (including me) to be moral.

• Therefore it is in my best interest for me to be moral.

All three statements are questionable. How are we sure
that it *is* in everyone's interest for everyone to be moral? It may
be that the collective interest of society is served by everyone
being moral, but does that necessarily apply to me as an individual? If I have committed a murder and am pursued by the
police, it would be much to my advantage if the police were

"Move him on, Bates, before I develop a conscience!"

to accept a bribe and let me go. The immoral acts of the police might not be to the good of society, but it certainly would serve my self-interest.

Moreover, why would it be in *my* interest for me to be moral when everyone else is? Surely this is a fallacy. If everyone else is following the rules of morality, it surely is best for me to use this opportunity to my profit. Suppose no other businessman sells arms to terrorists – it leaves the coast free for me to do so and make handsome gains. The fact that others behave in morally acceptable ways does not make it more profitable for me to do so. The opposite will often be true.[1]

---

1 G. I. Mavrodes, "Religion and the Queerness of Morality," in *Rationality, Religious Belief and Moral Commitment,* ed. R. Audi, Ithaca 1986, pp.221-222; R. Brandt, *Ethical Theory,* Englewood Cliffs 1959, pp. 375-378.

In other words, the self-interest theory collapses. Morality will only stand if I perform morally good acts because they have a value *in themselves,* whether I profit from them or not.

The general interest of the species may well have something to do with the origins of human morality. But could it ever be the ultimate ground for ethical behaviour? Who determines what *is* in the general self-interest of the human race? Baier's concern for the underprivileged could well be countered by the factual observation that in evolution the weak are eliminated ruthlessly and that by helping the weak we are hindering progress.

Read also ch.31

Morality exists because we are not the centre of the universe. We receive, but we also have *to give.* **We are called upon to respond to the gift of life by a free and responsible self-giving on our part, a giving which may demand sacrifices, but which is at the same time a giving that will make us share in what is greatest and noblest in the universe.**

Part Four

Encounter

38.

If *we* have a mind, God has Mind.

So far we have discovered God as the Ground of our Being, as the Ultimate Reality, the source of objective morality. The question we now have to address is: is God personal? Is God a Reality we can relate to on a person-to-person basis?

Jews and Christians may well want to take a short-cut at this stage. They may point to a direct experience of God in prayer and worship. "God knows me, God loves me," they may well say. "I'm sure of it, because I feel his response. I don't need any further proof. God himself confirms his personal interest in me." Such testimonies have, indeed, great value. In the context of this book, however, we have to proceed more gradually. We will discuss our direct encounters with God in the chapters that deal with God's self-manifestation. Believers too will benefit from pondering to what extent God can be known as personal even without revelation.

Read ch.44 to ch.47

Does the Ultimate Reality know us? Can we relate to him/her/it? Does he/she/it communicate with us? Can we respond to the Ground of Being in personal prayer?

The answer to such questions is not simple. In many ways God is impersonal. He is the God of the whole universe. He has a very unusual relationship to the universe which, as we have already seen, should not be conceived in terms of ruling a two-tier world. God is not the supernatural Architect, Manager, Lawgiver and Maintenance Person he/she/it has sometimes been made out to be in popular religion.

Read ch.17 & ch.49

That is why some people defend a purely impersonal God. Joel Friedman calls it "the Natural God," a God which is the evolving, unifying, maximizing Force of Nature.[1]

---

1   J. I. Friedman, "The Natural God: a God even an Atheist can believe in," *Zygon* 21 (1986) 369-388.

God is not like a person at all, Friedman says. He, or rather It, is more like energy. God is the power of Nature. God pervades the world as the evolutionary force that drives everything to ever higher states of perfection. God is the bond that unifies everything from the highest to the lowest. But God is not a person. It is not conscious. It is as blind as a bat and does not think. We cannot talk to It.

We must think of God, Friedman continues, as the poetic expression of the life energy in us. All creatures dance, and so do we. God is the dance in us. God is the Life Spirit. It is the poetic, mysterious, fascinating side of life. God is something to celebrate in us, to give free rein to, to live out in art and beauty and depth of feeling. But God is not a ghost who hovers around us and to whom we can talk.

Now Friedman is absolutely right in affirming the impersonal life-giving aspects of God. God is the energy that brings forth the universe and the dance in us. Friedman is also right in rejecting the hovering-ghost image of God. But Friedman is wrong in denying a personal side to God.

Seeing intelligence at work

There are many reasons that compel us to say that God, our deepest Self, our life Force, the Ground of our Being *must* be personal. One reason we will consider in this chapter.

We know that God must have *mind*. He/she does not have mind in the sense of having a brain, a human mind, but in a way of speaking God *is* Mind. And God's intelligence must surpass ours immeasurably. When we say God has "mind" and is "mind," we mean God can know and think, though God's knowing and thinking will be of a totally different order.

How do we know someone else has mind?

Think of the ancient Cro-Magnon people who hunted in the South of France around 35000 BC. We have never met them, but we know their paintings. In dozens of underground caves of the Dordogne they have left breath-taking pictures of

"Your Dad's going to be awfully cross!"

the animals they hunted: deer, swine, aurochses, mammoths, antelopes, ibexes and bears. On some of the mural pictures the artists have left imprints of their right hand, as a signature or a gesture of power. The art they produced is filled with mind. We know these people had intelligence.

In Britain we have Stonehenge, an impressive monument of huge stone slabs arranged in a circle. It was constructed in the second millennium before Christ. The builders carved the huge stones from quarries in Wales and in the Marlborough Downs, and transported them many miles to their present location. Some they erected as pillars, others, often 30 feet long and weighing up to 50 tons, they heaved on top of them as lintels. The axes of the circular construction were aligned with the rising of the sun at its solstices on the 22nd of June and the 22nd of December.

We have never met the builders of Stonehenge, but in what they have left we can see mind. We see thought, planning and organisation. We know that they possessed intelligence.

The fact is that we can never see mind or intelligence directly. We see mind in what people do, in their actions. We know other people have intelligence by looking at their faces, and seeing how they respond. When we hear them speak or see them act, we instantly know they can think. We do not even stop to reflect on it. And yet, we cannot see mind itself. We only meet people's mind in the thoughts, plans and actions they produce.

The same applies to God's being *Mind*. If we can see mind in other people's behaviour, in works of art and intelligence left by our ancestors, we can see God's mind in the fact of intelligence in the created world. For if God is the evolving, unifying and maximizing energy in everything, he/she must be the energy that produces mind. An effect cannot be larger than its cause.

Please, note that what I am saying differs from the classical argument from design. When people still thought everything had been created directly by God – without evolution, they would see God's design and planning in every detail of nature. For every flower, it was thought, God made a blueprint that specified shape and colour and matching insects to pollinate it. All the planning seen in nature was thus considered to reveal the mind of the Architect God.

Read also ch.21

We now realise that the argument is not valid. In the first place, the detailed features of everything in nature are determined by the forces of evolution. And secondly, if God is held directly responsible for what is successful in nature, he/she would be equally responsible for all its failures. In recent years whole forests have been destroyed by Dutch elm disease. The cause is the fungus *ceratocystis ulmi* which is spread from tree to tree by burrowing bark beetles. A design fault by the Master Planner? It shows that the idea of a supernatural Creator God does not do justice to the facts.

Read also ch.49

But the argument from intelligence in the world lies on a more fundamental level. It is more like saying that *if there is a software programme that can play chess, the person who wrote that programme can also play chess*, to say the least.

Intelligence in the universe

If God creates and sustains *our* intelligence from within, he/she must at least possess the intelligence that we have. In fact, God's intelligence must surpass ours immeasurably. That is why God is personal. God knows us. God relates to us and can communicate to us, but all the time working on a deeper level.

Think of it like this. God's creative energy pushes the world, from within, to ever higher levels of development. In evolution life begins to emerge. There are viruses and plants. All of these express God's creative energy, however imperfectly and partially.

Then *face* appeared.

Animals evolved to have intelligence, with their 'faces' as its outward sign. Worms and snails have faces of a sort, fish and birds, each with their level of intelligence. The mammals evolved even keener faces. They can convey a wide variety of responses which offer an amazing range of communication. When we look at the face of a chimpanzee, we can recognise personality and the beginnings of real thought.

The process culminates in human beings. Our faces reflect our inner personality. Our faces radiate mind. They help us relate to other people. Now, while God of course has no face as we have, nor a human brain, nor other personality features, it is God's fullness that is reflected in the intelligence that makes us persons. In that sense God too is personal. God cannot be less that what he/she produces in us.

Can he who created the ear be deaf?

He who created the eye be blind?

He who created the mouth be dumb?

On the other hand, we should not glibly call God *a person*, as we human individuals are persons. God is not a supernatural ghost who hovers about the world and has dealings with one individual after the other. In that sense God is impersonal. God is the creative power that supports everything that exists including the force of evolution. But that does not mean that God is blind, unconscious or incapable of communicating to us.

God is Mind. God is 'personal,' but not in the *anthropomorphic* sense of being 'a person.'

> *When we say that God is personal, we really mean that he is not less than what we experience as personality, in the sense that the perfection of personality must be in him in the only manner in which it can be in an infinite Being. . . .*
>
> *In that sense God is super-personal .* [1]

---

1 F. Copleston, *A History of Philosophy*, vol.II, Westminster 1962, pp. 396-397.

39.

God is personal because God is the Ground of our personal self.

What is the "self" in us that makes us individuals, aware of who we are and what we are doing? In recent years many studies have been devoted to a scientific understanding of human consciousness.

There is little doubt about the fact that self awareness is a feature that gradually evolved in animals as their intellectual capacities increased. It is also undeniable that our typically human self has identifiable biological and psychological components. It relies on a specific wiring of neurons in the brain. It utilises 'software programmes' such as culture and language for its full expression.

Read also ch.31

I tend to agree with D.C.Dennett that consciousness is a programme developed in the brain which allows intelligence, especially our working memory, to reflect on itself, a process of higher-order thought, that is: thought about thought. And our "self" is a construction of consciousness to help us function better, a web of words and deeds that becomes our 'centre of narrative gravity.'[1]

But do such physical facts exhaust the full reality of our individual self? I do not imply that we should postulate an immaterial soul separate from the body – which was the natural thing to do for those who believed in a two-tier world. But objects and people can have a higher reality even if their infrastructure is material. And our human reason and personality stand out as a spectacular spiritual advance.

Read ch.17

I cannot understand the shallowness of thought exhibited by those scientists who believe that their analysis of physical

---

1 D. C. Dennett, *Consciousness Explained*, London 1991, pp. 209-226 and pp. 412-418; see also A. Newell, *Unified Theories of Cognition*, Cambridge MA 1990.

and biological components demolish the "self" as a higher entity. When a pianist plays Beethoven's *Moonlight Sonata*, the sounds can be broken down as a mixture of complex waves. Yet as a piece of music it inspires us and moves us on a higher level. The Sonata is *more* than just vibrations of air. Rembrandt's painting *The Jewish Bride* can be correctly described as vegetarian pigments on canvass. Its complete nature, however, is infinitely more: it communicates a message of human tenderness that touches our hearts. In the same way our molecular, biological and psychological make-up as human beings does not prevent our individual "self" from possessing its own higher-level reality.

Dennett too falls into the materialist trap. He calls the self "an *imaginary* construction by Homo Sapiens." I cannot see what is imaginary about it. We are individuals. We are unique, each with our own history and our own specific desires and aims. For our progress in evolution it was natural and necessary for the human brain to develop the hardware and software to cope with our emerging individualities. Just as our brain evolved programmes to handle the light we see, the sounds we hear and the language we listen to – none of them imaginary! – so it evolved self-consciousness to deal with our emerging personalities.[1]

"You" make me an "I"

Let us now turn to our own experience. Being a *self* is presupposed in all we think, say and do. But our own identity is linked to that of other people. If we reflect a little, we will discover that our ability to relate to other people is by far the most exalted and absorbing experience in our life. We love, we hate, we fear, we care, we listen, we talk, we read: we are

---

1 For criticism on the narrow mechanistic analysis of consciousness, see A. Koestler, *The Ghost in the Machine*, New York 1967; K. R. Popper and J. C. Eccles, *The Self and its Brain*, Berlin 1977; Z. Vendler, *Res Cogitans*, Ithaca 1972, and *The Matt er of Minds*, Oxford 1984; TH. Nagel, *The View from Nowhere*, Oxford 1986; D. Rosenthal, *A Theory of Consciousness*, Bielefeld 1990.

continuously engaged in a process of exchange with others. Other people affirm us as persons, and we affirm them.

The process began when we were small. We became personalities in our own right because our parents treated us as persons and not just as objects.

I would like to deepen this reflection using the approach of Martin Buber, who has coined the expression "I-Thou" for any genuine relationship. "Thou" is an old word for "you," and I will translate it here as "you." Buber's thought may, at first, seem academic and involved. But if we take the trouble to reflect on what he says, we will grasp that he is making a valid and crucial point.

A room, a bed, a table, a book, etc., are things. We deal with them, but they do not enter our personality. They are for us nothing more than an *It*. With them we have a so-called *It* relationship. Sometimes we also look on people as if they were an *It*. Suppose I am waiting in the outer office of a lawyer and a stranger comes. I may hardly notice her. She is just like another object in the room – an *It*.

But when I discover that she is my younger sister, the whole situation changes. I will stand up and address her as *you*. She becomes more important than everything else in the room. I have with her what Buber calls an "I-Thou" relationship.

As long as I am dealing with things (with *Its*), I remain closed. To some extent I myself remain an *It*. My own relationship with other *Its* is bound to time and place. I am, so to speak, just one object among many others. But when I really get to know another person and open myself to the other, when I say *you* to the other with all its depth of meaning, a change takes place in me. It is as if I enter a new world. I am no longer bound by time or space, but have, as it were, a direct relationship to the other, irrespective of time or place. It changes me into a real *I*, into *myself*. Because only in as far as another person exists for me, do I become myself.

"If you don't help me wash up, it will be the end of our I-Thou relationship!"

At the moment when I really say *you* to someone else, I live the fulness of my personality. I experience the full intensity of being me. When I share myself with another person in close friendship and loving intimacy, my *self* reaches a peak.

But, however dear another person may be to me, I only have rare and short moments of "I-Thou" relationship with him or her. Very soon the person will again become a *he* or a *she* (and, therefore, a sort of *It*) *about* whom I think or speak and who is, therefore, again reduced to being just one among many *Its* around me.

Yet I have a strong *self* and I feel in myself a limitless hunger for *YOU*, Buber says. Limited human persons cannot account for the fulness of my personality. So there must be another, totally satisfying, unlimited, eternal *YOU* to which my soul is responding, and with whom I am in touch. This eternal *YOU* alone can explain the self in me and the *you* in other human beings.

Read also ch.56

My link to the infinite YOU

Buber's argument here may not convince you unless you perceive its intuitive force. It is based on the insight that some realities imply a counterpart to account for a perceived 'completeness.' An example from biology might show what is at stake.

In 1835 Charles Darwin, while studying flowers in Madagascar, was struck by the white Christmas orchid. This orchid has a honey-sack or "nectary" that is more than a foot long! The honey fills only one-and-a-half inch at the bottom. Darwin knew that the honey in flowers is meant to attract insects who pollinate the flower while sucking the honey. But no insect could be found with a proboscis long enough to reach such honey a foot deep.

After reflecting on the matter Darwin concluded that such an insect must exist. He said it should be a moth that operated during the night, as no daylight insects could account for the fertilization. Its tongue was to be a foot long. Many zoologists ridiculed the idea. But forty years later Darwin was proved right. The insect was found. It turned out to be a night-flying moth with a 10-inch tongue. It received the name *xanthopan morganii praedicta*, that is: "the moth that had been foretold."

Of course, this is just an illustration. But it shows how the existence of one reality (such as the openness of our inner *self*) can postulate the existence of its complementary reality (God, the Ground of all personality and self).

This is how Martin Buber puts it:

"The extended lines of human relations meet in the eternal Thou. Every particular Thou is a glimpse through to the eternal Thou. In every particular Thou, I ultimately address the eternal Thou."[1]

---

1 M. Buber. *I and Thou*, Edinburg 1937, passim; see also E. Brunner, *The Divine-Human Encounter*, London 1944.

What is the meaning of this in simple terms?

Read also ch.15 & ch.58 I become a person by other people affirming my identity. But I know that those people, however loving they are, cannot fulfill my deepest need of recognition. I carry in me a hunger to be realised by the whole of reality, by Ultimate Reality, by God. In fact, I know intuitively that the Source of all Being does affirm me and allows me to be me. And even if all other human beings would let me down and disown me, that affirmation by God constitutes me as a person. I also realise that it is this deepest affirmation that releases in me the ability to have other inter-personal relationships.[1]

God in us

Jan van Ruysbroeck, a mystic who lived in Flanders six centuries ago (1294-1381) expressed the same truth in poetic form. "God is more interior to us," he said, "than we are to ourselves. His acting in us is nearer and more central than our own actions. God works in us from inside outwards. Created beings work on us from the outside."

Why is each one of us an individual? "Because God has made us after his own image," Ruysbroeck said. The reason for our *self* is that each one of us is an expression, an imprint of the eternal *Self* of God.

> *Our essential and highest individuality lies in God. All creatures exist and live and are preserved by being united to God. The moment we were to be separated from God, we would return to nothingness. Our link to God is the self we possess, a self that reaches beyond ourselves: it is the origin and mainstay of our existence and our life.*
>
> *The essential unity of our personality with God is not of our own making. . . . Our spirit receives according to its most interior and highest being, in na-*

---

1 Borrowing a term from trinitarian theology, H. Ott calls this action of Ultimate Reality God's *perichoresis*, "intimate embrace" in us; *Gott*, Stuttgart 1971, pp. 10-16; *Wirklichkeit und Glaube*, Stuttgart 1975, vol. II, p. 178.

ked nature so to speak, the imprint of God's eternal image and God's own radiance – all the time without ceasing.

Created by God, we undergo every moment of our life the imprint of God's eternal image. Like an untarnished mirror we cannot fail to reflect that image.

The image God has of us, gives all of us life and existence. Our created being is anchored in that image as in its cause. . . . Thus our personality rests in God, and flows from God, and hangs in God, and returns to God as its eternal source.[1]

1   J van. Ruysbroeck, *The Spiritual Espousals*, London 1952, passim.

40.

The ultimate nature of our universe is personal.

We may well consider ourselves fortunate to live in our modern, technological age. We enjoy luxuries our ancestors would have envied. We take for granted a living standard undreamt of for ordinary people not so long ago: security, rights as citizens, material well-being, competent health care, fulfilment of individual aspirations, wholesome food and stimulating entertainment. But our secular, urbanised world also has its dark sides.

Our industrial and consumerist society destroys natural community. It breaks us up into individuals who have to manage on our own. Often it leads to indescribable loneliness and isolation, to people living within the four walls of their homes as in a prison from which they cannot escape.

A painful example of this came to my attention when I was visiting Vienna a few years ago. A taxi driver told me that in an inner-city flat the bodies of two elderly sisters had been found. They had both died of natural causes, and he told me some of the details.

The discovery occurred when the electricity board decided to install a new meter. The inspector could not obtain access to the flat. In the end he called in the police. They broke down the front door and found the dead bodies.

Medical examination established that the two sisters had died twelve years earlier (!) of old age. One of the sisters had outlived the other by about a month. She had rolled her sister in a carpet before she had herself died. No one had noticed their absence, the police had declared, because the two sisters paid all their regular bills for rent, gas and electricity by standing order.

"Another exciting day!"

Twelve years they lay dead and unburied, and yet no one noticed! What about the neighbours? What about family or friends? Did they not have any close acquaintance who *missed* them? And why was there no call for help when one of them fell ill and died? Was there no one whom they could trust and to whom they could turn for support? The taxi driver who told me this story was an immigrant from Turkey. "Allah forgive us," he said, "for building cities where all people are strangers to each other."

This may seem an extreme example, but it illustrates well the loneliness of many of our contemporaries. At the time when they are most needed, the traditional buttresses to our identities are being eroded:[1] the extended family, the parish community, cultural homogeneity, the friendly neighbour-

---

1 Ch. Lash, *Men in Darkness: Psychic Survival in Hard Times*, New York 1990.

hood, companionship in the workplace. People starve of a lack of intimacy and of healthy friendships.

We are "the lonely crowd." We are like Jean-Paul Sartre's bus passenger standing at a bus stop with twenty others whom we do not know and do not speak to.

On our own in the universe?

"My case is different," you may well say. "I have a loving family, pleasant workmates and wonderful friends." I do not doubt it. Fortunately, a good many people have. Personal relationships are necessary for survival. They can only be sustained by creating small clearings in our concrete jungle, clearings in which relationships can flourish. Such protected spaces include our home, our immediate neighbourhood, our circle of friends. Within the ocean of the faceless crowd that sweeps us along, we have our small islands of human friendship.

I have dwelt on all this to make you aware of how important relationships are for our human existence. In a manner of speaking, we live for them. It is intimacy, genuine love, being known by name, being needed by other human beings, that makes our life worth living.

If this is the case, if the *personal* aspect of existence means so much to us, why should we regard it as of secondary importance when considering the nature of the universe? Does our experience not rather show that the whole universe itself must ultimately be personal?

What I mean is this. A physical scientist may well describe you as a heap of atoms and molecules, but will that convince you that your experience as a person – the acquisition of knowledge, your awareness of self, your giving and receiving love – are of less account? Will you not rather think that your power of reason and your personality are of higher value than the biological infra-structure that supports them? Are you less a person, because you are made up of atoms? Do you feel human consciousness counts for little because the material earth is so much more bulky than we are?

Why then surrender to a view of the universe that is totally physical and mechanistic? Sure, the Big Bang was driven by nuclear forces. The galaxies are thousands of millions of stars made up of atoms that interact according to physical laws. But even if there were just one planet – our own earth – that has produced life and intelligent personalities like ourselves, does it not show that our universe is basically more *Read* than mechanistic, that it is capable of producing thinking and *also* loving persons, that it is ultimately personal? *ch.48*

Seeing the mystery of seeing

We can approach this in a variety of ways. The basic insight is to recognise the mystery in our own perception and thought.

Those familiar with physics may want to start with the strange influence which observation has on giving to indeterminate elements of a wave function a definite value. Physicists generally accept this so-called Copenhagen interpretation of quantum mechanics, but they cannot explain why measurement by an intelligent being should determine the outcome of something that is, in itself, not determined. Observation is thus regarded as something intrinsically different from anything else in nature. Does it not reveal a special role for intelligent life in the universe?[1]

In the Gospel Jesus Christ says:

Blessed are the pure of heart: they will see God![2]

and

I am telling you the truth, unless you are born a second time you cannot see the realm of God.[3]

---

1   F. Capra, *The Tao of Physics,* Wildwood House 1975; *The Turning Point,* Wildwood House 1982.

2   *Matthew* 5,8.

3   *John* 3,3.

Seeing the religious dimension, the dimension of mystery, the dimension of God, requires another level of awareness. It is like a re-birth, coming out of the womb a second time and looking at the world with fresh eyes!

It is difficult to describe this new insight. Perhaps we may call it the transition from seeing mere objects to suddenly discovering the *personal dimension* in reality. Hindus speak of shifting attention from hearing to the Hearer, from seeing to the Seer, from speech to the Speaker, from knowing to the Knower. They do not only mean a switch from reflecting on the mysterious fact of our own seeing and knowing, but on seeing and knowing as such. If we are a universe of seeing and knowing, then who is the ultimate Seer and Knower?

> *He who dwells in your understanding, yet is other than your understanding, whom your understanding does not know, whose body is your understanding, who controls your understanding from within – he is the Self within you, the Inner Controller, the immortal.*
>
> *He is the unseen seer, the unheard hearer, the unthought thinker, the unknown knower.*
>
> *There is no other seer than he,*
>   *no other hearer than he,*
>   *no other thinker than he,*
>   *no other knower than he.*
>
> *He is your Self, the Inner Controller, the immortal.*[1]

God meets us from all directions

If the universe is ultimately personal, then God, the source of all Being, is personal. In fact, "God is the personal depth of reality."[2] Yes, we experience something of the power of God in the eruption of a volcano or the explosion of a su-

---

1 *Bruhad Aranyaka Upanishad* III, 7, 22-23; see R. Panikkar, *The Vedic Experience*, London 1977, p. 709.
2 K. Ward, *Holding Fast to God*, London 1982, p.6.

pernova, but we equally meet God's tenderness in every intimate human embrace. It is because God is the personal depth
of reality that, as human beings, we are starved when we are
fed on bread alone. We need friendship.

When we discussed conscience, we met the same phenomenon in another form. We spontaneously respond to Ultimate Reality as to a person. In acknowledging our *Read ch.32*
responsibility for good and evil, we implicitly accept a deeper
relationship to a personal power who can judge us. In a
mechanistic universe we would owe nothing to any single
thing.

The most profound truth that can be stated about the reality of the world is that, in the ultimate analysis, it is a personal reality. Relationship, and especially genuine love, are *Read*
the highest aspects of our life. We have to conclude therefore *also*
that our Origin, our Ground of Being, cannot be a nebulous *ch.65*
force, a blind impersonal energy. He/She must be a reality we
relate to as a You, a "Thou."

*At the same time we must remember God is more
than a human Thou, more than just anybody.*

*If we imagine a Somebody, we imagine him or her
approaching us from one direction: from this place
or that, from the right or the left. It is then a limited
someone, a person.*

**But the Thou of God meets us from all directions,
from the roots of existence, from other persons,
from all that happens to us. God is the Source supporting us and meeting us from all directions.**[1]

---

1 See *A New Catechism*, London 1970, pp. 488-502.

41.

"It is perfectly logical to call God *a person*."

The element of body is not essential to personhood. God is, therefore, rightly called a person in the sense of God being a Pure Spirit, a personality without material defects.

God is a person without a body, i.e., a spirit, who is free, able to do anything, knows everything, is perfectly good, is the proper object of human worship and obedience, the creator and sustainer of the universe.[1]

Before I can reply to this question, I will have to define personhood more precisely. Some authors complain that it is 'fuzzy,' 'an untidy term,' 'a word often used sloppily.' So here we go. The term person carries at least five connotations in ordinary usage:

1. A person is **a thinking, intelligent being.** This is the classic definition favoured in the Middle Ages and much later.[2]

2. A person is **an individual who relates to other individuals.** We stress this feature when we say someone pays us "personal" attention, etc.

3. A person is **a character or role.** *Persona* was a mask worn by actors in classical drama. An actor or actress presented a *persona*, a character. We still use this original sense when we state someone acted "in the person of. . .," or someone "impersonated" someone else.

4. A person is **an individual with rights and duties.** This is legal language. Even companies and institutions can be "a person" in law.

---

1 R. Swinburne, *The Coherence of Theism,* Oxford 1982, p. 1; see also *The Existence of God,* revised edition, Oxford 1991. Similar definitions are found with D. High, *Language, Persons and Belief,* New York 1967, pp. 180-181; H. P. Owen, *Concepts of Deity,* London 1971, p.18; J. J. Shepherd, *Experience, Inference and God,* London 1975, p.4.

2 J. Locke, *An Essay Concerning Human Understanding* (1689 AD), ed. Oxford 1924, p. 188.

5. A person is **the body of a human individual.** This is clear from such expressions as: "No gun was found on his person." "She had a stately person."

I have already shown that God is *personal* in the first two of these five senses. God has intelligence and God relates to us. The Ultimate Reality is not just blind energy, not a dark chasm of nameless power, not an unechoing chasm of boundless infinity. God is personal. But is God *a person*?

Finding the right terminology

There are three main reasons why I believe we should *not* refer to God as "a person": (1) however much we try to avoid it, our concept of "a person" includes bodiliness; (2) the expression "a person" obscures the impersonal features of God; and (3) the concept of God as "a person" implies the outdated dualistic two-world view.

Firstly, however much we try to dematerialise our concept of God as a Person, we cannot avoid introducing inner-worldly, materialistic elements.

Given the use of 'God' as 'Pure Spirit,' we cannot understand what it would be for such a being to act and thus be loving, merciful or just, for these predicates apply to things that a person does. But we have no understanding of 'a person' without 'a body' and it is only persons that in the last analysis can act and do things. We have no understanding of 'disembodied action' and thus no understanding of 'a loving but bodiless being.'[1]

Secondly, using the expression "a person" may obscure impersonal features of God.

If God is conceived too rigidly under the individualistic aspect of "person," important qualities within the overall notion of God are lost. . . . God is

---

1 K. Nielson, *An Introduction to the Philosophy of Religion*, New York 1982, pp. 36-37.

*impersonal in his dealings with the whole of what
is. God does not show partiality. God's love is universal in scope and intent; particularistic love is
not. Surely an adequate conception of God must
view God as transcending the particularistic limitations that we as human persons experience in our
finite love. God's love is impersonal in that it is directed at the whole of creation and is not (just) intended or directed to individuals in themselves.*[1]

Last but not least, the concept of God as "a person" necessarily evokes the traditional two-tier world view which no
longer fits our modern, scientific understanding of the universe. As we have seen before, God as the supernatural Creator
and Maintenance Man is dead. When we define God as "a
person," we seem to imply philosophical concepts that contradict our modern world view.

*Read
also
ch. 17*

*I criticize not belief in a personal God, but certain
ways of expressing [that] belief. . . . Christians do
need to hold that God is personal: they do not need
to hold that God is a person. . . . Perhaps the big-
gest difficulty for bodiless theism is that the most
respected theologians for the church, ancient and
modern, have no use for the modern term 'person'
in relation to God. . . . More importantly God is not
called a person in the bible, not even by Jesus.*[2]

*God is not a person as a human being is a person.
The primal ground, primal support and primal goal
of all reality, which determines every individual existence, is not an individual person among other
persons, is not a superman or superego. The term*

---

1 C. D. Grant, "Personal and Impersonal Concepts of God: a Tension within
contemporary Christian theology," *Encounter* 49 (1988) pp. 79-91; here 81-82.

2 A. Thatcher, "The Personal God and the God who is a Person," *Religious Studies*
21 (1985) pp. 61- 73; here 70-71; J. MacQuarrie, *Principles of Christian Theology,*
London 1977, p. 116; see also G. Legenhausen, "Is God a Person?," *Religious
Studies* 22 (1986) pp. 307-323.

"person" also is merely a cypher for God. God is not the supreme person among other persons. God transcends the concept of person. God is more than person.

God is not less than a person. God is not neuter, not an "it," but a God of people. He is spirit in creative freedom, the primordial identity of justice and love, one who faces me as founding and embracing all interhuman personality.

It will be better to call the most real reality not either personal or nonpersonal but – if we attach importance to the terminology – transpersonal or suprapersonal.[1]

---

1 H. Küng, *Does God Exist?*, London 1980, pp. 632-633.

42.

"Doesn't Scripture present God as *a* person?"

On all its pages the Old Testament presents God as a living God. God's stated name, "I AM WHO I AM," expresses God's dynamic presence as someone who saves his people. God is a personal God. "I am the God of your fathers, the God of Abraham, the God of Isaac, the God of Jacob." God is a God who cares. He listens. He speaks. He guides the course of history.[1]

In the New Testament Jesus, too, presents God under personal images. He compares God to a landowner, a king, a judge. And mostly he calls him "Dad," "Father" – with all the connotations of authority, tenderness, parental care and intimate love the title implies.[2]

Does all this not show that God is "a person," in spite of all you have said?

No it does not. It shows that God is personal, not that he/she is *a person*.

Nowhere in Scripture is God called *a person*. It is true that many scriptural images reflect the two-tier world view that was prevalent at the time. God is imagined to sit on his throne in his heavenly palace. From there he rules the world, sending his angels to carry messages, unleashing locusts and famine as punishments, and changing the course of a battle when required. Though God is not explicitly referred to as *a person*, he is undoubtedly imagined as if he were a person in the supernatural world.

What we have to remember is that employing such *images* does not imply that the two-tier world view has to be taken as real. We too cannot help having to imagine God in terms that correspond to our immediate human experience. We

---

1 *Exodus* 3,6 and 3,13-15.
2 The Aramaic Abba *means* "Dad"; *Mk* 14,36; *Rom* 8,15; *Gal* 4,6.

"*Ee, by gum, mother – it's our Jim come 'ome.*
Open a tin of corned beef!"

may address God as "Almighty God" or "Father" – and *imagine* him/her in such a human form, without forgetting God's total otherness.

Yes, Jesus called God "Father" to articulate his experience of God's love. And never did he portray this better than in the parable of the Prodigal Son. The younger son, you will recall, had demanded his share in the family inheritance. Then he departed for a far country and squandered it all on drink and prostitutes. When he finally returned home, penniless and repentant, he found his father was waiting for him.

> *While he was yet at a distance, his father saw him and felt sorry for him. He hurried to meet him, embraced him and kissed him.*[1]

---

1   *Luke* 15,11-24.

Now John expresses exactly the same when he says: "God is love." He does not say: "God is a loving person," but "God is Love itself. God is the source of love. God manifests himself in every act of genuine love."[1] Where Jesus uses the image of a person, John points to the underlying suprapersonal Reality.

Read also ch.56

In spite of using human images about God, Scripture teaches that God remains a mystery. God is a hidden God.[2] And the Fathers of the Church teach the same. "If you think you understand God, it is not God," St. Augustine said.[3]

St. Thomas Aquinas, the uncrowned, medieval king of traditional theologians, came to the same conclusion.

The ultimate reach of our human knowledge of God consists in our acknowledging that we do not know him. For then we realise that what God is, surpasses everything we understand of him.

Our mind arrives at a better understanding of God the more we realise that the nature of God is above all that our mind can grasp in this life.[4]

Read also ch.4

Whenever we think about God, we have to think in images. Now it is natural for us to use personal images, images which represent God as a Father, a Mother, a King, a Friend, a Judge, a Lover. Scripture employs this language and we may rightly follow this example in our Christian worship. But we always have to remember that they are just images. God is not a human lookalike.

---

1 *1 John* 4,7-12.

2 *Judges* 13,18; *Job* 36,26; *Isaiah* 45,15; *Proverbs* 30,1-4.

3 *Augustine, Sermons* 52.6.16 and 117.3.5.

4 Thomas Aquinas, *De Potentia* vii, 5, ad 14; *In Boethii de Trinitate,* 1, 2, ad 1; more in CH. Journet, *The Dark Knowledge of God,* London 1948.

43.

"What about the *three* Persons in the Blessed Trinity?"

"You say God is not a person. What about your Christian faith in the Trinity? Don't you believe there are **three** *persons in God: Father, Son and Holy Spirit?" Instead of God just being one person, he is THREE!"*

Yes, Christians believe that there is one God who has revealed himself/herself as Father, Son and Holy Spirit. We know God as Father in his sovereignty, as Son in his self-communication in the incarnation, and as Holy Spirit in his self-communication to us in our daily life. Father, Son and Holy Spirit are three "Persons" in one God.

What we have to remember is the fact that the use of the term "person" in the context of the Trinity is unique, not to say idiosyncratic. It does not mean "person" in the way in which we use the term today. When we speak of a "person" today, we refer to an individual who can independently think, decide and act. If there were three persons like this in God, there would in fact be three Gods. But Christian doctrine, as laid down in early Church Councils, firmly holds that Father, Son and Holy Spirit are one God. They have one intelligence, one will, and one combined external action, if we may use such human terms about God. Father, Son and Spirit possess one divine nature and are not distinct in anything else except their mutual relationship to each other.

The use of the term "person" in the Trinity was introduced by the Greek Fathers of the Church as an equivalent of *hypostasis,* subsistence. What they were trying to express is that somehow, though God is one, he/she/it is not solitary. Within the one God there are mutual relationships, different faces as it were that reflect one another.

In human language this is sometimes expressed as the Father reflecting on himself and thus giving birth to the Son, and Father and Son reflecting on their mutual love which becomes the Holy Spirit. Since we are talking about God's deepest essence, we are dealing with first-class mystery, and human terms will always remain inadequate.

Christian belief in the Trinity emphasises the conviction that God is personal. In God's self-revelation to us in the incarnation and continued presence of God's Spirit, we experience a glimpse of enormous depths of relationships and love in God. In however small a way, we share in the richness of these relationships in God by our awareness of Father, Son and Holy Spirit in God.[1]

But the term 'person' is not a fortunate turn of phrase when we speak of the Trinity today.

> *The word person, because of the manner in which it is understood today, will almost automatically be misunderstood in the trinitarian formula. It will need to be extensively explained. Whenever possible, it is better to use the terminology we find in Scripture.*[2]

If I may sum up the meaning of our Christian belief in the Trinity in non-theological terms, it comes to this. God, cosmic Mind and uncreated Love, is so intensely personal that we experience him/her as caring parent, intimate brother/sister and inner spark in us, all at the same time. The personal dimensions in God are inexhaustible.

---

1 T. O'Brien, *Living in Personal Relationship with God, Father, Son and Holy Spirit,* London 1990.

2 K. Rahner, 'The Trinity' in Sacramentum Mundi, London 1971, vol.12; *Schriften zur Theologie,* Tübingen 19 vol.13, pp. 129-147.

44.

God makes contact with us
from the beyond within us.

The purpose of this chapter is to explain the Christian belief that God revealed himself/herself to us in a number of ways, culminating in God becoming human in Jesus Christ. Later we will examine reasons that make such a belief worthy of acceptance. Here I aim at clearing up misunderstandings.

Let me first explain some traditional terminology.

God is said to work on us, and in us, through *grace*. Grace comprises all the tangible and intangible things God does to us. He draws us to himself, encourages us, forgives us, heals us, enlightens us, comforts us, saves us.

When God communicates a message to humankind, it is known as *revelation*. When God assists human authors to write in his/her name, it is called *inspiration*. God is believed to have revealed information about himself/herself and about his/her intentions, in a gradual programme of revelation and inspiration that spanned the Old and New Testaments.

God's revelation of self culminated in the *Incarnation*. Incarnation means that the Son of God assumed human nature and lived among us as a human person. He was, as the creed says, 'truly God and truly human.' Because Jesus is both divine and human, he can save us from our sins, make us adopted children of God and give us his Spirit.

Christian doctrine, even in its traditional formulation, has never been naive. Incarnation has never been understood to mean, as some people think, that Jesus of Nazareth was not fully human. He was. He had a human body and a human personality, like us. He spoke a human language, Aramaic. He worked with his hands and walked with his feet. He had to sleep like us, eat like us, look after his health as we need to do. Jesus Christ was *not* a divine ghost in a human shell.

How can one person, Jesus Christ, be both human and divine? Bypassing for the moment the complex formulations devised in two thousand years of Christian theology, that belief may be best summed up in words of St. John's Gospel. God expressed himself faithfully in this human person – so that Jesus became an expression of what God is like. "Who sees me, sees the Father." "Who hears my words, hears the words of my Father." In Jesus, "God's Word became flesh," which we may translate as: in Jesus' humanity God expressed fully what he is like.[1]

Supernatural events?

In the traditional Christian language of Scripture and Sunday worship, revelation and incarnation have usually been expressed in images of a two-tier world. "In many and various ways God spoke of old to our fathers by the prophets, but in these last days he has spoken to us by his Son."[2] The Son of God came down from heaven, assumed human nature and lived among us as a human being.[3] The Father (= the Supernatural God) sent his Only Son into the world to save all those who would believe in him.[4]

Read ch.17 But such 'supernatural' imagery is not required to do justice to the belief in revelation and incarnation. In fact, as I have already pointed out, such imagery may pose serious obstacles to expressing faith adequately in our own scientifically-minded age.

In a two-tier world view, God's interventions are like dinosaurs that suddenly appear from nowhere, upsetting the balance of nature and changing the whole landscape by their unexpected intrusion. If God wishes to communicate with in-

---

1 *John* 14,9; 7,16; 1,14.
2 *Hebrews* 1,1.
3 *Philippians* 2,4
4 *John* 3,16-17

telligent creatures, could he/she not act in a more integrated manner?

A better image, therefore, is to picture the whole process as happening from within. In the course of human history God manifested himself by a series of ever more telling eruptions of divine awareness and divine revelation. They culminated in God's incarnational self-manifestation in Jesus Christ. They continue in the post-resurrectional presence of the Holy Spirit in people who are transformed by the Christ event.

Such a process of revelation and incarnation *from within*, or rather *from the beyond within us*, is not less objective and factual than interventions from above in a two-tier world.[1] For it is really God, Ultimate Reality, who breaks through into human consciousness and human life from within. It is not just an imaginary or fictitious awareness I am talking about. Just as God, the Creative Energy, caused eyes to evolve and mind to emerge, so God made spiritual openness and religious salvation erupt in the life of humankind.

This then is how we may imagine what happened.

Incarnation from within

God as the Ground of Being supports all growth. God is the Life Force that underlies the whole of the universe. God allows the forces of evolution to avail themselves of ever more exciting new forms of life. God opens avenues for intelligence to emerge. As higher and higher forms of intelligence arise, he/she permits and encourages the growth of the human self. God enables human freedom and autonomy to take hold in responsible personalities. God, the divine intelligence at the root of it all, recognises himself/herself more and more. God allows human personality to become, however faint, a mirror of himself/herself.

---

1   L. S. Thornton, *The Incarnate Lord*, London 1928, p.84.

Then the Ground of Being caused more direct awareness of its own existence to break through. Religion emerged. Sensitive people became mystics who were more conscious of Ultimate Reality than others. Some gifted individuals were so open to Ultimate Reality that they could convey messages on its behalf. They were the prophets. Finally, when religious consciousness had been sufficiently prepared, incarnation could happen.

In Jesus of Nazareth, Ultimate Reality found a human being so utterly open, so totally committed, so imbued with spiritual values that this human person could express God's purpose as never before. Jesus' humanity became 'the reflection of God's glory, bearing the stamp of God's nature.'[1] As the Son of God he made God's glorious love transparent and thus made the Father known.[2] Jesus Christ, while being completely human, was also divine as "the Word of God (= God's self-manifestation) made flesh."[3] As our high priest, chosen from among us and sharing all our human weaknesses, he could become our source of salvation.[4]

Christian belief is compatible with this image of *incarnation from within.*[5]

Two-tier world imagery is not the only imagery found in Scripture. Jesus himself used parables and comparisons that stress growth and God's hidden action from within.

The kingdom of God is not coming with external signs. People will not say: 'See, it is here!,' or 'See, it is there!' For the kingdom of God is within you![6]

---

1 *Hebrews* 1,3.

2 *John* 1,14-18.

3 *John* 1,14.

4 *Hebrews* 5,1-10.

5 I recommend in this context the Christology of the process theologians, especially N. Pittenger, *The Word Incarnate*, New York 1959; J. E. Barnhart, 'Incarnation and Process Philosophy', *Religious Studies* 2 (1967) pp. 225-232; D. R. Griffin, *A Process Christology*, Philadelphia 1973; L. S. Ford, *The Lure of God*, Philadelphia 1978; see also K. Rahner's evolutionary Christology in *Theological Investigations*, London 1970-1986.

6 *Luke* 17,20-21.

The kingdom of God is like this. A farmer scatters seed on the land. He goes to bed at night and wakes up in the morning, and the seed grows and sprouts – how, he does not know. The ground produces a crop by itself, first the blade, then the ear, then full-grown corn in the ear. But as soon as the crop is ripe, the farmer sets to work with the sickle, because harvest time has come.[1]

God reveals himself/herself to us, saves us and inspires us from within.

1   Mark 4,26-29.

45.

God's incarnation continues today in sacramental realities.

Suppose for the moment, that what we discussed in the previous chapter is true. God, the creative Life Force, communicated himself/herself to us *from within* by an ever more intense religious awareness. Finally God manifested himself/herself fully in a human person, in Jesus Christ. How does that make a difference to us?

After all, Jesus lived two thousand years ago. Even if he was the incarnate word of God, how would this improve my contact with God? Has it brought God closer to me – to someone who lives in the twentieth century?

The purpose of this chapter is to explain how the incarnation that took place in Jesus Christ continues to bring God present to me in undeniable, powerful realities. For Jesus' Spirit continues to live on in me.

The first key factor is my experience of newness of life and hope. As a Christian I believe that God revealed his/her deepest nature to be LOVE. This has enormous consequences for my understanding of the world and my place in it. I know that, somehow or other and in spite of apparent contrary evidence, the meaning of life is positive. I also believe that God, who is LOVE, heals me: he/she forgives my sins and accepts me fully the way I am.

Read also ch.56 to ch.59

The realisation that LOVE is of primary value in the universe changes my view on what happens in the world. I begin to see a deeper dimension in my relationship to other people. I assume more daring commitments, because I now grasp the value of such seemingly useless actions as selfless service, genuine reconciliation and forgiveness, overcoming violence with goodness, rating other people's needs above my own.

My belief in LOVE gives me hope that many wrongs in this world can be put right.

Jesus Christ, I believe, rose from the dead. The importance of this event is not the historical opening of the tomb in 30 AD. Its lasting impact lies in my Christian conviction that the Risen Lord lives and continues to live today. I meet him in other people whose lives have been transformed like my own. I experience his wisdom, his support, his concern in their fellowship and care.

This is not an empty statement. When I look back through my life I remember a long succession of family members, teachers, priests, friends, colleagues and casual encounters who each in their own particular way have been Christ to me.

This looking back into the past extends also into a much wider history. As a Christian I feel myself to be part of an incredible and wonderfully inspiring story – or should I say: complex of stories? I feel part of the heroism of the early martyrs, of the penances lived by the desert Fathers, of the search of generation after generation of theologians and scholars, of the generosity of people like St. Francis of Assisi and St. Vincent de Paul, of saints of every possible description, of the millions of Christian visionaries who spent a life of dedicated commitment in the service of the poor, the illiterate, the blind, the hungry and the naked. Aware of human shortcomings throughout this marvellous story, I am still gripped by the unmistakable presence of the Risen Lord in all these innumerable people. Their story is my story.

Read also ch.36

New life made visible

I feel joined to the Risen Christ also through the sacramental signs he left us. *Sacrament* means: 'a visual sign of an interior, spiritual happening.' The most pivotal of sacraments is the Eucharist.[1]

---

1 If you feel uncomfortable with some of the typically Christian terms I use, such as *sacrament* and *Eucharist*, I recommend a witty little handbook in which they are explained: *Wishful Thinking. A Seeker's ABC*, by F. Buechner, London 1993.

In the holy Eucharist the Christian community gathers to re-enact Jesus' passion and resurrection in the breaking of the bread and the offering of the wine. For me, the rite essentially expresses in symbolic form what I cannot say in words: my gratitude for existence, my trust in spite of fears and anxieties, my further commitment to God's programme of LOVE. And in holy communion, when I receive the consecrated bread and wine, I know myself confirmed by God in love.

I feel God's presence in many other sacramental realities: in the priest who forgives me my sins when I go to confession; in Gothic Churches with their high domes and stained glass windows; in hymns, in Gregorian chant and Bach's *Passion according to St.Matthew*; in Christmas celebrations with the crib under a candle-lit tree; in Church weddings and funerals; in informal prayers before meals. It is as if the Risen Christ has opened my eyes and my ears so that it is easier for me to reach out to God in what are, after all, just external symbols.

Read also ch.15 & ch.39

My heightened awareness also makes me see the whole universe in a new light. I read avidly about the latest scientific findings regarding galaxies, or quarks, or chemical reactions in living cells, or DNA, or archeological discoveries of our hominid ancestors. They all fill me with a sacred wonder – for I realise that they are all manifestations of how I myself came to be; of how God's creative energy enabled that long process of trial and error, of success and failure, of growth through suffering, that would result in the emergence of someone like me.

And the more I think about this, the more I am overwhelmed by its mystery and by a longing to live to the full the potential contained in my existence as a human being.

Read also ch.51

My realisation of LOVE also throws an entirely different light on hardship, disappointment, pain. I grasp that somehow even these negative experiences can be meaningful. I appreciate all the more that God's visible presence among us, Jesus Christ, shared our sufferings, and still shares them, somehow, in us.

I have not yet mentioned my moments of personal prayer. These take many forms: a walk in the park, a reflection on a Scripture passage, a few minutes in silence. Also, events and encounters can become a real prayer to me: meeting a person I love, a visit to a museum, admiring cloud formations when travelling on a plane.

Read also ch.61 & ch.62

This is what continued incarnation means to me. I realise that the experience will have unique traits for every individual. Others in my place might well highlight other realities and focus on additional areas of life.[1] I am sure that all committed Christians agree with me that **the experience of knowing the Risen Christ adds a new horizon to everything we are and everything we do.**

---

1 For other accounts, see: G. Carey, *Why I Believe in a Personal God,* London 1989; and M. P. Gallagher, *Where is Your God?,* London 1991.

46.

Religious experiences can be proved true or false by critical perception.

If Ultimate Reality is personal, we should not be surprised to find that he/she discloses himself/herself to us. And, in fact, religious experiences are far more common than is generally realised. In Western society two-thirds of people claim to be sensitive to religious realities, and one in ten to have had special religious experiences of one form or another.[1] God's self-manifestations always imply some level of religious awareness in us.

To indicate what we are talking about, here is a typical testimony:

> *I could not call myself a mystic, but on half a dozen occasions I have had experiences which for me made me certain of the reality of some supernatural Entity which, or whom, I label 'God.' One was among the foothills of the Himalayas near Simla, one at Vauxhall Station, one on a railway bridge at Woolwich, one in the lounge at a Swanwick Conference, and once at a Holy Communion service when the bombs were falling near us and we (the members of the City Temple Friday Fellowship) knelt on the rough boards of an upper room off Fleet Street lent to us by the Vicar of St. Bride's Church, the City Temple having been burnt to the ground by incendiary bombs. . . .*
>
> *I will try to describe one. Vauxhall Station on a murky November Saturday evening is not the setting one would choose for a revelation of God. . . . For a*

---

1 R. Stark and C. Y. Glock, *American Piety: The Nature of Religious Commitment*, Los Angeles 1968; D. Gerard, 'Religious Attitudes and Values' in *Value and Social Change in Britain*, London 1985, pp. 50-92.

*few seconds, I suppose, the whole compartment was
filled with light. This is the only way I know to describe the moment, for there was nothing to see at
all. I felt caught up into some tremendous sense of
being within a loving, triumphant and shining purpose. I never felt more humble. I never felt more exalted. A most curious, but overwhelming sense
possessed me and filled me with ecstasy. I felt that
all was well for mankind – how poor the words
seem! The word 'well' is so poverty stricken. All human beings were shining and glorious beings who
in the end would enter incredible joy. Beauty, music,
joy, love immeasurable and a glory unspeakable, all
this we would inherit. . . . All this happened over
fifty years ago but even now I can see myself in the
corner of that dingy, third-class compartment with
the feeble lights overhead and the Vauxhall Station
platform outside with milk cans standing there.*[1]

What to make of this? Can our awareness of God and
spiritual realities be trusted? Not all religious experiences are
peak experiences as described above, but all, in some way or
other, partake of the same directness of contact with Ultimate
Reality.

There are people who contend that a direct experience of
God is so powerful that it needs no further argument. "The
Christian experience of God in the nature of the case must be
self-authenticating and able to shine by its own light independently of the abstract reflections of philosophy, for if it
were not, it could hardly be the living experience of God as
personal."[2]

While they have a point, they overlook the fact that no
experience happens in a vacuum. Religious experiences usu-

---

1   Dr.Leslie Weatherhead in A. Hardy, *The Spiritual Nature of Man*, Oxford 1979, p.
    53.

2   H. H. Farmer, *The World and God*, London 1935, p. 158; criticised by R. W.
    Hepburn in *Christianity and Paradox*, London 1958, pp.24-48; see also A.
    Frossard, *God Exists. I have met Him*, London 1970.

ally presuppose that the reasonableness of belief in God has been shown by other arguments. Moreover, there is a danger of self-delusion.[1]

Is religious experience a mirage?

Wishful thinking often gives rise to self-deception, such as we find in day-dreams, neuroses, myths and superstitions. Our wishful thinking for something like God to exist is undeniable. This psychological need for God does not prove he/she does not exist, yet it should put us on our guard. Awareness of God's presence could be just the product of wishful thinking. A spiritual experience could be just a flight of fancy.[2]

Read also ch.3
We have hit here on a very real problem. Psychological needs exert a strong influence on religion and religion expresses itself first and foremost in our psychology. A religious experience is always of necessity also a psychological happening. A true perception of God's presence, which stirs us to the depths of our personality, may resemble, at least superficially, the state of mind of a person who is psychologically unbalanced.

For people travelling in the Sahara it is a well attested phenomenon that at times they see on the horizon the vision of a distant oasis. The oasis may look deceptively real, a lake of water surrounded by palm trees. Such a *fata morgana* is, however, an illusion and weary travellers are ill-advised to leave the beaten track in an attempt to pursue it. How can a traveller distinguish between a real oasis and a chimerical *fata morgana*? Fortunately for the traveller she need not persuade herself that every oasis she sets her eyes on is a projection of the mind; yet her problem remains: when an oasis comes into her field of vision, how shall she know whether to trust it or not?

---

1   D. A. Pailin, *The Anthropological Character of Theology*, Cambridge 1990, pp. 105-110.

2   J.C. Flugel, *Man, Morals and Society*, Harmondsworth 1955, p. 322.

"For heaven's sake, Mabel, it's probably a mirage!"

Such is the *fata-morgana* problem of religious experience. Some people maintain it cannot be resolved. If our own eyes deceive us, what eyes have we to correct them with? This is the way C.H. Berg approaches the question.[1] Religious experiences may be true or untrue, he says, but whether true or not, the evidence will remain inconclusive. We can always explain them in a natural way without having to invoke external supernatural factors.

If the *fata morgana* problem cannot be solved, are we then not condemned to go through life with the continuous fear that everything we experience is an illusion?

---

1   C.H. Berg, *Mankind. The Origin and Development of the Mind*, London 1962, p.17.

Can perception be trusted?

To tackle our problem in a positive fashion, it is necessary to work out the value of human perception. We are gifted with intelligence. Our mind is constructed in such a way that it is geared to perceiving and interpreting reality around us. We do not only reach the outside world through sight, hearing and touch; we also judge persons, objects and events in a continuous process of scrutiny and evaluation. Our survival depends on intelligent perception, and millions of years of evolutionary history have gone into equipping us with the faculty of being able to judge things and to judge them critically.

Of course, our perception is not entirely unconditioned. We do not see things as an indiscriminate blur of colours and lines, we do not hear an unstructured confusion of sounds. Whatever we perceive, we perceive within a *frame of reference*. This frame of reference is a way in which reality around us is already structured in a relevant manner. The frame of reference in which we perceive things is partly determined by inborn traits, partly acquired when we imbibe culture or order our own experience. The language we have learned to speak helps us to define experience in a particular way. In every perception our memory is present, laying down 'the rules of the game.'[1]

The frame of reference helps us to interpret the meaning of a situation, but it may also distort perception. Suppose we enter a church filled with people. While our eyes are still getting used to the subdued light inside, we see a person vested in a chasuble approaching the lectern. Immediately our mind jumps to a conclusion, to an interpretation of what is going on: 'The local parish priest is going to read from the Bible!' This 'hypothesis' of what is going on is due to our frame of reference: to the associations we have acquired about church, chasuble, lectern, and so on.

---

1 R. R. Blake and G. V. Ramsey, *Perception. An Approach to Personality*, New York 1951, pp. 123-126; L. E. Abt and L. Bellak, *Projective Psychology. Clinical Approaches to the Total Personality*, New York 1959, p.33.

However, as we continue to observe things, we may find we have been mistaken. The person wearing the chasuble may turn out to be not the local parish priest, but an Episcopalian minister, in fact an ordained woman priest. Although she is approaching the lectern, she may not read from the Bible, but from a collection of patristic writings. By continued perception we test the hypotheses suggested by our frame of reference. We either find them confirmed by further evidence, or reject them in favour of a better interpretation of events. This is the way perception works in life.

Critical perception

H.M.M. Fortmann, who specialised in studying religious perception and who published a four-volume report on it, suggests the following two principles as a key to solving the *fata morgana* problem.[1] 1. Perception as perception is never wrong, although inadequate perception may lead to wrong interpretations. 2. Perception itself is the norm for judging perception.

When we thought we were seeing the local parish priest on his way to the lectern to read from the Bible, it was not our perception that was wrong, because what we actually saw was the chasuble. The rest was interpretation. To correct our mistake, all we had to do was to continue examining the situation. It was our continued perception that judged the validity of our earlier assumptions.

W.P. Alston comes to a similar conclusion in his studies on 'perceiving God.' Critical perception can justify the experience, as long as we keep in mind that each kind of perception has its own rules which Alston calls its 'doxastic practice.' We judge things differently when handling a biological test in the lab, when checking the vision of our eyes, when analysing psychological feelings or when examining religious experi-

---

1 H. M. M. Fortmann, *Als Ziende de Onzienlijke*, Hilversum 1968; see esp. vol. 2, p.44.

ences. The experience of the divine should be critically tested according to its own requirements.[1]

R. Swinburne arrives at the same point via a different route. Like other experiences, religious experiences should be given a *prima facie* justification. They have just as much a claim to be taken seriously as sense perception has. However, subsequent examination should eliminate untrustworthy experiences as spurious, and should establish what can be taken to be genuine.[2]

The world around us is constantly sending messages to us. Who are we to say that these messages should only be taken seriously if they are of a particular kind, if they can be observed by the secular sciences? Reality is speaking to us in many more ways than can be understood by a telescope or a computer. Also, if these messages come to us from reality there can be nothing wrong with them or with our perception of them. We can only go wrong by giving them a wrong interpretation. This should be corrected, not by denying the messages or curtailing them, but by further critical perception. To deny the validity of perception itself is to strike at the root of our human contact with reality.

If, in a particular situation, we have the impression that something unusual is happening to us, that something of greater value is communicated to us, or in other words, if we feel we may have a spiritual experience, we should not react by rejecting the possibility of such an experience. Rather we should critically examine what is happening, being at all times determined to accept the truth. Imaginary experiences will always leave doubts; a correct perception of the Divine stands up to careful scrutiny. Whenever God touches us in some way

1 W. P. Alston, 'Perceiving God,' *Journal of Philosophy* 83 (1986) pp. 655-665; 'Religious Experience as a Ground of Religious Belief' in *Religious Experience and Religious Belief*, ed. J. Runzo, New York 1986, pp. 31-51; 'The Autonomy of Religious Experience,' *The International Journal for the Philosophy of Religion* 31 (1992) pp. 67-87.

2 R. Swinburne, *The Existence of God*, Oxford 1991, pp. 244-276; see also C. D. Broad, *Religion, Philosophy and Psychical Research*, London 1953.

"He's OK for the job – It's the ones who don't tremble you should worry about!"

or other, when God comes face to face with us in however passing a fashion, we know it and the confirmation of its truth will ultimately lie in the experience itself. The final confirmation of seeing is seeing itself.

The touchstone of truth

Scripture tells us the same. A prophet knows it is God who is speaking to him because the experience is so overwhelming that he cannot deny its reality even if he wanted to. Amos, who was just an ordinary shepherd in the village of Tekoa (750 B.C.) and who was called, much against his liking, to preach in the country of Judah, explains it as follows:

When a lion roars, who can avoid trembling?

When the sovereign Lord speaks, who can avoid proclaiming his message?[1]

Just as one cannot help trembling with fear when a lion roars, so one cannot help responding to God when he takes hold of us.

Hallucinations do exist. One way of identifying them is by applying the so-called negative norms, norms that show something is wrong. The woman in the desert who unexpectedly sees an oasis will be wary of trusting her eyes for a number of reasons: she may find that no such oasis is indicated on her map; she knows that light reflected on a mixture of heated air and dust can produce images resembling water. In the same way we will distrust religious experiences if we are under the influence of drugs or alcohol, or if we go through a period of emotional imbalance. We will also treat with the greatest suspicion whatever is in conflict with what we know about God and religion from reliable sources. Religious experiences cannot be genuine if they contradict good taste, common sense or sound advice. Experiences that unsettle us, make us unhappy, that rob us of concern for others or peace with ourselves, cannot be from God.

The spiritual life justifies itself to those who live it; but what can we say to those who do not understand? This, at least, we can say, that it is a life whose experiences are proved real to their possessor. Dreams cannot stand this test. We wake from them to find that they are but dreams. Wanderings of an overwrought brain do not stand this test.

I have severely questioned the worth of these moments. To no soul have I named them, lest I should be building my life and work on mere fantasies of the brain. But I find that, after every questioning

---

and test, they stand out today as the most real experiences of my life. [1]

---

1   J. Trevor in W. James, *The Varieties of Religious Experience*, London 1963, pp. 268-269.

47.

The validity of God's incarnation can be seen in its effects on our life.

As a Christian I believe that God has become human in Jesus Christ in a process of incarnation which I have described as happening *from the beyond within*. I also believe that as a result of my incorporation in Christ I share in his resurrection. I have become God's adopted child. My sins are forgiven. God's incarnation continues in me. His Spirit animates me.

The question arises: how do I know this is true? How do I know that my belief in the Risen Lord is not just an illusion? Do I have any proofs, and hard evidence, to substantiate my faith?

The answer is: Yes, I have. I have ample reason to justify my belief. In fact, I am convinced that I would betray my commitment to truth if I did not wholeheartedly subscribe to my faith. But the reasons that persuade me are lived and factual, not theoretical.

Let me explain what I mean by 'lived' and 'factual' in this context. It may be a general truth that electric trains can attain higher speeds than diesel trains. But if a particular diesel train travelled from London to Birmingham on Monday the 11th of January 1995 at an average speed of 123 miles per hour, then this is a *factual* truth. If I was present on the train and found it a smooth ride in spite of its speed, the experience becomes a *lived* as well as a factual truth.

How can we establish such a fact? Now suppose that I fall in love with a girl. She assures me that she loves me too. How am I to know she is telling the truth? Remember that this is a difficult reality to establish beyond doubt, not unlike God's presence in my life through continued incarnation. The girl could deliberately deceive me. She could flatter me with hypocritical words, play-act a sincere interest in me while being actually totally unconcerned. How can I *prove* she loves me?

The argument, I submit, will consist of three elements:

(1) I will carefully consider contrary evidence: facts that would prove the opposite of her claim. For instance, if I find she has lied to me, is dating someone else, slanders me behind my back, and so on, I will have reason to disbelieve her. This amounts to *eliminating contrary evidence*.

(2) If I am really in love with the girl and she with me, we are bound to experience a real meeting of heart and soul. This will be difficult for outsiders to assess, but the two of us will know when it happens. It changes our relationship for good. I call this element *transformative encounter*.

(3) In my continued dealings with her I will notice dozens of small happenings that confirm her real concern for me. She may stop attending a favourite show, to have time to be with me. I overhear her talk about me to a friend. I find she is keeping some snapshots of me in her purse. These acts seem insignificant in themselves, but altogether they present a strong case. It grows into *a convergence of affirmative evidence*.

The same kind of three-fold argument provides ample reason to accept the truth of God's continuing incarnation in my life.

Eliminating contrary evidence

If the accounts of the Gospel were to be untrustworthy, if the life of Christ or his teachings had no historical foundation, if the resurrection faith of the first Christians lacked reliable witnesses – in all such cases my belief in the continued presence of the Risen Christ would stand on loose sand. Studying the historical origins of Christianity is not a luxury.

Archeology, comparative literature, a critical analysis of the scriptural writing and other studies have given us a more complex picture of Jesus, his immediate followers and the sequence of events that led to the early Church. We can now recon-

"Of course, you're the only one, you silly boy!"

struct in more detail how Jesus' teachings were given shape in oral traditions before they coalesced to form the Gospels. We can discern better Old Testament, Rabbinical, Hellenist as well as Christian contributions to the original belief and worship.

Some scholars have rejected the reliability of the Christian sources on this account. But others have pieced together a picture that is human, but not in any way contradictory to a divine manifestation and incarnation. Their reconstruction is, in my view, supported by good historical evidence. It shows that the Christ event has firm roots in our own historical past.[1]

The transformative encounter

The Christian belief in incarnation seems to make heavy demands on our credulity. Is it not extremely unlikely that Ultimate Reality would manifest himself/herself in a human

---

1 See my own books on this: *Jesus For Ever. Fact and Faith*, London 1984; *Together in My Name*, London 1991. From among the vast literature on this topic, I further recommend these two compendia of modern scholarship: D. G. Reid et al. (ed.), *Dictionary of Jesus and the Gospels*, Leicester 1991, and G. F. Hawthorne et al. (ed.), *Dictionary of Paul and his Letters*, Leicester 1993.

person born in Nazareth two thousand years ago? It is not the kind of thing we would expect God to do, especially since we measure God with our own yardstick.

There is an enormous gap between the story of completely unselfish, loving God who 'becomes flesh' in the person of a carpenter and who allows himself to be crucified, and our own selfish, hardheaded commercialism. Incarnation thus becomes 'the most unlikely event possible,' a happening that goes counter to all our ordinary standards of probability.

Søren Kierkegaard has called this 'the absolute paradox,' a clash of expectations that makes faith an offence to natural thought. It can only be overcome, he tells us, by 'a leap forward,' a leap which is made possible because God himself provides a change through a first-hand encounter.

I remember seeing a film about the true story of a teenage boy from a socially deprived part of the Bronx in New York. At twelve he landed in a penitentiary for burglary, theft and carrying fire arms. When a family adopted him, he could at first not accept their sincere offers of friendship and kindness. It contradicted all his early experiences. But, when the mother gave him a small dog as a pet, there was a real *encounter*. It dawned on him that the impossible was possible, that real kindness did exist.

A transformative religious experience can provide the insight and energy for us to leap over the gap in faith. If we suddenly meet absolute, unconditional love, it may shatter our whole structure of preconceived attitudes and convictions. It may turn the tables totally. Instead of questioning the possibility of incarnation, we may come to question our own standards. We may then abandon our natural self-sufficiency and selfishness, turn to God in faith and accept his/her offer of love.[1]

Read also ch.56 to ch.59

---

1   S. Kierkegaard, *Philosophical Fragments*, Princeton 1985, ch.3-5; see C. S. Evans, *Fragments and Postscript*, Atlantic Highlands 1983 'The Epistomological Significance of Transformative Religious Experiences,' *Faith and Philosophy* 1(1991) pp. 180-192; M. Wistphal, *Kierkegaard's Critique of Reason and Society*, Macon 1987; R. Roberts, *Faith, Reason and History*, Macon 1986.

Meeting Christ

This transformative experience may be a dramatic face-to-face encounter. This is what happened to Simone Weil, the well known French philosopher (1909-1943). She had been educated as an atheist and had, by her own admission, never said a prayer.

As soon as I reached adolescence I saw the problem of God as a problem of which the data could not be obtained here below, and I decided that the only way of being sure not to reach a wrong solution, which seemed to me the greatest possible evil, was to leave it alone. So I left it alone.

The very name of God had no part in my thoughts.

In those days I had not read the Gospel.

I had never read any spiritual works because I had never felt any call to read them.

I had never prayed. I was afraid of the power of suggestion that is in prayer.

Until last September I had never once prayed in all my life, at least not in the literal sense of the word. I had never said any words to God, either out loud or mentally.[1]

The meeting with Christ came in the monastery of Solesmes in 1938 during Holy Week. Solesmes was famous for its Gregorian chant and perfect Roman liturgy. In spite of the splitting headaches she was suffering in those days, she enjoyed the beauty of the music and the meaning of the words. She was also helped by a young English Catholic who was a visitor at the monastery and who talked to her occasionally. In one of their conversations her new friend talked about English poets of the 17th century who had written mystical works and

Read also ch.60 & ch.61

---

1 J. M. Perrin and G. Thibon, *Simone Weil as We Knew Her,* London 1953, pp. 29, 42, 36, 37.

recommended them to her. Simone took the trouble to read them and was immediately intrigued.

During one of the times that Simone recited a poem she had a direct experience of Christ. Without her realizing it, as she confessed later on, the recitation must have assumed the virtue of a prayer. Then, unexpectedly, *"Christ himself came down and took possession of me. . . . In this sudden possession of me by Christ, neither my senses nor my imagination had any part; I only felt in the midst of my suffering the presence of a love, like that which one can read in the smile on a beloved face."* The experience took her totally by surprise. It had never occurred to her that this might happen.

Read also ch.51

> In my arguments about the insolubility of the problem of God I had never foreseen the possibility of that, of a real contact, person to person, here below, between a human being and God. I had vaguely heard tell of things of this kind, but I had never believed in them. . . . God in his mercy had prevented me from reading the mystics, so that it should be evident to me that I had not invented this absolutely unexpected contact.[1]

For most of us the experience will be less dramatic, but not, on that account, less real. For some it comes as a turning point in their quest of truth; for others as a series of successive insights and spiritual moments that together form a pattern. For those of us who were baptised as infants and who have to re-discover our faith, it may come as a gradual transformation by which we appropriate our Christian upbringing as truly our own. Somewhere along the road *encounter* will hopefully be there as a decisive event in our journey of faith.

Convergence of affirmative evidence

The evidence does not stop here. Rather, it gathers momentum. Swimming makes delightful physical exercise – but

---

1 J. M. Perrin and G. Thibon, *ibid.* pp. 35-36; see also J. Wijngaards, *Experiencing Jesus*, Notre Dame 1981, pp. 119-135.

how to persuade those who cannot swim that this is the case? Listening to music can transport us to ecstatic heights of pleasure, but what other proof is there than the listening itself, the willingness to learn and to be open and to vibrate with one's whole being in response to sound?

The proof of the pudding is in the eating, as the proverb says. The proof of the validity of Christian faith lies in the intense living of that faith, in the effects it produces. It is natural that we should want to see these effects in practice.

In fact, this is a norm Jesus himself referred to when he spoke about how we can distinguish true from false prophets. "By their fruits you shall know them," he said.

Thorn bushes do not bear grapes, and briars do not bear figs. A healthy tree bears good fruit, a poor tree bears bad fruit. A healthy tree cannot bear bad fruit, and a poor true cannot bear good fruit.[1]

If a religious practice confuses and disturbs us, if it results in anxiety or bitterness, it cannot be from God. But if it fills us with peace and joy, if it consistently helps to make us find happiness and meaning in our own life and bring love and forgiveness to others, we can be sure it derives from God the source of all good.

The Gospel message holds out a promise of an experience of inner peace, of knowing God's love, of spiritual development, of joy even in the midst of suffering, of living under the guidance of the Spirit. If such promises are fulfilled in our life, we may rightly see in their fulfilment an affirmation of religious belief itself.[2]

It should be noted that these affirmatory experiences receive their evidential strength from their *consistent affirmation*. This is precisely the way in which most of our valid

---

1 *Matthew* 7,16-18;see also *Galatians* 5,22.

2 D. Allen, *The Reasonableness of Faith,* Washington 1968; *Christian Belief in a Postmodern World; the Full Wealth of Conviction,* Louisville 1989;W. P. Alston, 'The Fulfilment of Promises as Evidence for Religious Belief,' *Logos* 12(1991) pp. 1-26.

convictions in life are formed. How do we know for sure that England, Wales and Scotland form an island? Few of us have been able to verify this fact directly, by, for instance, sailing around it. Yet we are sure it is the truth because we have been told about it on numerous separate occasions which, altogether, make a convincing argument.

Read also ch.25

> *"Most of what one hears, insofar as it is evidential at all about the world, is not systematic, controlled, or replicable evidence; and a person will never have an opportunity to verify more than a tiny fraction of it through more reliable means. . . . Yet it can lead to reliable, practical certainty."*[1]

John Henry Newman has called this 'the argument of convergence.' Even if we cannot see the hub of a wheel, we know its presence and location if we can see the many spokes that radiate from it.[2] From many various, positive and consistent experiences we can arrive at a reasonable and practical certainty that the Risen Christ is, indeed, present in our life. The proof of the pudding is in the eating.

---

1   J. Hobbs, 'Religious and Scientific Uses of Anecdotal Evidence,' *Logos* 12 (1991) pp.105- 121.

2   J. H. Newman, *An Essay in Aid of a Grammar of Assent,* London 1970.

48.

"If there is incarnation, why on earth? Why not on other planets in the universe?"

It is highly probable that there are planets elsewhere in our galaxy, or even in other galaxies, that have produced intelligent life. What about those creatures? God's incarnation in Jesus Christ is of no use to them. Will God reveal himself to them as well? And will they experience some form of incarnation?

Yes, although we have so far not had any direct evidence of intelligent life on extra-terrestrial planets, its existence is extremely likely. All our recent cosmic observations show that the same laws of nature that obtain here, apply throughout the universe. If life could evolve here, it can evolve elsewhere. It is calculated that our galaxy alone has 200,000 million stars. If they have an average of 5 planets each (a low estimate), and if one in a hundred million planets enjoys conditions favourable to evolution of life, our galaxy houses 10,000 planets like the earth, with life and, presumably, in time, intelligent life. And that is only our galaxy![1]

Read also ch.44 However, if we may legitimately extend our own experience of evolution to such other planets, we may equally extend our religious experience to them. We may presume that, as intelligent life evolves anywhere in the universe, an awareness of Ultimate Reality will also emerge. As on earth, this will lead to ever clearer self-manifestations of the divine, culminating no doubt in appropriate incarnations according to the understanding and the culture of the civilisation concerned.

If we are to learn from the history of religion in our own part of the universe, we can be sure that Ultimate Reality, which breaks through into intelligent consciousness *from the*

---

1   I. S. Shklovskii and C. Sagan, *Intelligent Life in the Universe*, San Francisco 1966.

"Beware of false prophets!"

beyond within, will everywhere respond closely to the specific characteristics of each particular group of intelligent beings.

It follows from this that the incarnation that took place in Jesus Christ is limited to humanity on our planet. It is the way Ultimate Reality communicated to us, human beings. Scripture calls Christ, 'the firstborn of all creation.' It gives him a cosmic role in the sense in which the universe was known at the time.[1] It does not say anything about extra-terrestrial life.

> *Incarnation is unique for the special group in which it happens, but it is not unique in the sense that other singular incarnations for other unique worlds are excluded. Humankind cannot claim to occupy the only possible place for Incarnation.*[2]

---

1 *Colossians* 1,15-20.
2 P. Tillich, *Systematic Theology,* vol.2, Chicago 1957, pp.95-96.

Part Five

Love

49.

We have to acknowledge squarely that evil is part of our evolving universe.

All of us, sooner or later in life, come to experience some tragic suffering that affects us deeply. It may be an illness that causes us much pain and anguish. It could be the loss of a close relative or a partner. It could be an accident we witness from nearby.

One occasion which I personally remember was the earthquake that destroyed the town of Agadir in Tunisia in 1962. I was passing through the Mediterranean on my way to the Lebanon at the time. I remember listening to radio reports on the rescue efforts: how some victims were dug up from below the rubble of stone and clay. But on the third day, when the stench of the corpses blew inland from the sea, the desert rats moved in. They scavenged the dead bodies and ferociously attacked whatever victims were still buried alive.

The picture not only filled me with horror, it also brought home to me the central question of suffering. Why is death part of human life? Why does death strike some people sooner than others? Why does it need to be so violent, so painful, so degrading to human dignity?

Almost naturally our thought then moves to God. Why doesn't he do something about it – that is, if he exists! Ever since the Greek philosopher Epicurus seized on human suffering to deny God's existence, doubters, critics and spiritual seekers, have counted suffering as an argument against God.

This is how the question is often formulated: *"If you were all-good, all-knowing, and all-powerful, and you were going to create a universe in which there were sentient beings – beings that are happy and sad; enjoy pleasure, feel pain; express love, anger, pity, hatred – what kind of world would you create? Try to imagine what such a world would be like. Would it be like the one which actually does exist, this world we live in? Would you create a world such as this one if you had the power and know-how to create any logically possible world? If your answer is 'no,' as it seems that it must be, then you should begin to understand why the evil of suffering and pain in this world is such a problem for anyone who thinks God created this world."*[1]

In other words, *we* would not create a world with earthquakes, Alzheimers disease, Down's Syndrome, droughts, locusts or whatever makes innocent people suffer. It is particularly *gratuitous suffering*, suffering that could be avoided, that is incompatible with the existence of an omnipotent, good Creator, we are told. Even the fact of one fawn trapped in a forest fire and suffering pain as she is burnt alive, suffices to show God does not exist.[2]

Traditionally, believers have attempted to defend God by pointing out that God is God, and therefore not obliged to follow our rules of kindness or justice. Moreover, God may have a greater good in mind. He may allow suffering because it somehow fits into a wider scheme of things which we, as human beings, are not aware of.[3]

But if there is a Supernatural Creator God who *uses* the suffering of innocent people for some other purpose in a master plan, it makes matters even worse. It would show that God has a 'corrupt mind.' *"If gratuitous suffering is inflicted on anyone, it is bad enough. But if it is inflicted for a purpose, to be planned from eternity – that is the deepest evil. If God is*

---

1   J. Cornman and K. Lehrer, *Philosophical Problems and Arguments*, New York 1974, pp. 340-341.

2   W. L. Rowe, *Philosophy of Religion*, Dickerson 1978 p.89; 'The problem of Evil and some varieties of Atheism,' *American Philosophy Quarterly*, 16(1979) pp.335-341.

3   Such traditional arguments can be found in J. Hick, *Evil and the God of Love*, San Francisco 1978, pp.70-78; J.M.TAU, 'Fallacies in the Argument from Gratuitous Suffering,' *New Scholasticism* 60(1986) pp.485-489; F. Swinburne, *The Existence of God*, Oxford 1991, pp.200-224; B. Davies, 'The Problem of Evil,' *Blackfriars* (1992) pp.357-375.

this kind of agent, he cannot justify his actions, and his evil nature is revealed."[1]

I think the objection has a point. The idea of a scheming Manager God who inserts bouts of suffering into a machiavellian master plan is repulsive. To pursue this line of argument would obviously put us on the wrong track. But is this the only way open to us?

God's awesome neutrality

Is it not obvious that our major problem lies with the image of God we have projected, the human look-alike imitation-king who rules a two-tier world? It would be better if we started from the facts as we know them.

In evolution all living beings compete for food, space and opportunities to grow. Hawks eat blue tits, blue tits eat caterpillars and caterpillars eat leaves. When a lion kills a springbok, it is bad for the springbok but a meal for the lion and its cubs. What is good for one creature is evil for another. So whose side is God on? Should we not say that God is not on anyone's side? He/she remains neutral.[2]

Ultimate Reality that keeps the whole universe in being, the Life Force that drives our world from within, supports the whole process equally, sharing in its successes and failures, in its triumphs and defeats. Hard though it may be to take for us, human beings, God's creative power was also in the earthquake that destroyed so many lives in Agadir and even in the rats that smelled an easy meal. It is the awesome, universal, impersonal, all-pervading presence of God.

Read also ch.21

Now suppose that in the course of evolution *pain* develops as a sensation that tells an animal something is wrong. Leaves do not feel pain as far as we know, but a squirrel does. Because it knows pain, it will avoid tearing its fur on thorns and will learn not to attempt ambitious jumps. Pain and sor-

---

1 D. Z. Phillips, *The Concept of Prayer*, London 1970, p.93; K. Surin, *Theology and the Problem of Evil*, Oxford 1986, pp.80-85.

2 B. Lonergan, *Philosophy of God and Theology*, London 1973.

row protect us. Visiting a leprosy hospital in India, I was surprised to see how many lepers had maimed hands and feet. This is not directly due to the leprosy, I was told. Because lepers lose sensation in their limbs, they do not notice when a spade hurts their foot or when their hand is scalded by fire.

So a fawn suffers pain in a forest fire not because some scheming God wanted to inflict evil, but because fawns themselves evolved pain to enhance survival.

Living in our kind of universe – where black holes gobble up stars, where one species preys upon the other and where an unwary pedestrian can walk under a bus, does tell us something about God. *"A genuine, religious defence of God begins by accepting creation as it is, including its evil, as a visible expression of God's nature, rather than dictating a priori what a divine expression must be like."*[1] It is small wonder that many natural religions attributed a darker side to God. Hindus revere Shiva as God's destructive power, and Kali as the goddess of death.

God's impersonal power is balanced by God's interest in us as persons, God's seeming harshness by manifestations of LOVE, as I will show in subsequent chapters. But there is no harm in dwelling a little on God's fearsomeness as it is revealed to us in reality. Since we are part of this world, we can be crushed by physical forces bigger than us. Since we are vulnerable biological systems, we are subject to disease, degeneration and decay. One day we will certainly die. These are facts. We do not improve matters by refusing to think about them. We have to acknowledge our fragility. We have to accept the *evils* that come our way – evils, that is, to us, though they may be good to other creatures.

Read ch.56 to ch.59

Laying a hand on our mouth

By acknowledging our fragility, we are actually admitting, in different words, that we are *contingent*, that we depend

---

1 L. Dupré, 'Evil – A Religious Mystery: a plea for a more inclusive model of Theodicy,' *Faith and Philosophy* 7(1990) pp.261-280; here p.267.

"Is the bus alright?"

in being, that we receive life as a gift, that in the last analysis we owe the life we enjoy to God. In religious terms, it means that we adopt an attitude of *humility*, of honestly assessing our total dependence while not minimising our human powers and our human dignity.

Read also ch.14

As autonomous human beings we will continue to improve the quality of our life as much as we can. We will do everything in our power to minimise human suffering – and the suffering of animals. But we will refuse to escape into a self-made dream that will one day be shattered. We will accept illness, accidents, disaster as part of our human condition. We will face death as the inevitable end of our life on earth. And we will, humbly and honestly, stand before God asking him/her what life is all about.

Read ch.28

Read also ch.61

In the Old Testament we find the fascinating story of Job, a prosperous farmer who loses his house, his livestock, his wealth and all his children. Covered with sores and scolded by his wife, he sits on a dung heap bemoaning his fate. Four friends come to console him. They accuse him of secret sins for which, they say, God is punishing him. Job strongly denies this. In the end he challenges God directly, complaining bitterly about his isolation:

Read also ch.62

> "*The night rocks my bones,*
>
> *the pain that gnaws me knows no rest.*
>
> *Suffering ties me like a tight garment,*
>
> *it chokes me like the collar of my tunic.* [1]

In the end God appears with his verdict. He condemns Job's friends for accusing him wrongly. Job's misfortunes were no punishment for sin. But God also chides Job. 'How do you dare to find fault with your Creator?,' God says. And God shows him the marvels of the world: the untameable ocean, the numerous stars, the variety of fascinating creatures. Job then humbles himself.

> *Behold, I am of small account,*
>
> *What answer can I give you?*
>
> *I lay my hand on my mouth.*
>
> *I have spoken once – I said too much;*
>
> *twice, but I will proceed no further.*[2]

Let us return to the question that was put to us earlier in the chapter: 'If you were God, would you create a better world than the one we have?' The temptation is to say 'yes' and to imagine ourselves to be the mythical divine Designer who dreams up a utopia for human beings – but do we really know what we are talking about?

---

1 *Job* 30,17-20; T. Royce, 'The problem of Job,' *Religion from Tolstoy to Camus*, New York 1961.

2 *Job* 40,45.

Granted, suffering is an enigmatic feature of our evolving universe. But do we know enough to balance its value against alternatives?

50.

We should own up to the evil which we, as autonomous free persons, inflict upon others.

As if catastrophes, accidents and diseases were not enough, much suffering befalls us on account of other people. It happens on a large scale, such as in the Nazi death camps that exterminated six million Jews, in the systematic genocide practised by the Khmer Rouge in Campuchea, and recently in the massacres of Tutsis by Hutus in Rwanda. It also happens on a small scale every day.

Sometimes we hurt others by our selfishness. Authoritarian parents leave deep scars on the consciousness of their children by refusing to affirm their growing need of adult autonomy. Sometimes there are traits of real cruelty and malice. Recently a college girl was humiliated and tortured by her 'friends,' till she died of the sheer loss of blood.

This is the worst kind of evil, the kind of evil that causes us much more sorrow and pain than natural causes ever could.

Predictably, God has been blamed for this evil too. For God made people who perpetrate evil. God could have created human beings who would always act virtuously, we are told. But what about human *freedom*, we might object? God could have created free persons who would, all the same, have never done any wrong, we are assured.

> *If there is no logical impossibility in a man's freely choosing the good on one, or on several occasions, there cannot be a logical impossibility in his freely choosing the good on every occasion. God was not, then, faced with a choice between making innocent automata and beings who in acting freely, would sometimes go wrong: there was open to him the obviously better possibility of making beings who would act freely but always go right. Clearly his*

failure to avail himself of this possibility is inconsis-
tent with his being both omnipotent and wholly
good.[1]

Well, if ever there was nonsense, it surely is this! What
does freedom mean, if not the ability to choose between two
alternatives. If God creates free persons, it implies they can *Read*
also
do wrong as well as right. Perhaps, we might question God's *ch.28*
wisdom in granting human beings autonomy and freedom – *& ch.29*
but asserting that God could make us truly free in such a way
that we would always be paragons of virtue is plain poppy-
cock. 'Evil presupposes freedom and there is no freedom
without the freedom of evil, that is to say, there is no freedom
in a state of compulsory good.'[2]

No freedom without merit and guilt

Again, we have started from the wrong end. If we look
at evolution, we discover how, gradually, human consciousness and human responsibility emerged. Human dignity, hu- *Read*
also
man freedom and human autonomy were new realities that *ch.31*
were carried forward to ever greater heights by the underlying
Life Force, by God. In freedom, growth comes by trial and
error. Mistakes and excesses are unavoidable in the process,
precisely because God, the Ultimate Reality, respected the true
nature of real human freedom.

God created the human search for freedom from within.
He/she allowed mind and intelligence to assert themselves so
that human beings could themselves work out the 'natural law'
that should guide them. In making human beings, God in a
way created creators – creators who depend on a divine source
for the exercise of their creative spontaneity, but not for its
determination.

---

1 J. L. Mackie, 'Evil and Omnipotence,' *Mind* 64 (1955) pp. 200-212; A. Flew, 'Divine
   Omnipotence and Human Freedom,' *New Essays in Philosophical Theology*,
   London 1965, here p.152.
2 N. Berdyaev, *The Divine and the Human*, London 1948, p.92.

"God's counted all your hairs? – Well, he's making the job easier for himself by the day!"

In spite of appearances, there is no contradiction in an overall responsible supporting Power creating smaller powers that have their own free responsibility. It is not unlike an army general leaving control of the details to commanding officers.

"Not everything that happens can be attributed directly to the detailed decision of God. Although he knows how many hairs I have on my head, he has not decided how many there shall be. He distances himself from the detailed control of the course of events in order, among other things, to give us the freedom of manoeuvre we need both to be moral agents and to go beyond morality into the realm of personal relations."[1]

But if we cannot blame God for making us free, we should be honest enough to blame ourselves.

---

1 J. Lucas, *The Future,* Oxford 1989, p.229. The reference is to *Matthew* 10,30: 'All the hairs on your head have been counted.'

As a human race we can point at many impressive achievements. We have a right to be proud of them. If so, we should equally be ashamed of our miserable failings. Even in our present day, with so much improved communication and a growing sense of solidarity, the rich nations refuse to share the world's resources equitably with the poorer nations. We in the West consume 15 times more per capita, and pollute the earth 20 times more per capita, than the developing nations. Our blindness, hardness and selfishness cause the inequality to continue virtually unchecked.

We should also be prepared to own up to our personal sins. We have a conscience and know what is right and wrong. Therefore, we do commit real sins. At times they may be small sins: like hurting people's feelings out of spite, or destroying their reputation through irresponsible small talk. At other times they may be sins with a capital S: when we take part in serious fraud; when we connive in the abortion of an innocent life merely to avoid some inconvenience; when we knowingly violate another person's integrity for our own selfish ends. *Read also ch.30*

It is so easy to cover our true inner sense of shame with lies.[1] We justify our actions with elaborate rationalisations. We project the blame on to others. We pretend there is nothing to answer for by losing ourselves in distractions. The only course of action that can save us as an integral human being is to be honest with ourselves, to uncover the lie, to admit one's wrong, to say 'I am sorry' and to seek forgiveness.

Breaking through evil

I do not suggest for a moment that we should be preoccupied with evil. Fundamentalist Christian preachers who describe modern society as a 'cesspool of indulgence, greed, gluttony and sex,' suffer from a mistaken and dangerous fixation. Most people, in fact, live decent and responsible lives, or try to do so. Shortcomings happen more through ignorance

---

1   M. Scott Peck, *People of the Lie. The Hope for Healing Human Evil*, London 1983.

*Read
also
ch.65* and weakness than though malice. We do not please God by running ourselves (let alone others!) down, we only please God by admitting what is true and by responding to love.

The marvellous thing is, actually, that since God is pure creative energy always looking for new opportunities of being, our human evil can produce unexpected good. Wars, though bad in themselves, have called forth great acts of endurance, courage and heroism. Unjust persecutions have allowed victims to attain extraordinary levels of human dignity, kindness and generosity. It is a paradox that has not escaped the notice of William Blake in *The Marriage of Heaven and Hell*.

"Without contraries there is no progression. Attraction and repulsion, reason and energy, love and hate are necessary to human existence. Good is the passive that obeys reason; evil is the active springing from energy."

The early chapters of the Bible also hint at this link between evil and progress. Adam and Eve lost their childlike innocence by eating the forbidden fruit; but it also opened their eyes and made them 'a little like God, knowing good and evil.'[1] Cain was the first murderer; he also built the first city. The warrior Lamech gave birth to a son who invented the skill of forging bronze and iron tools.[2] The evil we have done, regrettable though it may be, often contains the potential of turning into something useful and beautiful.

'Who never makes mistakes, doesn't make anything,' it is sometimes said. How true. Discovering our freedom and learning to be responsible involves trial and error. This applies to individuals, nations and the whole human race. But genuine progress requires that we acknowledge an error to be an error.

We can only face God and other people with dignity if we own up to our sins.

---

1 *Genesis* 3,5;3,22.
2 *Genesis* 4,1-22.

51.

God, the creative energy, shares our suffering and the suffering of all creation.

In the two preceding chapters I have tried to deal with the *intellectual* problem of evil. I have tried to show that evil is relative in an evolving world. What is good for one creature, is bad for another. I have also argued that it is rather silly to blame God for natural evil, or for the evil which we perpetrate as free human agents. We have to accept reality the way it is, and exercise our human responsibility in minimising suffering as much as we can.

But such thoughts are cold comfort to anyone who is actually affected by some acute suffering. A young husband and wife cycled home from a party. He got knocked from his bicycle by a drunken driver. He died in the hospital with a fractured skull. They had been an ideal couple. Understandably she was deeply upset by his pain, by her loss, by the sudden bolt from heaven that shattered their togetherness and her hopes for happiness. 'Why did God do this to Jim?,' she asked me. 'Why did he do it to me? What have we done to deserve this?'

Read also ch.62

Since God is personal, and since she felt she had a personal relationship to God, the question was not a theoretical one. It rightly challenged God directly: "What does this mean between you and me?" The real problem underlying a person's wrestling with suffering is: how can I trust God in a distressing world like this?

I have already mentioned more than once that the outdated image of the 'God up there,' who rules our world as a benevolent despot, lies at the root of many of our problems about God. God is the Ultimate Reality who supports everything we are from within. In this chapter I want to push this thought a little further. We can trust God because he/she is on

Read ch.17

our side. God is not the hidden oppressor. God suffers with us.

The idea of God's emotional involvement with creation is very biblical. *"I will recount the steadfast love of the Lord,"* we read in Isaiah. *"In all his people's afflictions, he himself is afflicted."*[1]

In the past, Christian theologians shaped their concept of God by Greek ideas of complete perfection. Since God was totally complete in his/her own being, God was absolutely immutable. Whatever happened to creation did not cause the least change in God. God's 'being afflicted' was written off as an *anthropomorphism*, a human way of speaking about God.

Read ch.4

God feels pain

In our century a whole new way of thinking about God is being rediscovered. It takes its starting point from the facts we experience, rather than from abstract philosophy. The physicist Alfred North Whitehead formulated a revolutionary new approach based on God's presence in evolution as the persuasive power that makes new developments possible. Though God is complete in one way, the events in creation enrich God in the sense that God experiences them as actual happenings. God is directly involved in every moment of creation.

Read also ch.44

God experiences every actuality for what it can be – its sufferings, its sorrows, its failures, its triumphs, its immediacies of joy – woven by rightness of feeling into the harmony of the universal feeling. . . . The revolts of destructive evil, purely self-regarding, are dismissed into their triviality of merely individual facts; and yet the good they did achieve in individual joy, in individual sorrow, in the introduction of needed contrast, is yet saved by its relation to the completed whole.[2]

---

1 Isaiah 63,7-9; see also *Isaiah* 49,15;46,3-4; *Jeremiah* 31,20; *Hosea* 11,3.4.9.

2 A. North Whitehead, *Process and Reality*, New York 1929, p.525. This approach is known as *process theology*. See also S. Ogden, *The Reality of God*, New York 1966; J. Cobb, *A Christian Natural Theology*, Philadelphia 1965; E. H. Cousins (ed.), *Process Theology: Basic Writings*, New York 1971.

The intense suffering of millions of people during the Second World War also focussed attention on God's involvement in the plight of the victims. The Japanese theologian Kazoh Kitamori came to the conclusion that, like any sensitive and loving person, God too feels pain. To express this, Kitamori uses the Japanese word *tsurasa*, the pain of a parent who loses a son. Tsurasa is the pain of having a deep relationship, which can lead to the sorrow of loss and sorrow of suffering with the other.[1]

Other theologians too returned to the original biblical way of recognising God's compassion, God's suffering with us. In particular, they grasped again with new clarity that Jesus' own passion and death illustrates how much God was on the side of the underdogs, of all who are rejected and all who suffer pain.

God showed himself in the man whose last words were: 'My God, why have you forsaken me?'

God emptied himself in the pain of love and died voluntarily a death of desperation.

What did God do in that despised human being?

God took upon himself all contempt we carry, including the chill in my heart.

What did God do in that misery of the world, also my incurable sorrow.

In the suffering and dying of Jesus, God bridged the distance between us, so that no one can any longer say: 'See – God doesn't care!'[2]

Whatever we think about God, we think in images. People have often experienced God as far removed from their trials because they imagined him/her as the heavenly ruler who from infinite splendour above looked down on us, poor mor-

---

1 K. Kitamori, *The Theology of the Pain of God*, Richmond 1965.

2 J. Moltmann, *De Taal der Bevrijding*, Baarn 1972, p.32; see also *The Crucified God*, New York 1974.

"Had it painted so I wouldn't have to visit it!"

Read also ch.4 & ch.17 tals below. They felt God was like a wealthy pit-owner in London who never even bothered visiting the mines in Wales, let alone go down into the pit to see, first hand, what the miners had to endure 2000 feet below ground.

We can now revise that image and replace it with another. God is much more like Alexander the Great, who was not only a good general, but who always personally led his troops into battle. When a fortress needed to be stormed, Alexander pressed forward among the front line, scaling the walls with them. His soldiers adored him for that reason. "He really knows our life," they would say. "He shares our hardships." It was in assaulting the city of Multan in 326 BC that Alexander was pierced in the side by a javelin. The wound never properly healed. He died two years later.

God is a God with us. God is the Reality within us that gives us all we are, that allows us to be free and autonomous persons and that enables us at all stages to grow and to flourish. God is also there to share with us our disappointments and failures, our searching and our sadness, our sins and our loneliness.

Read also ch.28

God's eloquent silence

Using human images, we can think of this as God choosing to incur a risk by creating us. Since God is personal and enables us to become persons, God takes on board all the fluctuations which such a relationship entails. God allows himself/herself to be affected by the evil and suffering which we, human beings, have to undergo.[1]

In us, God makes himself/herself vulnerable. God makes space in his/her life for us. God allows our experiences to enrich his/her own experiences. God accepts and undergoes our free response, our initiatives and even our resistance. It is as if God allows his/her omnipotence to step back, in order to respect the space he/she has created in us.

We can become aware of God's suffering with us and in us, if we listen to God in silence.

Simone Weil, who went through immense personal turmoil, tells us of her own experience. Though qualified as a lecturer of philosophy, she spent many years working in the Renault car factory near Paris to share the struggle of the working class. When the Nazis invaded France, she fled the country because of her Jewish ancestry and joined the French provisional Government in England. She refused to eat anything more than the rations given to her compatriots in occupied France, which may have contributed to her death of consumption in 1943 when she was only 34 years old.

When we are struck by some misfortune, Simone says, we ask the question: Why? Why are things as they are? Peo-

---

1 P. Bertocci, *The Goodness of God*, Washington 1981, p.267.

ple may point out the immediate causes to us, but these do not really interest us. They do not answer our real question. For our question 'Why?' does not mean 'By what cause?,' but 'For what purpose?' Here only God can answer.

God replies, not by indicating a precise purpose but by revealing his/her presence – in silence.

> *The person who is capable not only of crying out but also of listening will hear the answer.*

> *Silence is the answer.*

Read also ch.60

> *This is the eternal silence for which atheists bitterly reproach God; but atheists are not able to say how good people should reply to the silence. . . . The just person loves. He who is capable of both listening and loving hears this silence as God speaking to him. Created beings speak with sounds. God speaks through silence.*

> **God's secret word of love can be nothing else but silence. Christ is the silence of God . . . . When the silence of God enters our deepest self and penetrates it and joins the silence which is secretly present in us, from then on we have our treasure and our heart in God.**[1]

---

1 S. Weil, *Gateway to God*, London 1974, p.101.

52.

We may, paradoxically, experience that suffering has brought us great good, because it was transformed.

When soldiers are drafted into an army, they are subjected to a period of 'square bashing.' They are made to stand on parade in the icy cold. They are ordered to climb fences, jump from trees, run cross-country races till they almost faint from exhaustion. They are all the time kept under an iron discipline and severely punished at the least provocation. The philosophy is that hardship builds character and that demanding tests weed out unsuitable material.

Scripture ascribes a similar function to suffering:

Accept whatever happens to you
and show endurance in adverse circumstances.
For gold is refined in fire
and the elect in the furnace of suffering.[1]

Committed as they were to their image of an interventionist, supernatural Manager God, Christian preachers pounced on such texts to proclaim that God actually selects suffering to chastise, purify and perfect each specific individual. 'When suffering strikes you, render thanks to the Almighty. He sends special crosses to those he loves.' 'Your pain is just a shadow of a blessing – it is the shadow of a caring father's hand.' 'A valiant soldier does not complain about his wounds when he remembers it will grant him victory.' God was somehow reduced to being a strict parent disciplining his child, a sergeant drilling his troops.

We realise now that God does not plan suffering. Suffering happens as an inherent feature of evolution and growth.

---

1   *Sirach* 2,4-5; see also *Hebrews* 12,5-13..

"Take that scarf off – I'll tell you when it's cold!"

Read
also
ch.17
ch.28
ch.44
God, the Life Force who supports us in all that happens, shares in our joys and sorrows, our triumphs and defeats. Does God do more? Can it still be true that the furnace of suffering does refine us as gold? Can God, from the beyond within us, forge something useful and beautiful in that furnace of pain?

To consider this possibility on a spiritual level is not so far-fetched when we reflect on its occurrence all the time on a physical and biological level. Evolution turns seeming disasters into undreamt of new opportunities.

Creative violence

When the sun and the planets formed from a swirling cloud of dust 4.5 billion years ago, the earth rotated with a slow spin, like all the other planets. It spun around its axis only once every 300 days, so that the one side of the earth was completely scorched while the other was utterly frozen. Then a 'disaster' happened. A meteor as large as Mars hit the earth on one side. The impact was so overpowering that a cloud of debris was struck out that later coalesced to form the Moon.[1] Most of the earth itself was reduced to red hot fluid magma and it took millions of years before the gaseous atmosphere and the dust re-settled. But the impact also jolted the earth, like a whip lashing a top – and it acquired its present 24 hour day-and-night spin.

Because the earth began to spin as fast as it does now, its temperature became moderate – just right, in fact, for life to become possible. The giant impact was a chance happening in cosmic terms, utterly destructive in the eyes of any contemporary observer. But it created a new scene so that the force of evolution could grasp the entirely unforeseen possibility of life!

Many other examples can be given. Sixty-four million years ago another meteor, smaller but still 100 km across, struck the earth, gauging out the present Gulf of Mexico. The dust thrown into the stratosphere caused a 'nuclear winter' that killed off 70% of all animal species. It sealed the fate of the dinosaurs which had ruled the earth until then. It also gave a chance to a small warm blooded forest creature, who became the ancestor of all mammals, including ourselves. What looked like an ecological catastrophe that could wipe out all life, paradoxically created the environment in which our species would flourish.

Eight million years ago our ancestors the apes lived in Africa. Geological upheavals caused the continent to split into two halves: the western half retained lush, tropical forests; the eastern half turned dry and semi-desert. What was the result? The apes in the western part continued in their fixed life style. Today's chimpanzees in Rwanda and Zaire are their direct descendants. But the apes in the arid savannahs of East

---

1   J. F. Taylor, 'The Scientific Legacy of Apollo,' *Scientific American*, 271(1994) pp.26-33.

Africa were put under increasing duress. No trees to hide in. No fruits to collect. No safety from predators on the flat ground. It was the need to survive such new demands that led to those apes developing the traits that would gradually make them hominid, then human. It was the suffering, struggling, hard pressed apes that, by the unexpected discovery of new opportunities, found the way to human intelligence.

No doubt you may now see the paradox of suffering in a new light. For what happens in physical and biological evolution also happens on the plane of human awareness and religion. You should note, however, that suffering by itself does not bring progress. It only does so when it is *redeemed* by its being grasped as a new opportunity.

Drawing good from evil

W. Somerset Maugham has described his observations in a hospital ward:

At that time there was a school of writers who enlarged upon the moral value of suffering. They claimed that it was salutary. They claimed that it increased sympathy and enhanced the sensibilities. They claimed that it opened to the spirit new avenues of beauty and enabled it to get into touch with the mystical kingdom of God. They claimed that it strengthened the character, purified it from its human grossness, and brought to him who did not avoid but sought it a more perfect happiness. . . . I set down in my notebooks, not once or twice, but in a dozen places, the facts that I had seen. I knew that suffering did not ennoble; it degraded. It made people selfish, mean, petty, and suspicious. It absorbed them in small things. It did not make them more than human beings; it made them less; and I wrote ferociously that we learn resignation not by our own suffering, but by the suffering of others.[1]

Left to itself, human suffering is degrading. But Somerset Maugham overlooked the element of redemption. As his-

---

1 Quote in D. Z. Phillips, 'The Problem of Evil,' in *Reason and Religion*, ed. S. Brown, London 1977, p.114.

tory shows, the awakening religious consciousness of human beings discovered that suffering *does* offer new opportunities, provided one has the right attitude. Hindu *yogis* saw the potential of suffering for self discipline. Buddha taught that suffering can lead us to detachment, and Lao Tzu that it changes our priorities. But the fullness of redemption came when Ultimate Reality, in Jesus Christ, used human suffering to express God's nature of LOVE and to transform, once for all, the potential of all human suffering for some higher good.[1]

Read also ch.47

We Christians believe that, through Christ, God offers redemption in many ways. If we repent, God wipes out the guilt of our past sins by total forgiveness. God allows us, through the sacramental sign of the Eucharist, to align ourselves with Christ's act of resignation and Love, thus making our life part of his sacrifice for the world. Whatever hardships we endure, Christ gives us the grace and comfort to bear them with a sense of meaning.

Read also ch.57

Dietrich Bonhoeffer, a Lutheran pastor imprisoned by the Nazis for his opposition to their regime, experienced deep comfort from Christ's suffering:

> *Herein lies an essential difference with all other religions. People's natural religious sense brings them in their need to turn to God's power, to expect help from him as from a deus ex machina. But the Bible refers people to God's powerlessness and passion; only the suffering God can help.[2]*

Victory of the Spirit

To stay with the Nazi concentration camps, a Jewish doctor, Victor Frankl, has left us a valuable testimony of what helped people face and overcome their suffering in the most appalling and humiliating conditions. After describing his

---

1   M. McCord Adams, in *Rationality, Religious Belief and Moral Commitment,* ed.R. Audi, New York 1986, pp.248-267.

2   D. Bonhoeffer, Letter of 16 July 1944, in *Prisoner of God: Letters and Papers from Prison,* London 1951.

horrific experiences in Auschwitz and Dachau, he comes to the following conclusions:

(1) *It was people's inner resources that saved their dignity.*

"Even though conditions such as lack of sleep, insufficient food and various mental stresses may suggest that the inmates were bound to react in certain ways, in the final analysis it becomes clear that the sort of person the prisoner became was the result of an inner decision, and not the result of camp influences alone. Fundamentally, therefore, any person can, even under such circumstances, decide what shall become of oneself – mentally and spiritually."[1]

Read also ch.11

(2) *The death camps offered new opportunities.*

"There was a danger of overlooking the opportunities to make something positive of camp life, opportunities which really did exist. People forget that it is just such an exceptionally difficult external situation which gives us the opportunity to grow spiritually beyond oneself."[2]

(3) *It was religious meaning that gave him the strength to survive.*

"We were at work in a trench. The dawn was grey around us; grey was the sky above; grey the snow in the pale light of dawn; grey the rags in which my fellow prisoners were clad, and grey their faces. I was struggling to find *the reason* for my sufferings, my slow dying. In a last violent protest against the hopelessness of imminent death, I sensed my spirit piercing through the enveloping gloom. I felt it transcend that hopeless, meaningless world, and from somewhere I heard a victorious "YES" in answer to my question of the existence of an ultimate purpose!"[3]

Read also ch.19 & ch.58

---

1 V. Frankl, *Man's Search for Meaning*, New York 1959, p.87.

2 V. E. Frankl, ib. p.93.

3 V. E. Frankl, ibid. p.60; see also his *The Unheard Cry for Meaning*, New York 1978.

I cannot close this chapter without remembering another victim of the Nazi death camp at Auschwitz, Father Maximilian Kolbe. On July 31, 1941 the guards discovered that a prisoner had escaped. In retaliation ten inmates of his block were to be sent to the starvation bunker. While the inmates stood on parade, ten of them were taken at random.

When Franciszek Gajowniczek, a Polish sergeant, was chosen, he shouted in despair: 'What about my wife and children!'

At that moment Kolbe stepped forward. 'Take me instead of him' he said, 'I am a Catholic priest. I have no wife or children.'

The guard agreed. The ten were then driven naked into the bunker. After fourteen days the guards found four were still alive, including Father Maximilian Kolbe. They were executed on the spot.[1]

Kolbe died a horrible death. Yet I am sure that, in spite of all his agony, he died with a sense of *fulfilment*. Redeemed suffering can, paradoxically, bring us good that we could otherwise never obtain.

---

1 Fr. Kolbe's life is described by D. Dewar in *Saint of Auschwitz,* London 1982. Compare also the heroic death of Dr. Janusz Korszak who refused to leave Jewish orphans entrusted to his care in the Warsaw ghetto. He accompanied them to the death camp; B-J. Lifton, *The King of Children,* London 1989.

53.

"How can a good God allow
innocent children to suffer?"

*In our world we see many small children suffer and die.
Some are born in abject poverty and starve. Some are tortured
and beaten to death by their own parents. Some are cruelly
put to death in war. Dostoevski's character Ivan Karamazov
cried out that he would never forgive a Creator God for such
injustices. For these children have not deserved such suffering. And nothing else can justify it, not even the eternal punishment in hell of those who harmed the children. I agree. No
just and good God could ever be forgiven for tolerating such
a situation.*[1]

The pain and suffering of even one young and innocent
child does, indeed, bring home to us the fact of sin, evil and
injustice in our world. And when we think of children, we
should, perhaps, extend consideration of their plight to all
members of society that are weak and vulnerable: the underdogs, the poor, the handicapped, in some cases women and the
elderly. It is usually these weaker members of society that
bear more than their share of the hardships that come our way.

Fyodor Dostoevsky (1821-1881) is frequently quoted in
atheist literature because of the eloquent pages in which he
raises the problem of innocent suffering. However, atheists
always omit to report on Dostoevsky's own attempt at answer-
ing the question in the legend of the Grand Inquisitor, presented by the same speaker, Ivan Karamazov.[2]

Dostoevsky posits that absolute human freedom of
choice is God's first priority. But has God not overestimated

---

1 Bruce Russell, 'The persistent problem of Evil,' *Faith and Philosophy* 6(1989) pp.121-139.

2 F. Dostoevski, *The Brothers Karamazov*, London 1950, vol 1, part II, book v; read both chapters 4 and 5!

human beings? he asks. The majority would, perhaps, prefer just to be given food to eat and be told what to do, rather than having the responsibility of building up a just world. God's mistake, if any, lies in expecting people to be autonomous and to develop a mature conscience. "Thou didst crave for a love that is free and not the base raptures of a slave before the might that has overawed him for ever."

Dostoevsky also points to Christ, the mystery of God suffering with the underdog. The Grand Inquisitor condemns him to be burnt at the stake, together with witches and heretics. But Jesus, who is nothing but goodness, does not defend himself. He remains silent and embraces even the Inquisitor. This is how Dostoevsky describes him: "He moves silently in the midst of people with a gentle smile of infinite compassion. The sun of love burns in his heart, and power shines from his eyes, and their radiance, shed on the people, stirs their hearts with responsive love."

Solidarity

The closest we can come to understanding unjust suffering from God's point of view is, perhaps, to think of ourselves as parents seeing our children grow up. We want to give them freedom and autonomy. We want to allow them to become adults. We cringe when they make mistakes. We share the agony of our children as we try to patch up the scars they leave. And we rejoice all the more about their triumphs and successes. *Read also ch.28 & ch.29*

In the same way God, creative Reality in us, cares deeply about everything we do and endure, without interfering with our personal autonomy.

But God's involvement does not stop there. In the Gospel, Jesus teaches God's profound concern for the marginalised and downtrodden. God is on their side.[1]

Happy are you poor; the kingdom of God is for you!

---

1 *Luke* 6,20-25.

*Happy are you who are hungry now; you will be
filled!*
Happy are you who weep now; you will laugh . . . !
*But how terrible for you who are rich now; you have
had your comfort!*
*How terrible for you who are full now; you will go
hungry!*
*How terrible for you who laugh now; you will cry
and weep!*

At the last judgment, when all human beings will stand
trial before God, God will punish those who have not helped
the underdogs. The reason is: "What you failed to do for the
least of my brothers or sisters, you have failed to do to me."
But the just and the merciful will be rewarded.

*Come and enter the royal status I prepared for you
since I began to create the world. For I was hungry
and you gave me food, thirsty and you offered me a
drink; I was a stranger and you welcomed me in
your home, naked and you clothed me; I was sick
and you nursed me; in prison and you visited me."*

*The righteous will then answer him: "When, Lord,
did we see you hungry and feed you, or thirsty and
give you a drink? When did we ever find you a
stranger and welcome you in our homes, or without
clothes and we dressed you? When was it we saw
you sick or in prison, and we visited you?"*

*The King will reply: "I assure you, whenever you
did this for one of the least important of these brothers and sisters of mine, you did it for me!*[1]

God, the creative energy who supports us in being, cares
deeply about fairness, justice and love. The mystery is that

---

1   *Matthew* 25,31-46.

God wants this goodness to come about through our own conscious decisions.

Children, the weak, the poor are part of us. They belong to our families and our society. They suffer with us. They experience even more than the rest of us do, our human fragility and dependence. In their successful growth or untimely death we see the unfolding of God's experiment with intelligent and free beings, an experiment we know as creation. **Rather than blame God, should we not do our bit to make the experiment succeed?**

Read also ch.64

54.

"Only a cruel God could design a Hell."

Many Christians still believe in Hell. They claim that sinners will be tortured there in an unquenchable fire for all time to come. Surely this is not only ridiculous, but reveals traits of sadism. What glory can God derive from a sinner's torments? And, however shocking human crimes can be, could they ever deserve punishment for all eternity?

There are many popular misunderstandings about the Christian concept of hell – which explains why about twice as many people believe in heaven as in hell.[1]

To begin with, the fire of hell is a scriptural *image*, not a literal description. The image derives from the valley of Gehinnom outside Jerusalem where rubbish was dumped and burnt. Hell, the place where the misfits of humanity end up, was called after it: *Gehenna*. The scriptural authors did not claim to know the actual form and shape which hell would take; as little as they claimed to know this about heaven.

Secondly, and perhaps most of all, it is wrong to think of God as the one who is responsible for assigning people to hell. Christian doctrine throughout the centuries has always stated that it is the sinner himself/herself who refuses to accept God and thus condemns himself/herself to hell. God, with generous and merciful love, is always prepared to forgive.

The sinner chooses damnation by rejecting goodness and love. "It is not God who casts off the sinner. He casts off himself."[2]

Hell is much more a condition of painful separation from God, the source of all goodness, which people impose on

---

1 According to the *European Values Study,* heaven 41%, hell 23%.
2 St. Ambrose, *Commentary on Psalm 43.*

"I trust you won't get any funny ideas down here!"

themselves. As Christopher Marlowe's devils confess in
Faustus, they carry hell with them wherever they go.

> *Hell hath no limits, nor is circumscribed in one*
> *self place; but where we are is hell, and where*
> *hell is there must we ever be. And, to be short,*
> *when all the world dissolves, and every creature*
> *shall be purified, all places shall be hell that*
> *are not heaven.*

Final separation from God's love, i.e., 'hell,' is one of the
alternatives a person can choose. It is an alternative simply
because God takes human freedom and autonomy utterly seriously. If some people live on in God after death because they
opted for what is good, others can opt to be separated for ever
from that love. Belief in heaven and hell underlines the importance of the life we live now and our fundamental moral
choices.

*Read
also
ch.28*

In the third place, since we talk about *fundamental* choices, we should not imagine that many people end up in hell. The vast majority of people basically mean well. They make mistakes through a mixture of weakness, cowardice and ignorance. There is an ancient conviction among Christians that such sinners are given a last chance. Before meeting God they are purified – perhaps, through a final act of shame as they see their life in its true light. This is known as *purgatory*, a process of punitive cleansing.

Read also ch.59 In fact, many theologians are convinced that, though hell exists as a real possibility, in fact no single human person will be consigned to hell on account of both mitigating circumstances in the crimes committed and of God's great mercy. There is much to recommend itself in this view, especially the insight that God differs from us: *I am God, not human. I am the Holy One. I have no wish to destroy.*[1]

Read also ch.65 Finally, to clear up a last misunderstanding: Hell is sometimes thought to be the place which God reserves for pagans, heretics, members of other religions. Nothing is further from the truth. Every person determines his or her final fate on the basis of one's own conscience. I am sure that in heaven we will meet people from all beliefs and Churches, and also many who declared themselves atheists and agnostics.

> *God will reward every person according to what he or she has done.*

> *Some people patiently do good, seeking what is splendid, honourable and immortal; God will grant them eternal life.*

> *Others are selfish. They refuse to obey the truth and turn to evil. They will inherit anger and fury.*

---

1 *Hosea* 11,9.

*There will be upset and pain for all who do evil . . .
but glory, honour and peace for everyone who does
good. . . . For God shows no partiality.*[1]

---

1 *Romans* 2,6-11.

55.

"Prayer of petition is riddled with contradictions."

Christians often ask God for specific favours. They rely in this on Jesus' promise: "Ask and you shall receive. Seek and you shall find. Knock and a door shall be opened to you!" (Read the whole of Luke 10, 5-13!). But the whole exercise makes no sense. For if God is truly Love and has the best intentions for each individual, why does he only grant the favour when he is asked for it? If he is almighty, why did he not create a better world to begin with, rather than adding bits and pieces afterwards? Petitioning God for a particular favour makes no sense![1]

I must confess that I feel a good deal of sympathy with the person who formulated this objection. Yes, some Christians do have crude ideas as to how petition works.

We may reduce God to being some kind of *Superman-ager* who has made a bad job of the world. Our petition helps God to 'patch up' some of his mistakes. In this world of ours many people fail exams. By reminding God at the right time of our child's special case, we give God a chance to patch it up by making him or her pass. Many people fall ill and all of us will die sooner or later, but by putting in a word on behalf of some of our friends, we give God a chance to give some extra life to them. Many regions of this ugly globe on which we live do not receive sufficient rain. But by timely prayer now and again, we help God to prevent some disasters that would otherwise have occurred.

By our prayer of petition we hope that God will do some minor miracles that will take the sharpest edge off our human suffering. Whenever God does the minor miracle, it seems to us that God shows special love to us.

Read also ch.4 & ch.17

---

1 D. Basinger, 'Why petition an omnipotent, omniscient, wholly good God?,' *Religious Studies* 19 (1983) pp. 25-42.

What is left of God in such a concept? How inefficient is God to have made such a rickety world to begin with! How cruel is God since hard-hearted people like us are more easily moved to compassion than God is! How partial since God only helps those for whom his friends pray, and not the many millions about whom no one cares! Atheists and agnostics are quite right in rejecting a God of this nature. Moreover, if this was the true idea of God, we Christians would have no answer concerning human suffering. Christian faith would be in a sorry state if it rested on confidence in this repair-style miracle-working anthropomorphic God.

The right approach

Our first religious act when encountering God, should be to accept what we are: human beings. We should accept ourselves with all our possibilities *and* limitations. If God has given us two hands, we should not demand to have four. And suffering is part of our human nature. Because we depend on food, because we age and grow older, because our bodies are frail and weak, we necessarily decay and suffer. Our fundamental disposition should be to accept this condition and all its consequences as part of our nature. When God became human in Jesus Christ, God did not eradicate our human limitations. Rather God lifted up suffering and gave it a new meaning. *Read also ch.49*

Scripture teaches us that God loves every person equally, whether he is rich or poor, young or old, Jew or Gentile. It is a theological blunder to see the special love of God in things we possess: in riches, comfort, fame and health. Jesus teaches just the opposite: *"Woe to you rich . . . Blessed are you poor."* God shows his/her fundamental love for each person by giving us life, by granting us a free will and so making us an image of God, by calling us to adopted childhood in Christ. *Read also ch.47*

Of course, it is right that we do our utmost to secure our own well being and that of others. But the accidentals of health or sickness, riches or poverty, success or failure, do not bring us nearer to God. Christ wants us not to be anxious about these things and, therefore, not to pray for these accidental things as if they are of primary importance. *"Seek rather the Kingdom of heaven and these 'accidental' things will be given you in addition."*[1]

Christ recommended prayer of petition. But it was not for accidental things he wanted us to pray. When saying that we should ask with great faith, that we should importune God as the unhappy widow did, or as the friend who needed loaves for his guest, Christ is thinking of the graces of the Kingdom which we should pray for. For God is anxious to give us these gifts. If fathers on earth give what is good to their children, *"how much more will your heavenly Father give the Holy Spirit to those who ask him."*[2]

When Christ says that the Father will grant 'whatever we ask in his name,' he does not expect us to ask for relatively trifling things, such as food, or clothes or health, in his name. He expects us to pray for the gift of "living in him and he in us" and the other petitions expressed on our behalf in his high-priestly prayer.[3]

Read also ch.45 & ch.61

If we pray for conversion, for grace, for the Holy Spirit, our prayer will certainly be heard. Because through our prayer we predispose ourselves to receive these gifts. We take away the obstacles in ourselves that impede the divine light from entering our inner selves. We provide the psychological soil in which the seed of divine action can bear fruit. In this way, through our prayer of petition, we do not change God, but change ourselves.

Being persons with a free will, we have to open the windows: but the light comes from God, the Sun. On account of our human solidarity also, prayers for religious gifts for others

---

1 *Matthew* 6,33.
2 *Luke* 11,13.
3 *John* 15,16; 17,1-26.

partake to some degree of this inner psychological preparation.

Why ask God for favours?

Being the creatures we are, we experience the presence of God in every event that happens to us. When things go well, we grasp God's generosity in them. When we suffer, we feel our dependence on God. If such is our fundamental disposition, will there still be room for petitioning God for material favours? Not in a mythological and magical sense, as I have explained. But there will be in other ways.

First, we should not exclude God's freedom. We are free and responsible. So is God. We can achieve many of our objectives in spite of the limitations put on us. So, humanly speaking, can God. There is no reason to exclude God being able to make use of our prayer in ways beyond our immediate understanding, in order to guide a course of events in a particular direction without a crude magical interference with nature. Employing the image of a laser beam that brings photons to oscillate in phase, God's interaction can be understood as the tuning of the divine and human wills to mutual resonance through the collaboration of prayer.[1]

Read also ch.38 to ch.40

The accidentals of sickness, drought, failure and death are so upsetting, that it is natural for us to raise spontaneous prayers to God asking him/her to safeguard us from these evils. We do not expect God to do a minor miracle on our behalf. But accepting our human condition and realising God's love whatever may happen, we express our dependence on God in the form of such a petition.

In this case the petition is unconditional as it has the function of expressing our dependence. The utter need we feel becomes a *disclosure situation* in which we spontaneously reach

---

1 I highly recommend in this context the sensitive discussion of this issue by the scientist-theologian John Polkinghorne in *Science and Providence*, London 1989, esp. pp. 45-68 and 69-76; as also the classical treatment of it in C. S. Lewis, *Miracles*, London 1947; *Letters to Malcolm*, London 1966.

out to God. God from his/her side opens the way for us to deal with the situation constructively, and perhaps, prepares an unexpected resolution.

A model of prayer of petition

The best example of such prayer is given by Jesus himself. Although he knew he would have to undergo suffering and death, and although he had already accepted this sacrifice, his human nature made him spontaneously pray: *"Father, let this chalice pass me by."* By praying in this way to his Father, Jesus disposed his human nature to receive the strength it needed for the passion.

Read also ch.51 ch.61

As could be expected, Jesus' petition was not granted in the literal sense of the word. He himself did not want it to be granted on his own terms. He said: *"But not my will but your will be done."*[1]

Is this not the pattern for prayer of petition which Jesus wanted to teach us? *"May your will be done on earth as it is in heaven."*[2]

The remarkable outcome of Jesus' prayer only became apparent in Christ's resurrection. His new life in God was totally unexpected from a human point of view. It made Christ's suffering meaningful. It fulfilled both what God wanted and what Jesus, as a human individual, really wanted in terms of bringing wholeness to the world.

God's ultimate *rule* of events often lies beyond our grasp; as it was on Calvary. It means that God will have the last word, and that prayer has been heard and will be answered, in God's own way.[3]

---

1 *Matthew* 26,39; *Luke* 22,43-44.

2 *Matthew* 6,10.

3 F. De Grijs, 'About the question of God's Government of the World,' *Bijdragen* 4 (1989) pp. 358-372.

56.

God's being Love reveals a structure of mutual dependence in our universe.

Christians believe that God has made known something about himself. In a nutshell it comes to this: God is Love.

God is Love. We could be forgiven for thinking: What's the big deal? What difference does it make? In this chapter I will tackle this question. I will show that understanding God as love does, indeed, make a great difference.

To make myself clear I will dispense with the niceties of theological language and paint a picture in starkly contrasting colours. I use the comparison with 'painting' deliberately. You will remember that when we speak about God, we can only do so in images. Anything we say is like a painting that resembles God more accurately, or less so.

Read ch.4

Roughly speaking, there are two ways in which we relate to other people. There is the relationship of power or the relationship of love. We either control and are controlled. Or we share in a friendship that involves give and take. The same applies to God and God's relationship to us.

Traditionally, people have defined God in terms of power. As the absolute Creator, God was thought of as exercising absolute control. Being infinitely greater than we are, God was thought to be utterly removed from us. Nothing we did, could really harm him. As omnipotent and patriarchal ruler, "he" could do with us as he liked. If we opposed him, we would face eternal punishment which would still be to God's greater glory. For everything that happened, was to God's greater glory.

This was the picture of God as the Boss. God's nature could then be summarised in the phrase: God is Power. Everything was seen in the light of God's omnipotence. Our basic relationship to God was expressed in terms of dependence and fear.

It is hardly surprising that human beings constructed this basic image of God. As we have seen earlier in this book, our experience of living a fragile existence in a hard world tends to highlight our dependence on God. God was judged by the hard realities of life: the earthquakes, droughts, famines and disasters that befall us. Since there is no escape from such a harsh treatment which was ascribed directly to God's detailed decisions, God was reckoned to be a hard taskmaster.

Read also ch.19

But that was not all. In previous centuries practically every form of authority was exercised in a paternalistic and autocratic manner. Emperors and kings ruled their countries with a heavy hand. Fathers and grandfathers dominated their families with strict control. Small wonder that people expected God, the King of kings, to wield power of the same kind.

Another influence derived from Greek philosophy, which left a deep mark on religious thinking in the Middle Ages. Since the Greeks considered everything material as inferior, God was conceived of as infinitely superior to, and removed from, our material world. God was not really interested in the universe as such; all he was after was to receive the worship and praise of 'purified' human souls.

The image of God as the Supreme Power, though pre-Christian in origin, thus succeeded in casting a lasting shadow on the spirituality of many Christians.

The voice of the Lord bellows upon the seas.

The God of glory thunders.

His voice echoes on the ocean.

The voice of the Lord resounds with might.

The voice of the Lord reveals majesty.[1]

---

1   *Psalm* 29,3-4.

"A whisper of love from above? – What does he mean?!"

Jesus Christ, however, revealed a totally different picture of God: God is Love. If we love another person, and it is genuine love, there are some important consequences.

Vulnerability

The first of these is that we relinquish control. We cannot fully love a person and yet retain the final word about what that person should do or say. Genuine love implies such a respect for the person we love that we may not overrule that person, or manipulate him or her to make the loved one do what we want. A parent, who may have to restrain a child for some time for its own good, will ultimately grant the child the support it needs to become a free, autonomous person.

If God is Love, if love and not power is God's basic relationship to us, we should expect exactly the same attitude. And this is precisely the case, as we have seen in the section on Conscience. It was God who, in his creative love, made us evolve into free and autonomous human beings. God gave us reason so that we can work out what is right or wrong for ourselves. God does not dominate us. He respects us. He allows us freely to respond to the opportunity of becoming moral adults.

Read ch.28 & ch.29

If we love another person, we also lose some of our independence. For the other can disappoint us or hurt us, as well as please us and make us happy. Love makes us vulnerable. It is impossible to extend genuine love and goodwill to someone else without running the risk of being wounded in the process.

Read also ch.50

The belief that God is Love implies precisely the same for God. Since God loves the universe which God creates, he/she invests part of his/her own being in the outcome. Speaking in human terms, God rejoices with all that comes out well. God is sad about whatever fails. God triumphs with all successes and suffers with all setbacks.

Read also ch.57

The compass of love

When we speak about love in this context, we do not refer to love in a reduced sense: to romantic love, or sexual love, or the way in which people are said to love their porridge, or love their pets. Love stands for our human capacity to reach out to another human person in his/her totality, and to establish friendship with that person – which, obviously, may include romantic and sexual love. Love aims at the full, authentic self-realisation of each of the two persons. The person who loves generously gives from his or her own fullness of life and looks forward to receiving from the other the kind of response that makes the friendship mutual.[1]

---

1 For penetrating studies on the full meaning of love see A. Nygren, *Agape and Eros*, London 1953; G. Outka, *Agape and Ethical Analysis*, New Haven 1972; M.

The love we talk about is substantial. It embraces the other person in his or her totality and seeks their total well being. A parent's love for a child, for instance, shows itself in concern for the child's health, education, social integration, its finding a good job, and so on. The parent feels rewarded in love by the child's happiness and progress. The stuff love is made of is fact and deed, not only talk and feeling. *Read also ch.64*

The expression 'God loves the world'[1] should be interpreted in such an all-round and substantial way. It means: God shows that he cares about us by giving us life, autonomy, freedom to be ourselves, space to expand. God cares by giving us others to relate to, and by revealing something about himself to us. By caring about us, God made himself vulnerable.

Scripture uses the expression: God *emptied* himself. This applies especially to God's becoming human in Jesus Christ. *"Though he was in the form of God, he did not count equality with God a thing to be grasped, but emptied himself, taking the form of a servant, being born in the likeness of human beings."*[2] In a wider sense it applies to the whole of God's relationship to us. God, who is overflowing with inner fulness, empties himself/herself when creating, because God is a God who loves: *Read also ch.47*

God, in his love, is totally expended for the being of his creation – so that he is helpless under its weight and barely survives for its everlasting support. In the tragedies of the creation, in its waste and rubbish, God himself is exposed to tragedy: so that the creation is sustained at the cost of the agony of One who is buried and almost wholly submerged with the depth of it.[3]

D'Arcy, *The Mind and Heart of Love,* New York 1947; R. Hazo, *The Idea of Love,* New York 1967; S. Say William, *The Spirit and the Forms of Love,* New York 1968; J. Toner, *The Experience of Love,* Washington 1968.

1   *John* 3,16.
2   *Philippians* 2,6-7.
3   W. H. Vanstone, *Love's Endeavour, Love's Expense,* London 1977, p.72.

If God is not a detached Power, but deeply involved in and concerned with the well-being of the universe, then God can truly be recognised as the source of our own concern for the universe. Our discovery that 'God is love' confirms our own basic responsibility for the welfare of human beings and of the world we live in.

"In this love of neighbour, in its claim for eternal validity and finality, it becomes clear to contemporary people for the first time what is meant by God. They come to see the existence of God in a way that was not required in earlier times."[1]

---

1   K. Rahner, *Theological Investigations,* London 1980, vol.9. p.193.

57.

God's Love offers us forgiveness

Most of us are not criminals. Most people sincerely try to be just, honest and kind. Most people also know how to cope with their own shortcomings and failings. But we do not have to be villains and guilt ridden to realise that we need *forgiveness* all the same.

We need forgiveness as individuals because we have done wrong, on occasion. A friend of mine told me how she had left home after a row with her mother. She felt so angry and frustrated that she had vowed never to see her mother again. Her resolve was tested when her mother was taken to hospital with a suspected tumour in the brain. Her mother sent a message for her to come. She refused. When her mother died after the operation, she suddenly realised what she had done. Her teenage rebellion had been justified, she knew. But failing to give her mother a moment of comfort when she needed it most had been an act of cruelty. 'How can I ever be forgiven?' she said to me.

All of us carry the scars of our mistakes and sins. We have been cowards, mean, dishonest, unfair, unjust, unkind. Some of our faults stand out in our memory. Others merge in the background of our general imperfection and selfishness. Of course, quite rightly, we do not always dwell on our shortcomings. We try to forget them, at times deny them. But as we grow older we may become more and more aware of the chances we have missed. My friend's question may then assume a wider and profounder implication: "How can I ever be forgiven?"

Read also ch.50

The question applies to us all the more when we reflect on our share in the structural sins of our time. There are racial inequalities through which minority groups do not receive the support, the education, the opportunities for work and the re-

"Father, I have sinned – It was me wot mugged you!"

spect they are entitled to. I am not personally responsible for all this injustice, but as a member of a society that perpetuates the injustice, I too share the guilt. I share the social guilt of our unfair consumption of the world's resources, of the profitable sales of arms to Third World dictators, of our commercial exploitation of poor nations and similar injustices. As a citizen of a world in which children starve in one part while harvests are destroyed in another, where violent crimes, wars and massacres are commonplace, and where the rich become richer and the poor poorer, I cannot disown complicity. Here again I may rightly feel: "How can I ever be forgiven?"

We Christians believe that such forgiveness is offered by God as the first step in a process of transformation. The word we use is *salvation*. Salvation does not take away our responsibility to mend our ways and continue to improve our world.

It makes this responsibility easier by giving us a fresh start, by healing the wounds of the past and giving us a new vision to work from.

In Jesus Christ God manifested himself as Love. It is as if God tells us: *"I know you. I understand you. I accept that you are sorry for all the things that you have done wrong. As the first gift of my love, I offer you forgiveness. Since I am the creative power that allowed you to become what you are, I can heal your past, wiping away your sins as if they never existed. I can make you new by the touch of my Love."*

Baptism is the sacramental expression of God's forgiving touch of Love. If I may use traditional language, in baptism God both forgives *original sin* (the communal sin we share with the whole human family) and *personal sin*, and God establishes a new relationship by making us his adopted children.

If, later in life, I need forgiveness again, this is available to me in the sacrament of reconciliation. Provided I am truly sorry for my sins, I may confess my sins to a priest who will then forgive me in the name of God. *"Whosoever's sins you shall forgive, shall be forgiven (by God)."*[1] *Read also ch.47*

Reconciliation

If we have been healed by Christ, we ourselves can become instruments of reconciliation. For there are many deep divisions between people that can only be healed by a miracle of love.

An act of injustice will provoke the victim to vengeance and retaliation. Murder leads to counter-murder. Contempt leads to hatred, and hatred in turn to deeply ingrained hostility. Human history is full of escalations of violence and counter-violence, of the never ending spiral of hurt and revenge. Think of the conflicts between Arabs and Jews, between Protestants

---

1   *1 John 20,23.*

and Catholics in Northern Ireland, between neighbouring tribes in Africa.

Only an act of radical reconciliation can break the cycle of conflict. Jesus spelled out his recommendations in the Gospel.

• *"I tell you: do not take revenge on someone who wrongs you. If someone strikes you on the right cheek, let him strike your left cheek too."*

• *"Blessed are the peacemakers. God will call them his children!"*

• *"If someone sins against you seven times on the same day, and each time he comes to you saying 'I am sorry', you must forgive him."*

• *"Love your enemies. Do good to those who hate you. Bless those who curse you, and pray for those who treat you badly."*[1]

We must read these texts carefully. Jesus did not advocate that we give free rein to criminals, or neglect to protect ourselves when prudence requires it. But he suggests that we transcend the human rule of *quid pro quo*, or *tit for tat*, which dominates our relationships. Instead, he proposes a higher principle, the principle of love, which can heal the past and create a new future.

Read also ch.64
Apart from being eminently practical in resolving conflicts, it makes sense in a universe which is, ultimately, founded on love. *"Dear friends, if this is how God loves us, then we should love one another. No human being has ever seen God, but if we love one another, God is present in us and his love is realised in us."*[2]

---

1 *Matthew* 5,39;5,9; *Luke* 17,3-4; 6,27-28.

2 *1 John* 4,11-12.

God in our home

In the book of Revelation, Christ is presented as speaking in these words:

I know the kind of person you are. You are neither hot nor cold. If only you were cold or hot! But because you are lukewarm, and neither cold nor hot, you make me want to vomit!

You say: "I'm rich. I'm doing well. I don't need anything." Do you not realise that you are pathetic, pitiable, poor, blind and naked?

Therefore I advise you to buy from me gold refined by fire, as well as white garments to clothe you and cover the shame of your nakedness; and oil to anoint your eyes, that you may see.

The fact that I criticise you and challenge you shows my love for you. So come to your senses and be sorry.

Look, I stand at your door and knock.

If you hear my call and open the door, I will enter your home and share your food, and you will share mine.[1]

The poet George Herbert (1593-1633), vicar of Bemerton parish, was very much struck by this image. He imagines us being invited by Christ to share a meal with him. Christ accepts us as we are. He welcomes us to sit at table with him and become his friend.

Love bade me welcome: yet my soul drew back,
*   guilty of dust and sin.*
But quick-ey'd Love, observing me grow slack
*   from my first entrance in,*
*   drew nearer to me, sweetly questioning:*
*   "Do you lack anything?"*

---

[1] *Revelation* 4,17-20.

"A guest," I answer'd, "worthy to be here."
Love said, "You shall be he."
"I, the unkind, ungrateful? Ah, my dear, I dare
not look at thee."
Love took my hand, and smiling did reply, "Who made
the eyes but I?"
"Truth Lord, but I have marr'd them: let my shame
go where it does deserve."
"And know you not," says Love, "who bore the
blame?"
"My dear, then I will serve."
"You must sit down," says Love, "and taste my
meat!"
So I did sit and eat.[1]

---

1   G. Herbert, "Love," in *The Temple: Sacred Poems and Private Ejaculations,* ed. N. Ferrar, London 1633.

58.

God-is-Love means that we have been made capable of giving and receiving real happiness.

What is the source of human happiness?

To give flesh to this question, allow me to tell you of a stark contrast I once came across. I passed through Nairobi in Kenya on my way to give a course deeper inland. I was staying with some English friends who owned a magnificent house in the richer outskirts of the city.

My hostess, whom I will call Liz, was anything but a happy person. She complained bitterly to me about her husband ("He is *always* away on business"), about her grown-up daughter ("She *never* bothers to write"), about her health, about mosquitoes and a thousand other aspects of life. She told me all this while we were sipping cool beer and relaxing in armchairs on her spacious verandah with its breathtaking view of a colourful African garden. Later that evening we had supper in her colonial-style dining room where a black cook served a four-course meal that would have given credit to any upper-class hotel.

That same week the parish priest of Showry Moyo, one of the slum quarters of Nairobi, introduced me to Mamma Lucy, the head of a small Christian community. The contrast could not have been greater. Her 'house' was just one bare room, furnished with a low bed and a rickety chair. Her 'kitchen' consisted of an assortment of battered tins surrounding a kerosene cooking pit. But her face radiated happiness. Every now and then a warm smile creased her grooved features and made her eyes twinkle.

Mamma Lucy took me on a walk through her slum. In her broken English she told me about the men and women who belonged to her community. Unemployment was the scourge for men, prostitution for girls. Disease was endemic, with no proper sanitation and few medical facilities. Wherever Lucy entered she ignited a spark of excitement and happiness – as in one shed shared by three unwed mothers and the eight children they had between them! "People love her," the parish priest told me, "because she is always there when there is someone in need."

Don't think for a moment that I believe that the poor are happier than the rich, or Africans happier than Europeans. The contrast between Liz and Mamma Lucy rather shows what all of us instinctively know: that happiness does not reside in what we own, it resides in us. A UNESCO report has recently exposed three major causes that divide human beings into haves and have-nots: wealth, race and sex. As a poor black woman, Mamma Lucy should be firmly classified as belonging to the world's most underprivileged. Yet, she was a happy person.

What then makes for happiness and what for unhappiness?

The gift
The only thing that can really fulfil us as a human being is the affirmation of our personality by another person. If someone else accepts us the way we are and offers us love and friendship, so that we in turn can offer genuine love and friendship to that person, then we know ourselves affirmed as a human being and we enjoy all the goodness that arises from our friendship.[1]

Read also ch.9 & ch.40

Modern society makes us unhappy by presenting the wrong goals to us. Capitalism tells us we need money; of course we do, but it is not the key to happiness, witness the human failure of so many millionaires. Competition forces us to become achievers; but hard work is no more than an escape

---

1 Affirmation as the root of human happiness has been extensively documented by A.A.A.Terruwe, *Neurosis in the light of Rational Psychology*, New York 1968; *Geef Mij Je Hand*, Lochem 1972.

for so many successful, unhappy executives. The media hold out fame, but without inner substance fame is a soap bubble that does not last. Popular culture sees happiness in satisfying the appetites through food, drink and sex, omitting to warn us that the enjoyment of such pleasures can only really fulfil us when we have been granted our self-worth.

We can make ourselves rich, famous, successful and pampered – but we cannot make ourselves happy. Happiness is a gift that we need to be given by others. The gift is usually extended to us, on terms of greater or lesser generosity, by our parents. Even here things often go wrong. What matters to the child is not just the physical care for our health and the opportunities of growth and education, but the personal love received and being accepted for what one is. Good parents who are really happy with the child, give it one of the most precious gifts in life: the genuine feeling of self worth and the ability to give a generous response of love in return.

Read also ch.18

Once the capability of friendship has been awakened in us – and all of us possess it to a lesser or greater degree, we can find love and friendship with other people. Meeting our marriage partner will be a high point in this growth and sharing of ourself. Having our own children opens another succession of chances to give and receive love. Our colleagues at work, the neighbours who live next door, people who share our concerns: all offer opportunities to develop real friendship, and, therefore, true happiness.

The reach of affirmation

In the past, people's worlds remained limited to their own clan or town. In the present time our horizons have widened enormously. The society we live in is cosmopolitan. It includes people of many different races and social classes. We also belong to larger political units. Through the media and through international institutions we somehow relate to people on the furthest parts of the globe. Here again we meet chances to affirm other human beings and to be affirmed by them, even if the channels are less direct than personal contact.

As human beings we have always possessed a social dimension, since we are social by our very nature. Today, however, not accidentally but structurally, the advent of the international community extends and intensifies this dimension. The international community too has human value and is therefore, the medium and the object of love. Human love also walks along 'tedious' paths: the systems of distributive justice and administrative structures.[1]

Read also ch.64

In other words, by politically supporting the cause of underdogs in a faraway country, or by collecting funds to support an irrigation project for a Third World village, we affirm other human beings, and are being affirmed through their increased well-being and response.

But is there any substance in this game of mutual affirmation? Are the love and friendship we receive and offer more than just an emotional illusion, a trick of nature to reconcile us with our fate? When other people show us love, does it mean that we are really lovable, or is it no more than the correct social response in a troop of intellectual apes?

The substance in affirmation

It is here that the belief that God is Love makes a fundamental difference. It means that the mutual love given and received by human beings reflects a deeper Reality that lies at the root of all life and all evolution.

Read ch.15

Yes, everyone of us is fundamentally *lovable* because God has made us so. The love shown us by other human beings is a reflection of God's love for us.

In Scripture we read:

---

1 M. D. Chenu, 'Les masses pauvres,' in *"glise et Pauvret,"* ed. G. Cottier et al., Paris 1965, p.174.

God is Love.

Whoever loves, knows God.

Whoever does not love, does not know God.[1]

The text does not only tell us that we are in contact with God whenever we give or receive love; it tells us that our experience of love is in line with the whole purpose of the Universe.

We are used to paying with metal coins and paper. When we handle a $10 bill, we somehow take for granted that is worth $10. But how do we know? What gives us *the trust* to accept a slip of paper that costs no more than a penny, as a token worth $10? The only reason is the fact that the government Bank guarantees to pay the value of the banknote in gold if we were to require this, and the fact that the same Bank has tons of gold in its vaults to back up the promise. We all know what can happen to money when it devalues!

The revelation that God is Love backs up all the paper money of human loving with an incredible permanent value. In a mechanistic universe, human loving would still be worthwhile. But it would not go beyond the comfort given to us by intellectual prisoners, trapped like us in a dark world of blind forces. In a universe in which love is the manifestation of what Ultimate Reality is all about, love receives a deeper, higher and more permanent quality. *Read also ch.33*

Scientists have not been able to explain fully the phenomenon of self-sacrifice. Yes, animals are often programmed to give up their own food, or even their own life, for the sake of offspring or kin. The preservation of the species is a deeply ingrained social instinct. Such an instinct certainly plays its part in examples of selfless love displayed by men and women. However, it does not explain it all. *Read also ch.31*

---

1   *1 John* 3,7-8.

Love is stronger than death

In 1980 Archbishop Oscar Romero of San Salvador strongly condemned the unjust practices of the totalitarian government of his country. He appealed to the army and the police who were involved in the indiscriminate killings – twelve thousand people in the course of that year alone!

• *Dear brothers and sisters, you belong to our people, yet you kill your own brothers, the farmers. God's law which says: 'Thou shalt not kill,' ranks higher than the order of any human leader who makes you kill.*

• *No soldier is bound to execute an order that contradicts the Law of God. No one is obliged to implement a code that is immoral. It is time for you to own up to your own responsibility, to obey your own conscience rather than a sinful command.*

• *In the name of God, in the name of our suffering people whose cries rise up to heaven every day with greater exasperation, I appeal to you, I beg you, I order you in the name of God: stop your killings!*

On March 24th of that year a murder squad burst into the cathedral while Romero was preaching. They shot him with bullets from four submachine guns. The Archbishop, who was a quiet unassuming man, had been warned by friends that such an attack was imminent. 'Why should I hide myself,' he countered, 'when my poor people can't?'

Jesus said: *'No one has greater love than he who lays down his life for his friends.'*[1] Indeed, giving up one's own life for the sake of others is the highest affirmation one can give of the value these others have. Does such a sacrifice make a person happy? Yes, it does, in spite of all the pain, confusion, humiliation the actual death may imply.

---

1 *John* 15,13.

   Archbishop Romero died a happy man because he gave his all for his people. And his generous act had real value because it was backed up by God, the Ultimate Reality who is Love.

59.

God's love guarantees life beyond death

Death is an event most of us naturally fear. Not only are we programmed to want to survive, we dread the pain and loss death entails. We feel the decay of our body. We regret the parting with all that is dear to us. As Woody Allen once remarked: "I don't mind dying. I'd just rather not be there when it happens!"

The unsettling circumstances of our future death unnerve us. Underlying it all, however, is an existential anxiety, our fear of being reduced to nothing, of being obliterated in a darkness in which we cease to be. This anxiety has been heightened in our secular age. After all, if one adheres to a mechanistic view of the universe, death is literally for us the end of everything. All we have been, our hopes, our struggles, our achievements, only leave scratches of love or hideous scars on the world we lived in. But then we are gone for ever.

In the words of Arthur Schopenhauer (1788-1860), *"people, burdened with fear, want and sorrow, just dance into the arms of death, wondering what the tragic comedy of life is supposed to mean – and finding out it ends in nothing!"*

If death is understood as the annihilation of oneself, it becomes enemy number one. Thinking or speaking of it has to be repressed by a social taboo. It has to be fought with every possible means. Medical science is seen as a chief ally, even though medicine can only offer delay of execution, not a permanent victory over death. The unspoken strategy is to escape from death's awesome and terrifying reality as long as possible.

Read ch.49

The discovery that God is Love can free us from the lies and fears surrounding death. It can help us accept death as a natural completion of our life. It can make us aware of the dimension of love in death. And it opens the perspective of continuation beyond death. As research has shown, Christian faith does make a noticeable difference to people's coping with death.[1]

Dying is natural

The will to survive is strong in us, but we also have, if only we learn to be open to it, a readiness to die. I myself have known quite a number of people who, by their own admission, were prepared to die. "I am grateful for every day of life," one seventy-year old told me, "but now it is time for me to go. I have lived a full life, as far as I could. I feel I have accomplished my task. Don't grieve for me. I'm dying a happy person."

Such a gracious bowing out is made much easier by the recognition that life itself has been granted to us as a gift in the first place. If we consider the universe as a hostile place in which we owe our existence to a chance quirk of evolution, we are tempted to adopt a stand of defiance. We adopt a position of unlimited autonomy. We act as if we own the whole universe. But, of course, we don't. While having legitimate autonomy as free human beings, we are at the same time completely contingent and dependent.

Read also ch.14

Our greatness as human beings does not only lie in becoming independent, acquiring control, understanding managing, organising, harnessing nature and shaping the future; it also lies in accepting the truth of dependence, relinquishing control, trusting without understanding, adopting oneself to the managing and organising of others, being open to an uncreated and unpredictable future.

Our most fundamental religious act is to acknowledge the debt we owe to God for life and to accept all the limitations inherent in the gift. This also means accepting our death. Rounding off our business and having said farewell to our relations, we can then, like the patriarch Jacob, "draw our feet

Read also ch.28

1 P. A. Mabe and M. Dawes, 'When a child dies – the impact of being a Christian,' *Journal of Psychology and Theology*, 19 (1991) pp. 334-373.

up onto our bed" and breathe our last breath peacefully.[1] But that is not all.

Dying can be an act of love

If we grasp what 'God is Love' means, our eyes may be opened to a very curious connection between loving and dying.

We can measure the degree of our love for someone else by what we are ready to give up for that person. If we really love another person, we give of our time, our energy, our possessions and our own self. The French philosopher Gabriel Marcel has rightly pointed out that every real act of love, implies a degree of dying to ourself.[2]

Read also ch.52

It is true that our acts of human love are always an imperfect mix: we give of ourself, but we also take; we may even use the other person for own selfish ends. We benefit from our giving to the extent that it fulfils our own wholeness. And yet, the paradox stands. We grow in love to the extent we learn to die to ourself. And since loving is the fullness and peak of life, we live to the extent we learn to die.

"If you want to come after me, deny yourself, take up your cross and follow me."

"If you seek to save your life, you will lose it. If you lose your life, you will save it."[3]

Read also ch.64

When we love, we acknowledge that the centre and meaning of life is not ourselves, but someone else. By giving up what is most precious to us from a limited human point of view: our time, our strength and personal health, our privacy and intimacy, and ultimately our life, we give a new centre to our existence, which is another human person and ultimately God. This is the kind of 'dying to find real life' Jesus is speaking about. To learn to move off the centre of the stage, to make

---

1 *Genesis* 49,33.

2 G. Marcel, *Presence et Immortalit"*, Paris 1959.

3 *Matthew* 16,24; *Luke* 17,33.

room for others, to expend oneself for others, to serve a cause that benefits mainly others are all forms of creative dying.

If we have learned such a self-denying love in our life, our physical death itself will become the culmination of that love. Instead of just undergoing death as a necessary evil, we can make dying a conscious act of final surrender, of making room for others in love, of completing one's task of selfless service.

"Dying is our first completely personal act. It is, therefore, by reason of its very being, the place above all others for the awakening of consciousness, for freedom, for the encounter with God, for the final decision about our eternal destiny."[1]

This is the reason why the death and resurrection of Jesus is the central mystery through which God revealed to us the ultimate meaning of life. Jesus' death on the cross is representative of all the worst features death can have for us: pain, abandonment, scandal, despair and shock. And yet, Jesus made it the supreme gift of himself in love. Jesus' death has thus become a measure by which our deaths can be judged.

> *"The death of Jesus has become for Christians the mode of discernment of the degree of maturity of the human person. To die humanly is to complete the project of one's life and being as a self-gift. To die tragically or subhumanly is to succumb to biological death, still trying vainly to make oneself the end and purpose of one's own existence."*[2]

The dung beetle of Egypt, the sacred scarab, was venerated as a symbol of eternal life because the ancient Egyptians saw the adult beetles creep into holes before the dry season, and rise again when the rains returned. The Egyptians did not realise that what they saw was a 'dying for love.' The mother beetle creeps into a deep hole where it lays an egg near a heap

---

1 L. Boros, *The Moment of Truth*, London 1973, p.84.
2 M. K. Hellwig, *What are they saying about death and Christian hope?*, New York 1978, p.47.

"Beer tastes a bit off, guvenor!"

of dung it has prepared beforehand. It then dies to allow its offspring to live. As Jesus said: *"Unless a grain of wheat falls to the ground and dies, it remains alone; but if it dies, it bears much fruit."*[1]

But what about resurrection, and after-life?

Death can be the transition to life in God

The Gospel assures us that, once we are risen with Christ, through baptism, we possess eternal life. We have passed from death to life.[2] If we share in the Eucharist, we will live forever. Christ will raise us on the last day. For Christ is our

---

1   *John* 12,24.
2   *John* 5,24.

resurrection and our life. Even though we seem to die, we shall keep on living.[1]

It does not mean that heaven is an imitation earth, somewhere up in the sky, where earthly life carries on, on a happier note: business as usual, but now with angels in attendance, and food, drink and other pleasures served on the house. The Scriptural texts about heaven present *images*, not accurate descriptions. If our life with God were to be just a replica of what we live on earth, death would be a farce and heaven a degrading parody of responsible living. *Read also ch.54*

The life after death which Scripture promises is something of an entirely higher nature. Somehow or other we will be taken up into God.[2] There will be granted a much more direct experience of God's Reality.

"Beloved, we already are God's children now, but it is not apparent yet what we shall become. When Christ appears (on the Last Day) we shall be like him, because we shall see him as he really is."[3]

In some unspeakable manner we will be transformed so that we can share in God's life. The precise form this will take escapes human imagination. *"What no eye has seen, no ear heard, nor human heart has conceived, is what God has prepared for those who love him."*[4] *Read also ch.52*

Some theologians express our new life in God as our living on in God's memory. This has not to be understood, in Buddhist fashion, as one being a drop of water that is returned to the ocean of spirit and dissolves in it. It is rather a final seal of approval which God puts on our identity and our life so that from now on we are part of God's own experience.

Since God is love, in God's tender care nothing precious can be lost. And our having become 'a pulse in the eternal

---

1 *John* 5,24;6,47-58;11,25-26.
2 *Kohelet* 12,7; *Wisdom* 3,1.
3 *1 John* 3,2.
4 *1 Corinthians* 2,9.

Mind and Heart' does not preclude further consciousness on our part in some form or other. For God's way of remembering is active, dynamic and life giving. [1] After all, God is not a God of the dead, but of the living.[2]

I conclude with a scriptural passage that presents heaven as a city of joy and light. The image is poetic and stresses the absence of earthly suffering and God as the source of our fulfilment and happiness.

> *I saw the Holy City, the new Jerusalem, coming down out of the sky from God, prepared and ready, like a bride decked out to meet her husband. I heard a loud voice proclaim from the throne: 'Now God is making his home with humankind. God will live with them, and they shall be God's family. God himself will live in their midst and will be their God.*

> *He will wipe away all tears from their eyes. There will be no more death, no more grief or crying or pain. For the old order had disappeared. . . .*

> *People will see God's face, and God's name will be written on their foreheads.*

> **There shall be no more night, and no one will need lamps or sunlight, because God himself will be their light. And people will live as kings and queens for ever and ever.**[3]

1   N. Pittenger, *After Death. Life in God*, London 1980, esp. pp.58-70.
2   *Matthew* 22,32.
3   *Revelation* 21,2-4; 22,4-5.

60.

Still the lake of your mind.

All the major religions of the world agree on the need for inner *stillness* if we want to heighten our awareness of reality.

Usually our mind is so preoccupied by thoughts and emotions that we cannot pay attention to the wider perspective of reality, to the things that really matter. The Hindu scriptures call the turmoil in us the *samudra samsara*: the ocean of anxiety. It is as if desires and emotions rage in us like a storm, churning high waves and throwing up a spray of froth. To become truly aware of ourselves and of reality around us we need to calm the turmoil.

We have to still the storm within us.

"A heavy squall arose and the waves beat against the boat till it was all but swamped.

Now Jesus was in the stern, asleep on a mattress. The disciples woke him up and said: 'Master, we are sinking! Don't you care?' He stood up, shouted at the wind and to the sea he said: 'Hush! Be still!' The wind dropped and there was a dead calm."[1]

We have to turn our mind into a lake that is so still that it can reflect reality like a mirror.

Still water is like glass.

Look in it and you will see the bristles on your chin.

It is a perfect level that carpenters can use.

If water is so clear, so level,

how much more should be the human mind?

The heart of a wise person is tranquil.

It is the mirror of heaven and earth

---

1 Mark 4,37- 39.

"I asked my gardener to show me the way –
'Seek and ye shall find!,' he told me!"

reflecting everything.
Emptiness, stillness, tranquility,
reserve, silence, non-action:
these mirror heaven and earth.
This is perfect Tao.
Wise people find here their point of rest.[1]

To achieve such inner stillness, go to some quiet place and sit down in a comfortable position. Close your eyes and begin a process of gradual withdrawal. At first you are aware of the external sounds you can hear and of the environment in which you find yourself. Take note of it, then let it go. After a while you become aware of the inner turmoil in yourself: the

---

1 Chuang Tzu, 13,1; see B. Watson, *The Complete Works of Chuang Tzu*, New York 1968. *Non-action* does not mean total inactivity here. It means remaining interiorly detached, not getting embroiled in one's actions.

memories you carry in your mind, the feelings that accompanied your actions. Try to detach yourself from them. Let them go.

Do not feel under pressure. Do not suppress anything with violence. Acknowledge it all. Let it be there. Just gradually pull away from it so that you feel a new tranquility and peace take hold of you.

Some people find it useful to pay attention to their breathing. It helps them withdraw interiorly. Others lie down during the exercise – which is fine as long as you guard against falling asleep. We are not looking for drowsiness, but a heightened level of awareness.

Begin in a quiet and secluded place. Once you have learned the practice of inner withdrawal and mental composure, you can achieve the same effect even when surrounded by people or subjected to external noise. You can experience such inner withdrawal when travelling by bus or by train, for instance, provided people sitting next to you are not engaged in a distracting conversation.

Inner withdrawal is not an aim in itself. It only represents a first stage.[1] It creates a wider openness, a keener perception, increased attention, intensified awareness, a state of mind in which we can reach out beyond ourselves and experience things in a new way.

Even this first step has its own reward. The inner peace we can acquire will be a treasured possession we would not gladly give up. Gradually it will make us aware of the Ultimate Reality that underlies everything, yes, that lies even at the basis of our own search.

Read also ch.14 & ch.15

---

1 The method described in this chapter is worked out more fully in a book and video *The Seven Circles of Prayer* by J. Wijngaards, London 1987, available from Housetop, 39 Homer Street, London W1H 1HL.

61.

Think aloud in the presence of God

Some people find it quite difficult to speak to God in prayer. It may seem to them an awkward, perhaps even childish thing to do. It may somehow seem to make God small too. If God is the invisible Life Force in us, how can we pretend to have a conversation with him/her?

A prayer without words can be an excellent prayer. Often we can say more through a silent meditation than we could express otherwise. So we should not force ourselves to adopt anything we are not ready for, anything artificial.

We can learn from what occurs in marriage. A happily married couple who experience a dramatic event in life: the birth of a child, the loss of a close relative, the enjoyment of a new home, do not need to express their feelings and thoughts aloud. Since they understand each other so well through their mutual love, they can communicate volumes in perfect silence, just by being together. And then, at other times, they will feel the need to talk.

The same is true about us and God. On one level we communicate with God all the time in silence. But on another level, since God is personal it is natural for us to respond in words when we build up a relationship with God. God does not need to speak, but we sometimes do. We need to express the thoughts and feelings we have, so that we can clarify our relationship to God.

How can we do this in a dignified and responsible manner?

Speaking to oneself

As a first step I suggest that we adopt what psychologists call *private speech*. It consists in talking to ourselves, in verbalising what we feel or what we intend to do.

There was a time when it was thought that 'talking to yourself' was somewhat abnormal, a sign of mental instability. Now we know that just the opposite is true. We do it all the time. And we need to do it because we cannot function properly without it.

Professor L. Vygotsky of Russia was the first to demonstrate convincingly that we use words to organise complex operations. Sometimes these words are spoken almost audibly in our mind, at other times the words lie hidden in our thoughts.

When a soccer player dribbles with the ball in front of the opponents' goal, he works out the tactics in his mind which he expresses to himself in inner words: "Turn on my left foot, push the ball to the right, swerve to the left to deceive the goalie, kick hard with my right foot," and so on.

Granny, when baking a cake, runs off a similar sequence in her mind: "Take the flour packet from the cupboard, pour out half a litre into the bowl, put the flour packet back, take the milk bottle from the fridge, etc, etc."[1]

Private speech is also important in relationships. We all know only too well how we rehearse in our mind what we plan to say when proposing marriage or when confronting our boss. By talking to ourselves about what we want to say and what not, we clarify the relationship and prepare our next step. Private speech is a form of self-education.[2]

Prayer of thinking aloud

Now read the following passage from a Jewish writer in Alexandria in the second century BC.

I considered all the injustices perpetrated on the earth. I saw the tears of the oppressed, and there was no one to give them comfort. The oppressors

---

1 L. Vygotsky, *Thought and Language*, New York 1962.
2 R.M. Diaz and L.R. Berk (ed.), *Private speech: From Social Interaction to Self-Regulation*, Lawrence Erlbaum 1992.

enjoyed power. No one was there to defend the un-derdog.

That is why it struck me that those who have already died are often better off than the living. And even happier than they are people who have never been born. These have been spared all the evil that happens on earth!

Again I observed all the toil people inflict on them-selves by ambition and rivalry against their neigh-bour. It is utterly useless and a chasing of wind!

Another useless thing I have seen is a man who is totally alone. He has no relations – neither a son nor a brother, and yet he works himself to death. His eyes are always greedy for more riches, but he never stops to think: 'For whom am I killing myself and depriving myself of all joy in life?' This too is a stupid and miserable existence!

. . . I have seen everything that happens on earth. It is all useless and a chasing of wind. What is crooked cannot be made straight. What is defective will not be repaired. [1]

I do not know what went through your mind when you read that passage. The moanings of an incorrigible pessimist perhaps? May be. The interesting point is that it is part of the Bible and – that it is a prayer!

When we think aloud in the presence of God we are ac-tually praying. And the more truthful and honest we are, the better. Our thoughts will often be a mixture of wonder, doubt, indignation, gratitude, anger, you-name-it! That is the stuff of real prayer, of genuine communication with the Source of all we are.

---

1 *Kohelet* 4,1-8;1,14-15. This book is also known as *Ecclesiastes*.

Also, there is only a small step from such a 'thinking aloud' to addressing our thoughts directly to God – if we want to do so.

Starting you off

There are a number of ways you might want to begin your 'talking to yourself' in the presence of God. Allow me to suggest a method that involves a mirror, since mirrors can at times help us make our *private speech* explicit.

People in the Middle Ages knew a form of meditation called *speculation*, literally "gazing into a mirror." We will try this approach. Place yourself before a mirror. Adopt the inner withdrawal in silence described in the previous chapter. Then open your eyes and look at yourself.

First you take in your general features, those you are familiar with and, perhaps, others which you have never paid attention to. Then focus on your face, and especially on your eyes. Look as it were inside yourself. If it is possible, study your own reflection on the pupil of your eye. The experience will affect you in a strange way. Do not be afraid to face the reality of what you are. You may have defects, as all of us have. You also have personality. You are unique. You can be proud to be you.

Spend some time to reflect on your history, the struggles of your life, your achievements, your search. There will never be anyone else in the world exactly like you. You are unrepeatably unique.

Then move on to the inner world that is in you, the world of mind and heart that expresses itself in you. This requires a new way of looking at yourself, and observation with spiritual eyes. According to the Bible, understanding ourselves will, somehow, mean understanding *God* of whom we are a reflected image.

It is like this: when I was a child, I spoke like a child,
thought like a child and reasoned as a child does.

But when I became an adult I put aside my childish ways.

In the same way, I am now only seeing things dimly, looking in a mirror; then I will see face to face.

Now I know in part, then I shall understand fully, just as God understands me.[1]

Then express your thoughts to yourself. Begin to 'think aloud.' Tell yourself what you feel. Put into words what is most important to you.

And remember all the time that you are in the presence of God whose image you are.

---

[1] *1 Corinthians* 13,11-12.

62.

Talk to God by talking to friends.

Years ago a friend and I were making a long train journey together. In the course of the day our conversation drifted into profound topics. We talked about spirituality, faith, boredom, mediocrity. "I find it difficult to pray," my friend confided to me. "I wish talking to God was as easy as talking to someone like you."

"Thanks," I told her. "But I'll tell you something even more amazing. While talking to me you *were* actually also talking to God."

She laughed, "Ah! You're pretending to be God!"

"You know I'm not," I said. "I may be conceited, but not to that extent! All the same, I am serious. When people like us discuss spiritual things, God is very much part of it. He listens and speaks in both of us."

There is a marvellous story in the Gospels about the risen Christ appearing to two disciples who were on their way to Emmaus. As they were walking along, a stranger joined them. Soon they were involved in a deep and lively discussion about Jesus' death in Jerusalem and how it agreed with Old Testament prophecies.

When they arrived at Emmaus where the two disciples were going to stay for the night, the stranger prepared to take leave. "Stay with us," they said to him. "It's late. You may not easily find lodgings elsewhere." He agreed. And when they had supper together, the stranger took a loaf of bread, gave thanks and broke the bread. The scales then fell from the disciples' eyes and they recognised that he was Jesus, the Risen Christ.

Christ disappeared before their eyes. Then they realised that they had actually been talking to Christ all day without having been aware of it. *"Didn't our hearts burn when he talked to us on the road?," they said to each other.*[1]

The story is purposely narrated in the Gospel to make us understand that God is often present in our encounters and discussions when we talk about the religious, ultimate questions of life.

This does not mean that God takes the disguise of some stranger (as we might read from the Emmaus story), but that God is present in and through the people we are talking to. As Christ said: *"Where two or three of you are gathered in my name, there I am in your midst."*[2]

Human mediation

The simple fact is that God understands our human need to relate to him in a human way. That was the whole reason of his incarnation, his living among us in a human individual, Jesus Christ. It is also the reason why our friends and companions do at times represent God in their dealings with us.

Read ch.44 According to our Christian belief, some people may be specially called upon to speak on God's behalf in specific circumstances. They are known as *prophets*. Priests and ministers represent God by preaching his word and administering the sacraments. But speaking for God is not a monopoly. All sensitive and responsible people do at times mediate God. *"Who hears you, hears me,"* then applies to them too.[3]

God speaking to us

One obvious implication of what we have seen is that we should be open to the possibility of God trying to tell us something through another person.

Suppose we have had an interesting conversation with someone we trust, in the course of which we touched on profound spiritual truths. I may often feel depressed, for instance,

---

1 *Luke* 24,13-35.
2 *Matthew* 18,20.
3 *Luke* 10,16.

*"Love your enemy? Of course, padre –
but can you do it singlehanded?!"*

and my friend, who is a convinced Christian, has spoken about
the unique worth of every single individual in the eyes of God.
What she said struck a cord in me. Could something like that
really apply to myself? I wonder.

When I reflect on it afterwards I may, with good reason,
feel that it was not just my friend who spoke, but that God too
was in the discussion. God was trying to tell me something
through her. Instead of it being just her words, it was God who
told me: "Of course, you too are a unique and lovable person.
You mean a lot to Me. Yes, *you*!"

The same may happen when I am reading a book about
spiritual matters. I may always have imagined God to be a
stern and demanding Father, who watches me at every step to
see if he can find fault. By what the author says it may suddenly dawn on me that that is not what God is like at all. The

image of God as a loving, caring and tolerant *mother* is so much more appropriate, I realise.

> *Can a mother forget her own baby and not love the child she gave birth to? Even if a mother should reject her child, I will never reject you. I have written your name on the palms of my hand!*[1]

Having this new insight is just the first step. The second is to recognise that God himself/herself is addressing me directly through this passage. It is as if God, as a loving parent, says to me: "Hey, my child. Why do you hang on to those wrong impressions you have of me? Come close to me. I want to embrace you. I want to make you feel happy in my love. Why don't we make a new start?"

Of course, we should not be carried away in all this. We should not begin to think that God is sending us thousands of messages through everything people tell us or through every page we read.

In particular, I recommend two safeguards. The first one is that the person who talks to us, or the author whose book we read, should be a sensible person. God does not normally speak through bigots, fanatics or people who are emotionally unbalanced.

Secondly, listen to your heart. If God is speaking to you, he/she will touch you interiorly. His message will resonate in you. Like the disciples of Emmaus you will be saying: "Didn't my heart burn when so-and-so was speaking to me?" Deep down you will know: this is more than just a human being talking to me.

Our speaking to God

Another consequence of human mediation is that, when we feel we would like to talk something over with God, we

---

1 *Isaiah* 49,15-16. The mystic Juliana of Norwich even called *Christ* our mother, "in whom we are endlessly born and out of whom we shall never come!"; *Revelations of Divine Love*, New York 1978, p. 292. On the importance of female imagery of God for women, read K. Fischer, *Women at the Well*, London 1989, pp. 75-92.

might decide to put the matter to some friend whose judgment we trust.I know from my own experience as a priest how many people are helped by a frank discussion about some question that bothers them.

• *"When I pray, I hardly say a word. Is God happy about that?"*

• *"I lecture in physics and have said goodbye to many traditional concepts of God. Am I wrong?"*

• *"I can see the point of religion, but I'm put off by the official Church."*

• *"Does God really back me up when I follow the honest assessment of my own conscience?"*

In many cases people are intensely relieved when they can discuss their thoughts and feelings openly, and know that somehowthey were actually speaking to God and receiving his/her mediated answer. And speaking to a human person about matters that concern our relationship to God does not stand in the way of our speaking to God directly. It prepares us for it. It flows from personal prayer. It makes our prayer complete.

63.

Join a community of believers

It is much easier to pursue a particular interest when we join a group of like-minded people. The same applies to us in the matter of religion. Others can give us much needed inspiration, support and advice.

Read also ch.44

There is even more reason for joining a community of believers once you have become aware of God's *sacramental* (symbolical) presence among us. Because we cannot see or touch God directly, God expressed his/her presence in a human individual, in Jesus Christ. Through him it has become much easier for us to relate to God in truly human ways: through sight, hearing, touch and all forms of human interaction.

Read ch.45

God's tangible presence in Jesus Christ continues through signs and symbols today. These consist of shared worship, a common meal of thanksgiving, forms of inner healing, the support of the community, the guidance of spiritual leaders, days of remembrance and celebration, religious functions at turning points in our life and other useful helps.

There is absolutely no reason why you should not enter a church building to say a prayer whenever you feel like it, or attend a service. These churches have been constructed specifically to be open places for any member of the public. You do not need to be a 'registered member' to enjoy the religious ambience they provide.

Joining a Christian community as a full member is less traumatic than people often imagine. Most parishes have well-tried procedures to welcome new members and to make them feel at home. If you want to make an approach, ask one of your friends whom you know to be a committed Christian to perform the necessary introductions for you. Otherwise, simply attend a Church service and contact the priest or minister at the end of the service.

There are many Christian denominations, "Churches," to choose from, and all of them, in their own ways, offer community support and a link to Jesus' sacramental reality. However, if I may give a word of personal advice, it is not a waste of time to give thought as to which Church you eventually decide to join.

In general, it is advisable to join one of the mainstream Churches. The smaller the community, the more likely it is to have restricting beliefs, customs and practices. The international Christian Churches have centuries of experience and you are bound to benefit from their 'catholicity,' their wider vision, their riches of spiritual traditions. To use a comparison, if you have to settle abroad, will you not find more space and choice in a large country?

This brings me to my second point. Within the larger Church, find your niche. Make contact with like-minded groups that can give you the support you need. You may feel more at home in one parish than in another. You will feel inspired by this Christian weekly rather than that. You will come across a wide spectrum of interest groups, some of which will offer you the inspiration and companionship you may need.

To come back to our comparison: if you were to migrate to a country as vast as Australia, would you not consider in detail where within the country you will take up residence? A village in the outback may not suit you; does that mean you rule out Sydney as well? On the other hand, you may prefer the outback to Sydney!

Finally, you will need to give some time to studying the human features of the Church you are joining. It will require some familiarity with its history. All human organizations are mixtures of miserable failings and marvellous achievements. Overstatements and prejudices may need to be cleared up, the *Read ch.10 ch.35 & ch.36* reasons for specific practices and customs explained. It is very much like tracing the history of one's own family or nation.

The fundamental reason why Churches exist is that we are social beings. We cannot live on our own. Also in our search for God and our attempt to respond to God, we need the support of community. That is why what happened in Jesus Christ makes a difference to us. God came close to us in him. God continues to come close to us in people.

64.

Make the gift of selfless love your highest priority in life.

Each one of us has the unspoken aim to make the most of our life. We want to find and assert our worth. We want to be affirmed as being a unique and lovable person. We want to live to the full all the power of our creative and emotional potential.

Paradoxically, we will achieve these aims best by turning outwards, by making others, rather than ourself, the prime target of our efforts.

Love is the principle that expresses this paradox. The belief that God is Love means in practice that the paradox of love provides the key to our self fulfilment. Allow me to work this out in seven concrete suggestions.

1. Try to make others happy

Making love our priority means that instead of focussing attention on ourselves, we think of others first. It requires an altruistic attitude.

In a family situation, for example, we ask ourselves: `What will make my wife/husband happy? What can I do to make my children happy? What can I do that would really please my ageing parents?' I look at the situation from their point of view. I try to do honestly what is best for them, never mind the inconveniences or discomforts it brings me.

Read also ch.11 & ch.58

I am not suggesting that we should simply become a doormat, or that we should injudiciously try to satisfy everyone's dreams and wishes. Concern for people's true happiness requires prudence and discretion. Yet life becomes crucially different when I myself no longer feature as the focus of my endeavours, but the happiness of others.

The same should obviously apply to other relationships: my colleagues at work, the people I serve, my companions when I travel, my fellow tourists when I am on holiday, and so on.

By being an altruistic person I will, unexpectedly, find a lot of happiness myself.

2. Affirm others in their self-worth

The principle of genuine love will take me a step further. In all my dealings with other people I will attempt to affirm them whenever the opportunity arises.

Affirmation requires that I let another person know that I respect his or her dignity, that he or she is a unique and lovable individual. I will not utter these precise words of course, nor will I need to use words all the time. Affirming people is also effectively done through the gift of time, attention, respect, friendship, genuine admiration.

Wanting to affirm people should be kept clearly distinct from mere diplomatic gestures. Diplomatic flattery and related techniques are tricks to manipulate the other person. Genuine affirmation springs from respect for the other's individuality, and seeks to strengthen the other in his or her autonomous self worth.

3. Bring quality to your service

The priority of love requires from us also that in every transaction with people, we give them of the best that is in us. Each one of us has tasks and responsibilities through which we render a service to others. The quality of what we do matters to those people. By assuring that quality we are contributing substantially to their welfare.

Suppose you are an optician. People depend on you for your professional assessment of their eyesight and for your honest advice as to what is best for them. If love is your priority, you will take extra care to be up to date with the latest academic studies. You will give each customer the attention he or she deserves. You will not sell products which you know to be inferior or unnecessary, simply because you would make more money on the sale.

Again, the paradox works. Even though it may seem that your adherence to quality and truth is costly to you, it will pay off in other ways. It may well increase your clientele, for instance. And, within a wider perspective, if you can be trusted in your service, there is a better hope that you can trust others in the services they render to you. But most of all, by delivering real quality, you are being true to yourself and will thus be a happier person.

4. Make sex a means of expressing tenderness and genuine love.

Sexual intimacy can be such a wonderful way of relating to another person. In its fulness, sex leads to the creation of new life. We should do everything in our power to keep sex subservient to genuine love and life.

Sex corrupts when we reduce other people to being mere objects that give us pleasure. In all contemporary Christian Churches a much needed debate is going on regarding sexual morality: What freedom should be given to homosexuals? When, if ever, is abortion allowed? What forms of contraception do justice to respect for love and life?

Underlying the debate is the strong Christian conviction that genuine love requires that we restrain our sexual impulses. Fidelity to a partner does matter. Voluntary celibacy to dedicate one's life more fully to serving God and the neighbour make sense for those who have the gift. Even within a married relationship voluntary restraint is frequently a sign of genuine love.

Such a basic disposition is not a denial of sex, but an attempt to raise it to its full human dignity and potential. Sex is an area in which each individual should formulate his or her own principles of action, in order that the priority of genuine love is safeguarded.

Read also ch.29

"Among your sermons this is the one I like best, Vicar!"

5. Defend the rights of the weak.

In our society it is the poor, the weak and the marginalised who are the most at risk. They are subject to multiple disadvantages. They neither have the knowledge, the skill, the capital nor the social support to fend for themselves.

Defending their rights is a sacred duty. If in any way we ourselves are directly involved, we should unhesitatingly take their side, even if such support can only be given at a cost. Love may well require us to join a campaign, march in a demonstration or engage in political action. The cause we fight for could well extend beyond national borders – for instance to secure human rights for a minority group in a distant country.

If *we* do not abandon the underdog, God and others will not abandon us.

6. Be generous to the needy.

If love is our priority, we will often have to go out of our way to help people in need. As we come to know a particular need, we should dig deeply into our purse and share of our wealth.

Often, much more is required. We may be called upon to contribute our personal skill, our time, our confidence, our enthusiasm which alone can give the human support that will truly help. We should then be willing to volunteer our services, if it is within our power to do so.

Sharing the life of people in need can bring us marvellous benefits. Children with learning disorders, patients in hospital, the handicapped, the mentally ill and other disadvantaged groups can give us so much more in return than we could ever give them by the service we render. A friend I knew spent a Christmas looking after homeless people in an urban shelter. He expected it to be hell. In fact, he told me, it was the best Christmas he had ever had.

7. Give thanks for the gift of life.

If we are able to give and receive Love from other people, it is only because we received all we have and whatever we are from God, Ultimate Reality. God is personal and God is Love. What is more appropriate than for us to respond to God in our own human way – with a personal gift of gratitude and love?

And if we go through a spell of suffering or sadness, what is more natural than to entrust ourselves firmly to God's care? Our gratitude will be mingled with a cry for help.   *Read also ch.51*

We can express our feelings to God in a personal prayer, in the ways I have outlined before: by thinking aloud in God's presence, by talking to friends and by speaking to him/her directly.

Our prayer will be a prayer of love if it contains all the elements I described in this chapter: concern for others, commitment to high-quality service, attention to human needs.

Read also ch.55 We will talk about all these things to God, expressing our own relationship to him/her as the reality that gives ultimate meaning to our life.

Read also ch.45 Since words can only express our thoughts and feelings inadequately, and since we would like to draw strength from the sacramental gifts of God's love, we will also, if at all possible, take part in the communal acts of thanksgiving that celebrate God's love among us.

65.

Appreciate God's presence in all the love you come across, all the time.

Judging one's own time correctly is notoriously difficult. This applies especially to religion and morality. A mood of despondency seems to have descended upon our present-day society. People feel unease and disgust at the spate of violent killings, at marital breakdown, at corruption and fraud, in general at the decline in standards of decency and humanity. Public debate regarding moral questions often lacks inner conviction, conducted as it is by politicians and journalists whose stated intentions are so often known to conflict with vested interests. It makes honest folk feel depressed.

Modern life is often too glibly perceived to be the main culprit. *What can you expect from a culture in which everything revolves around the self instead of around God?* It would seem to me that the reality is more complex.

Our modern, secularised society carries many precious values that manifest the inner workings of God: sensitivity about human rights, the ideal of honesty in much of the media, the rigorous quest of truth by the sciences, and the dedication of professionals to improving the quality of life, to mention just a few. It might be worth exploring the presence of God in such tangible forms. After all, a spiritual renewal of human society needs to build on our own experience of God, rather than on foregone models.

The point I want to make in this chapter is that we should not be too hasty in condemning our contemporaries. *"Do not judge others. Then God will not judge you. For God will judge you in the same way you judge others."*[1] And in any case, the

---

1 *Matthew* 7,1- 2.

norm we should use for any assessment is the one suggested in Scripture:

> *Love comes from God.*
> *Whoever practises love is born of God and experiences God.*
> *Whoever does not practise love has no experience of God.*
> *For God is love.*[1]
>
> *No one has ever seen God.*
>
> *But if we love one another, God shows that he lives in us. Yes, it is his love that flourishes in us. By this we know that God and we share the same life because he gives us his own Spirit (of love).*[2]

Scripture is not first and foremost speaking of romantic love, or 'making love,' though these are not excluded. Love means wishing another person well and showing it in deeds. Love implies a readiness to give, to make sacrifices, to perform humble services.

The question is: Do we find such love in present-day humanity? I believe we do. We find it in the most unexpected places. I visited Taiwan in 1993 and would like to use my findings as an illustration. Half the population of Taiwan has lost its religious past and is utterly secularised.

A desert without green shoots?

The traditional religion of the Chinese in Taiwan, most of whom are immigrants from mainland China, is a Taoist mix of superstition and polytheistic worship. The Lung Shan Temple in Taipei still draws ageing crowds of believers who offer food to Kuan-Yin, the goddess of mercy, and burn incense sticks to an assortment of gods and goddesses whose idols fill the shrines. Buddhists gather for prayer and ritual chants in pagodas or in private homes. But such religious activities belong to

---

1   *1 John* 4,7-8.
2   *1 John* 4,12-13.

the past. They do not reflect the interests of the young, the intelligentsia or the country's industrial elite. I asked myself: do the latter have any 'religion' at all?

Our traditional Christian response has often consisted in judging people *from outside,* by applying to them norms derived from the past. God, however, as Creator and Spirit, fills the world and all people *from within.* The Pharisees had already condemned the sinful woman who wiped Jesus' feet with her hair; Jesus saw her great love and made it the basis for her renewed turning to God.[1] The thought takes me back to Taiwan and an unusual encounter.

I was interviewing actors and actresses for parts in an international co-production. Since the projected film portrays our present-day search for God, empathy with religious values hardly seemed a luxury, but I found it a commodity in short supply. One actress, whom I will call Fong Shoa-li, spoke for many when she said: "Religious people inhabit an alien world." I inquired about her own world and was invited to visit her home.

Read also ch.44

Fong's husband is an engineer. She herself earns an additional wage as a part-time actress. They have two children who go to primary school. The precious fragments of time not claimed by work or by endless traffic jams are spent on watching TV at home, visiting friends or, rarely, taking the family to a park. A visit to the temple does not feature on the programme.

"I have never said a prayer in my life," Mrs. Fong told me with disarming candour, "nor do I feel the need to." Asked about God, she replied she had never given the matter much thought.

"Will virtue be rewarded and crime punished?" I asked her.

---

1   *Luke* 7,36-50.

"Yes," she said after some hesitation; but she could not explain how. Providence, judgment, after-life had no place in her vocabulary. For her and her husband life had to be lived now, with economic solvency, health and good relations as their chief objectives. Then, almost as an afterthought, she pointed at a framed calligraphic text that adorned the living room wall.

It was a quotation from Hung Ying-ming's *Ts'ai Ken T'an* (around 1600 AD) which she translated for me.

> *While performing your public office, remember two words of advice. Be impartial, and you will gain respect. Be honest, and your authority will grow. While residing at home, remember two words of advice. Show love, and emotions will be at peace. Work hard, and what you have will be sufficient.*

On further probing it turned out, in fact, that values such as impartiality, honesty, love and hard work were purposely cultivated in the Fong family, and especially love. I was impressed by the mutual respect and affection between Mrs. Fong and her husband, and their warmth and dedicated commitment towards the children. Mrs. Fong was also involved in neighbourhood services, such as taking a handicapped child to the bus and shopping for a bedridden pensioner.

Read also ch.34

The Fongs, I began to realise, though living in what Peter Berger has described as "the pervasive boredom of a world without gods," may unknowingly experience and radiate the exciting presence of God.

On returning to England, I retrieved an English translation of Hung Ying-ming's work and found in it another appropriate verse.

> *"In every household there is a true Buddha, in every life you will find people of the Way (Tao). If a person is sincere in his heart, harmonious in spirit, joyful in countenance and kind in words, if he will serve his parents and siblings, laying aside selfishness in*

"I know you're an atheist – but do come in!
You've done the right things!"

body and spirit, and adjusting himself to those
around him, such a person will be far superior to
those who regulate their breathing and practise
meditation."

It reminded me of Jesus' own puzzling priorities.

God *is* love

When Jesus described the last judgment, he pointedly
omitted the saying of prayers or the observation of the Sabbath
as decisive norms. Instead, the Judge will ask: *"Did you*
clothe the naked, feed the hungry, nurse the sick and visit
criminals in prison?"[1] For not only is love the greatest commandment, God is love.

---

1   *Matthew 25,31-46.*

Wherever we find love, we know it comes from God. It is impossible for a human being to see God directly. It is by seeing love at work in ourselves and in others that we come face to face with God. Love is the clearest manifestation of God's presence.

When the New Testament speaks of 'love,' it points to the best in our human nature. Love means respect for the other, an openness leading to selfless commitment. It is love that makes us overcome our inborn egoism, urging us to serve rather than just be served. If we love people, we tell the truth even if it embarrasses us; we put up with other people's failings and forgive them; we turn the other cheek rather than take revenge; we pray for those who curse us and treat us badly. The love we talk about here is deeper than emotional attraction, and more resourceful. It engenders respect for who and what people are, not for what we can get out of them. It expects us to make sacrifices, yes, even to give our life if this be necessary.

We meet such love even in the midst of our secular society. We find it exemplified in individuals and in some characteristic virtues of our time. Whenever we do, we should realise we are walking on sacred ground. For *any* manifestation of genuine love is a manifestation of God, even if it comes wrapped in a secular envelope.

Making sense of life

The principle of love provides us with the most trustworthy norm to assess what is healthy or not in our own culture. Fortunately, there is a lot to be proud of. Both on an institutional and personal level, the face of practical love shines through. We should remember that an explicitly religious motivation is not required here. At the last judgment we will not be grilled about our deepest conscious motives, but about whether our actions were humane, positive, and thus loving.

Christians are not hostile to the present world. Christians want to build on God's self-manifestations in present-day ide-

als and commitments. Our duty as believers is to render ex- *Read*
plicit what is latent in people's collective and personal con- *also*
sciences: that selfless love makes sense. *ch. 15*

Love is not a waste of time because there is a deeper dimension to reality, a reality we call God whose essence is love and who reveals himself most clearly in love. Love makes sense because God makes sense.